Copayments and the Demand for Prescription Drugs

T0298759

Increasing prescription drug cost-sharing by patients—in the form of increasing copayments—is one of the most striking developments in the health sector over recent years. Debate over the exact nature and use of copayments by healthcare insurers continues to be hotly debated by experts in the private and public sectors.

Differential copayments for medically equivalent alternatives is one strategy insurers use to affect the choice of one drug over another when they face different prices for each drug. This book's results suggest that differences in copayments influence choice, shifting market share in these drug markets. This detailed and meticulously researched study is one of the first of its kind: it examines the influence of copayments on the choice of prescription drugs. Relative copayments for therapeutically equivalent drugs, imposed by insurers, are shown to have a significant impact on consumer choice—the implication being that physicians are acting in patients' financial as well as medical interest.

Unlike much work in this area, *Copayments and the Demand for Prescription Drugs* is not sponsored by any drug company; its up-to-date results, established on a firm scientific basis, are entirely unbiased. Its results have applications for the private insurance and pharmaceutical sectors as well as the public sector. It will be of great interest to professionals and researchers in the fields of health economics, economic and healthcare policy-making, and microeconomics.

Domenico Esposito is a Researcher at *Mathematica Policy Research Inc.* in Princeton, New Jersey, USA. He is a health economist whose specialty is in the economics and policy of the pharmaceutical industry.

Routledge International Studies in Health Economics
Edited by
Charles Normand
London School of Hygiene and Tropical Medicine
Richard M. Scheffler
School of Public Health, University of California, Berkeley

Copayments and the Demand for Prescription Drugs

Domenico Esposito

Routledge
Taylor & Francis Group

LONDON AND NEW YORK

First published 2006
by Routledge
2 Park Square, Milton Park, Abingdon, Oxon OX14 4RN

Simultaneously published in the USA and Canada
by Routledge
711 Third Avenue, New York, NY 10017

First issued in paperback 2012

*Routledge is an imprint of the Taylor & Francis Group,
an informa business*

© 2006 Domenico Esposito

Typeset in Times New Roman by
Newgen Imaging Systems (P) Ltd, Chennai, India

All rights reserved. No part of this book may be reprinted or
reproduced or utilised in any form or by any electronic,
mechanical, or other means, now known or hereafter
invented, including photocopying and recording, or in any
information storage or retrieval system, without permission in
writing from the publishers.

British Library Cataloguing in Publication Data
A catalogue record for this book is available
from the British Library

Library of Congress Cataloging in Publication Data
A catalog record for this book has been requested

ISBN13: 978–0–415–64895-0 (pbk)
ISBN13: 978–0–415–70145–7 (hbk)
ISBN13: 978–0–203–79937–6 (ebk)

Contents

Illustrations

Acknowledgments

Some portions of this research were previously published in the Journal of Pharmaceutical Finance, Economics, and Policy (volume 14, number 2, 2005 pp. 39–57) as "Prescription Drug Demand for Therapeutic Substitutes: The Influence of Copayments and Insurer Non-Price Rationing." The results are reproduced here with full permission of the journal. The Journal of Pharmaceutical Finance, Economics, and Policy is published by the Pharmaceuticals Product Press (an Imprint of Haworth Press, Inc.; Binghamton, NY: 13904–1580).

1 Introduction

Pharmaceutical companies have long been the subject of controversy for their ability to set high prices for patented prescription drugs. The United States popular press often cites the rise in average wholesale prices (AWP) for pharmaceutical products over time as contributing to decreased patient purchasing power and escalating prescription drug expenditures. Public advocates argue that drug prices are unaffordable to the average American consumer, particularly the uninsured elderly. However, with the exception of Medicare beneficiaries without drug coverage and the uninsured without Medicaid, much of the US population has some form of drug insurance benefit and rarely pays a price as large as AWP for necessary medication. Rather, these people purchase prescription drugs based on a schedule set by insurance companies, not pharmaceutical firms.

In 2001, nearly two-thirds of Americans (177 million people) had employer-sponsored health insurance (United States Census Bureau, 2002) and 98 percent of those also had outpatient prescription drug coverage (Kaiser Family Foundation, 2001). In fact, more than 75 percent of all persons with health insurance in the United States have a pharmaceutical benefit (Kaiser Family Foundation, 2001). Individuals in this large group normally pay for their pharmaceutical products under a predetermined scheme set by their insurer and are primarily responsible for a nominal copayment at the point of drug purchase. In some cases, they pay a fixed percentage of the actual cost, but often much less than the AWP.

Increasing coverage of prescription drugs by insurers has coincided with considerable growth in pharmaceutical spending. According to data compiled by the Centers for Medicare and Medicaid Services (CMS), from 1993 to 2000, expenditure on outpatient prescription drugs was the fastest growing component of US health care. Over this period, CMS reports that drug spending grew more than 13 percent annually. Interestingly, the composition of spending growth on pharmaceuticals throughout much of this period was skewed more towards increased utilization than price changes (see Dubois *et al.*, 2000 and PhRMA, 2000 for further exposition). Yet, some of the more utilized, though innovative, drugs are also the most expensive.

As a result of this expansion in the use of costly prescription drugs, a variety of organizations from AARP (Gross, 2001) to Families, USA (McCloskey, 2002) to the National Institute of Health Care Management (Findlay *et al.*, 2002) have called for increased government intervention to combat high drug prices with affordable benefits for the elderly and uninsured. Many proposed solutions for limiting the growth in drug spending, or providing coverage to those without it, call for the use of managed care type financial incentives and non-financial strategies to influence pharmaceutical choice.

However, little is known about the impact of these types of drug benefit programs on drug choice. Much of the literature on the demand for pharmaceuticals ignore the choice of one drug over another and focuses on the amount of total drug utilization. Moreover, there is scant evidence concerning the impact of non-price rationing on choice behavior in the pharmaceutical market. Most importantly, these pharmacy benefit packages often require patients to purchase drugs based on copayment schedules that mask the true cost of the drugs. As a result, it is not clear if these "prices" set by insurers behave like real market prices and affect the allocation of goods as one might expect in a normal market setting.

To study this issue, this research examines the impact of patient copayments on the demand for drugs within one therapeutic class. While there is some evidence concerning the substitution of generic drugs for brand names, given differential copayments, multiple patented products that perform similar functions at different levels of efficacy and cost-effectiveness makeup many prescription drug markets. One of these is the market for antihyperlipidemic agents, drugs that treat high cholesterol and medical conditions known as coronary heart disease (CHD). Most of this market belongs to the hydroxymethylglutaryl coenzyme A reductase (HmG CoA) inhibitors, commonly referred to as the statins.

Statins and coronary heart disease

Three major medical indicators of a patient's risk for CHD and detrimental cardiac events such as a myocardial infarction (heart attack) or stroke are low- and high-density lipoprotein cholesterol (LDL and HDL) and triglyceride levels. LDL, known as the "bad" type of cholesterol, consists mostly of fat, travels from the liver, and collects in the walls of the arteries, causing atherosclerosis (hardening). Medical experts consider a level of LDL below 100 milligrams per deciliter (mg/dl) desirable for people with a history of heart disease as is a level of below 130 mg/dl for those free of prior heart problems National Cholesterol Education Program, (NCEP, 2001).

HDL consists mostly of protein and helps to clear LDL from the bloodstream. An HDL level of 35 mg/dl or more is desirable while experts consider a lower mark to be a risk factor for CHD and future cardiac events (NCEP, 2001). Triglycerides are a form of fat that the body uses for energy that can build up in artery walls and cause atherosclerosis much like LDL; levels less than 200 mg/dl are normal (NCEP, 2001).

Drugs in the statins class primarily act by inhibiting the action of an enzyme in the liver that the body uses to produce cholesterol; the liver responds by absorbing more cholesterol from the bloodstream, reducing cholesterol levels throughout the body (Gotto, 2002). Statins are particularly effective at reducing levels of

LDL while moderately raising HDL and lowering triglycerides. In addition, recent medical research has demonstrated that statins lower serum C-reactive protein, a sensitive marker of inflammation, independently from lipid levels (Strandberg *et al.*, 1999).

The first statin introduced to the marketplace was lovastatin (also known by its brand name, Mevacor) by Merck in September 1987. It was an important medical advance because it allowed patients to supplement diet and exercise therapy used to control unhealthy levels of cholesterol with a drug to be taken once a day. Due to the prevalence of high cholesterol and CHD in the United States[1] and the success of Mevacor, other statins followed. In November 1991, Bristol Myers Squibb brought pravastatin (Pravachol) to the market while Merck introduced simvastatin (Zocor), in January 1992. In April 1994 and February 1997, Novartis and Pfizer followed with fluvastatin (Lescol) and atorvastatin (Lipitor), respectively. Bayer introduced Cervistatin (Baycol) in 1997 but removed it in 2001 when the drug was found to be linked to deaths resulting from the muscle disease rhabdomyolysis and severe kidney failure (Baycol Recall Center, 2002).

Statins are an important class of drugs to consumers and insurers alike. In 2002 and 2003, according to IMS Health, statins were the third most prescribed drugs in the United States behind non-injectable codeine and selective serotonin reuptake inhibitors (SSRIs), but the largest in terms total dollar expenditures. In these years, consumers spent more than $12.5 billion and $13.9 billion on statins, more than 6 percent of all US prescription drug spending. Moreover, response to the newest cholesterol-reduction guidelines by the National Cholesterol Education Program (2001) is expected to nearly triple the number of statin users in the United States (Liebman, 2001).

Given that statin use is both widespread and costly, insurers certainly have a motive to manage their utilization. To accomplish this, health plans create financial incentives to encourage use of one drug over another, such as the example provided in Kessler (1999). Whether or not these inducements alter a consumer's choice of a statin, and act like prices in the market setting, is the subject of this research.

Organization

The remainder of the monograph is organized in the following manner. First, it reviews much of the established literature pertaining to the demand for pharmaceuticals and related topics. The next two sections explore the relationship between CHD and the statins as well as economic differences in an attempt to ascertain the level of substitutability among the drugs in this class. Following this is a discussion of the structure of demand for prescription drugs in the United States. Afterwards, the study examines consumer choice behavior for prescription drugs and proposes an econometric specification for the primary economic questions. The subsequent sections explain the data source and method of sample selection, along with caveats for the use of medical claims data, and also provide descriptive statistics and multivariate regression results. Finally, the reader will find a discussion of the results with suggestions for future research and a conclusion.

2 Previous literature on prescription drug demand

Little economic research on the demand for pharmaceuticals addresses markets where there are no generic equivalents for branded drugs. In fact, a significant portion of the field investigates issues surrounding both firm and consumer behavior after drug patent expiration (Grabowski and Vernon, 1992, wrote the seminal paper in this area; Ching, 2002, extends this field of inquiry). Moreover, only a limited portion of the established empirical economic literature can also account for the impact of a patient's insurance type on choice behavior.

Interestingly, although much is known about the pricing of pharmaceuticals by drug firms, research on the determination of copayments and drug benefit plan structures is sparse in the economic or insurance literature. One potential explanation for this deficiency is that, historically, copayments for drugs in the United States were not differentiated among products other than generic and brand name drugs until the early 1990s. Prior to this time, most insured patients paid a fixed amount for any prescribed medicine that was not a generic formulation. Second, only recently have expenditures on prescription drugs become an increasingly important portion of insurers' spending. As a result, escalating financial pressure exerted by an acceleration in pharmaceutical prices has spurred insurers to actively manage pharmacy benefits by differentiating copayments among therapeutic substitutes and, in some cases, restricting access to some alternatives altogether. Thus, until recently, the decisions underlying copayment and pharmacy benefit design have been rather uninteresting.

Today, however, the process through which copayments and drug benefits are determined is based largely on bargaining between insurers (or their agents) and pharmaceutical companies. Drug firms offer discounts and hidden rebates to insurers in return for favored benefit status. Often this selected status means a lower copayment for their drug compared to rival products or a preferred position on an insurer's formulary. While this is certainly a topic that demands a stylized economic interpretation, it is beyond the scope of this literature review.

The existing literature on prescription drug demand is focused primarily on measuring utilization changes when consumer cost-sharing is instituted or modified and estimating price elasticity of demand for pharmaceuticals. Prior to the early 1990s, research on these topics was scattered and based primarily on medical information about patients covered by public, state-sponsored insurance.

However, the collection of healthcare data in large insurance databases coupled with increasing public policy and management interest have caused the literature on demand and utilization of prescription drugs to expand rapidly.

Prescription drug utilization

Much of the early research on prescription drug demand focuses on utilization by Medicare or Medicaid recipients (Brian and Gibbens, 1974; Nelson *et al.*, 1984; Smith, 1993; Smith and Garner, 1974; Soumerai *et al.*, 1987). These studies confirmed what one may expect from economic theory: total prescription drug utilization increases with the initiation of a benefit program while a small copayment for services holds down the cost and decreases utilization of drugs among recipients. Reeder and Nelson (1985) also find that the imposition of a copayment decreases utilization among some therapeutic classes, including cardiovascular drugs, but does not change usage among other groups such as analgesics or antihistamines. It is possible that this latter result is a function of the brand name-generic mix in the particular therapeutic classes examined by the authors as well as the therapeutic usefulness of the drug class.

Liebowitz *et al.* (1985) use data derived from four Rand Health Insurance Experiment (HIE) sites to examine the effect of cost-sharing on the use of prescription drugs and compare the response for drugs with that of all ambulatory medical expenses such as outpatient or hospital expenditures. The HIE was a panel study that tracked medical expenditures, health, and demographic characteristics of an enrollee group where families or individuals were randomly assigned to an insurance plan for a 3- or 5-year period in six different areas of the United States. The authors find that individuals with more generous insurance bought more prescription drugs, drug use per capita differed markedly across the six sites, and the proportion of brand-name drugs among all drugs purchased was not a function of insurance plan generosity. In addition, they find that the cost-sharing response for drugs was similar to that for other medical services in all sites except for Dayton, Ohio. The peculiarities surrounding drug utilization in this one site were not analyzed further; however, these results were most likely due to small area variation in the use of medical care services as documented in other studies (Bennett, 1973; Bennett, 1975; Paul-Shaheen *et al.*, 1987; Wennberg and Gittelsohn, 1982).

Overall, the study confirmed the belief that more generous insurance for prescription drugs induces greater use (moral hazard). Consumers facing 95 percent of the costs of drugs up to a maximum dollar expenditure used only 57 percent as much as persons whose drugs were free. However, the data is not able to pinpoint use of particular drugs within a health plan and cannot account for differences across various therapeutic classes. Moreover, the HIE imposed the same benefit structure for drugs as for other health care and was not designed to account for disparate drug benefit packages set by insurers.

Research utilizing data from the United Kingdom National Health Service (NHS) (Birch, 1986; O'Brien, 1989) and other private US data sources

(Harris *et al.*, 1990) also, not surprisingly, find that increasing copayments are associated with a significant reduction in prescription drug utilization per capita. However, the aggregate health care data from the NHS can not account for the intricacies of many different therapeutic classes. Moreover, Harris and colleagues do not use claims data to examine drug choice but rather to test the effect of an imposition of a new cost-sharing plan on the overall utilization of drugs. Why one might expect this behavior to differ considerably for a privately-insured population from that of a publicly insured one is unclear.

Coulson and Stuart (1995) analyze the influence that health insurance has on elderly individuals' decisions to use prescription drugs. They employ a dataset from Pennsylvania's Pharmaceutical Assistance Contract for the Elderly (PACE) program which provides supplemental insurance for drugs to Medicare recipients. Using survey data from Medicare recipients, they measure the influence of insurance on purchases of pharmaceuticals (total prescriptions, any prescription, and prescriptions per drug users). Not surprisingly, PACE beneficiaries filled more prescriptions than other elderly patients without drug coverage suggesting moral hazard behavior.

Johnson and colleagues (1997) examine the impact of increased prescription drug cost-sharing on medical care utilization and expenses of elderly health maintenance organization (HMO) members in the northwest United States. Among HMO enrollees, prescription drug utilization dispensing grew at a slower rate annually when copayments rose. Moreover, after controlling for patients' health status, there was no consistent relationship between drug cost-sharing and medical care utilization or expense among elderly HMO participants. Thus, the introduction of higher drug copayments or cost-sharing on the part of these HMOs did not appear to increase the number of outpatient, inpatient, emergency room visits, or total expenditures among elderly patients.

Hellerstein (1998) examines why physicians continue to prescribe brand-name drugs when less expensive generic substitutes become available. While her results demonstrate persistence in the prescribing behavior of some physicians, she also shows that doctors with a large number of HMO or other pre-paid insurance plan patients are more likely to prescribe generics. This suggests that insurers can independently influence the prescribing decision of a medical professional. Her research also uncovers wide regional variation in the physicians' propensity to prescribe generics which is not attributable to state laws that mandate generic dispensing when the option is available.

Lundin (2000) examines whether a physician's choice to prescribe a generic or brand-name drug is subject to moral hazard by utilizing data before and after a 1993 change in Sweden's country-wide prescription drug reimbursement scheme. The alteration in policy amounted to a reduction in drug coverage of brand-name drugs up to a specified reference price which is set by adding 10 percent to the most inexpensive generic version available. Physicians were less likely to prescribe brand-name drugs to patients with large out-of-pocket costs than persons receiving greater reimbursements. Results also suggest noteworthy moral hazard in prescribing behavior before and after the introduction of reference pricing.

However, insurers' large drug cost differentials do not influence physicians' prescription decisions in the same manner as do consumers' out-of-pocket expenses. While the likelihood of prescribing a brand-name drug fell with increasing patient costs, it was unaffected or *rose* when insurers' costs were substantial.

Motheral and Fairman (2001) examine the effect of an imposition of a three-tier prescription copayment system on pharmaceutical utilization and expenditure, medication continuation, and use of other medical resources by preferred provider organizations (PPO) enrollees. They investigated these outcomes for drugs in four different therapeutic classes, including antihyperlipidemics, for a sample of patients whose pharmacy benefit changed from a two-tier to a three-tier structure. Differences in medication continuation rates before and after the intervention were not attributable to the switch to a three-tier plan and they also found no differences in office, inpatient, or emergency room (ER) visit rates. Three-tier prescription drug benefits modestly lowered prescription utilization and expenditure while considerably reducing net costs to the insurer primarily by shifting costs to patients.

Joyce and colleagues (2002) also investigate the impact of multi-tier formularies and mandatory generic substitution (MGS) programs on total costs to insurance providers and out-of-pocket payments to beneficiaries. Not surprisingly, their simulations of consumer behavior suggest that an additional level of copayment, increases in copayments, and a MGS requirement reduces drug payments overall. Results further suggest that this drop in total expenditures disproportionately benefits insurers because the percentage of drug costs paid for by enrollees rises significantly while insurers' share of drug costs drop. However, it is unclear why this result is surprising since patients with chronic medical conditions will not, and often cannot, cease pharmaceutical care due to changes in out-of-pocket costs.

Prescription drug price elasticity

Early studies on prescription drug price elasticity employ aggregate monthly data sources outside the United States (Lavers, 1989; Phelps and Newhouse, 1974). The estimated elasticity of prescription drug demand with respect to price in the Lavers study ranged from -0.15 to -0.20. These values can be interpreted as representing a portion of the intertemporal population demand curve that is relatively inelastic. This may appear to run counter to the notion that profit-maximizing, drug-producing monopolists produce and price in the elastic portion of their demand curves; however, the data analyzed by Lavers are charges to the patient, not prices set by firms. Moreover, the aggregation of many drugs and classes of drugs in the data make it impossible to analyze elasticity at the single drug or therapeutic class level.

Ellison and co-authors (1997) extend the drug price elasticity literature considerably by modeling demand for four cephalosporins (a type of anti-infective agent) and computing own- and cross-price elasticities between branded and generic versions with data from the late 1980s. Modeling demand as a multistage budgeting problem, they find large elasticities between generic substitutes as well as significant elasticities between different therapeutically equivalent options.

Mortimer (1997) examines the effects of insurance coverage on demand for prescription drugs in the antidepressant and beta-blocker markets among the insured and uninsured and estimates price elasticities as a function of insurance provider type. Her dataset allows for an investigation of both therapeutic and generic substitution patterns. She finds that uninsured patients are the least sensitive to drug prices, suggesting a physician may not be a good agent for patients in terms of evaluating the effect of drug expenses on them. Her results also indicate that demand in managed care sectors (patients covered by HMOs and Medicaid with a managed care component) is more elastic than for other insurance types, particularly in the beta blocker market. Elasticity estimates for beta blockers as a class of drugs in managed care sectors range from -1.7 to -1.5 while the measure in other markets is no larger, in absolute value, than -0.4. However, its reliance on average retail drug prices to estimate elasticities limits this study. Patients with insurance rarely face these prices when they purchase a prescription and these prices would not accurately reflect their true out-of-pocket costs to patients, which primarily are copayments set by their insurers.

With the exception of Ellison and co-authors (1997), there is little to no knowledge of the effect that actual patient copayments have on the choice of a drug within specific therapeutic classes. Yet, some of these markets represent an important portion of overall health care expenditure in the United States. Moreover, few studies can account for differences in patients' insurance type and the impact of one kind of insurer compared to another. A study incorporating these aspects of the US pharmaceuticals market would provide valuable information to decision makers at insurance and pharmaceutical firms as well as in the government.

3 Coronary heart disease and the statins

Coronary heart disease (CHD) is a leading cause of death in the United States; approximately half of men and one-third of women will develop CHD by the age of 40 (AHA, 2001). The American Heart Association estimates the annual incidence of CHD in the United States at greater than one million cases, and more than 45 percent of people experiencing an acute cardiac event will die (2001). The direct medical costs of CHD create a large economic burden on the US health system. Cumulative costs of outpatient, inpatient, and pharmaceutical care for patients with CHD over a 10-year period have been estimated at more than $125 billion in 1995 dollars (Russell *et al.*, 1998) while the average cost per episode of care in 2000 has been calculated at more than $22,000 (Managed Care Measures, 2001).

Major medical advances in understanding the origination of acute coronary syndromes such as myocardial infarction, unstable angina, and coronary death have recognized the importance of atherosclerotic lesions (plaques) (Constantinides, 1990; Davies, 1990). The rupturing of these lesions largely contribute to the development of acute cardiac events. However, research has demonstrated that medical intervention reduces the risk of plaque rupture. The cessation of smoking, lowering of blood pressure, and addition of low-dose aspirin therapy also decrease the incidence of acute coronary episodes. Moreover, major clinical trials have established that the statins significantly reduce the risk for cardiac events independently and through the abatement of serum cholesterol.

This section will explore the clinical properties of the statins to determine the extent of their medical substitutability. The statins are powerful lipid-lowering agents that reduce the risk for coronary events and mortality; however, in multiple clinical trials and controlled studies, these drugs have displayed differing effects on cholesterol and risk for CHD. To create an appropriate context, the connection between cholesterol and CHD will be discussed first. Then, the relative substitutability of statins will be investigated in terms of CHD risk reduction, cholesterol modification, and adverse side effects.

Serum cholesterol and CHD risk

Clinical trial evidence has demonstrated that higher levels of low density lipoprotein cholesterol (LDL) and triglycerides as well as lower concentrations of high density lipoprotein cholesterol (HDL) are all indicators of risk for CHD (Gordon *et al.*, 1977). In addition, more recent medical evidence has established a significant relationship between CHD risk and C-reactive proteins (Anderson *et al.*, 1998; Haverkate *et al.*, 1997; Maseri, 1997; Mendall *et al.*, 1996; Ridker *et al.*, 1998).

The first randomized clinical trial to establish that lower cholesterol resulted in a reduction in nonfatal Myocardial infarction (MI) or sudden CHD death was the Lipid Research Clinic-Coronary Primary Prevention Trial (LRC-CPPT). In this study, patients were prescribed either cholestyramine resin or a placebo and followed for an average of 7.4 years (Lipid Research Clinics Program, 1984a). Cholestyramine resin is a bile acid resin employed to reduce cholesterol; approximately 50 percent of the full sample of patients (3,806) in the LRC-CPPT were in the treatment group. Among those treated with cholestyramine resin there were 17 percent less nonfatal and fatal MIs attributable to lower lipid levels compared to the placebo group. There was also a significant dose-response relationship between cholesterol reduction and lower risk for MI. Patients who reduced their LDL levels by more than 25 percent had a 64 percent abatement in risk for heart attack. Moreover, a 1 percent drop in LDL corresponded to a 2 percent decrease in risk for MI (Lipid Research Clinics Program, 1984b).

Findings from the Multiple Risk Factor Intervention Trial (MRFIT) demonstrated that the relationship between cholesterol levels and CHD is continuous and dose-related (Stamler *et al.*, 1986). Prior to this study, it was believed that the association between cholesterol and CHD was a threshold one. However, MRFIT results on a group of 356,222 men aged 35 to 57 refute this notion. For example, when broken down into serum cholesterol quintiles, persons in the highest four quintiles had CHD mortality rates 29 percent, 73 percent, 121 percent, and 242 percent larger than the lowest cholesterol grouping.[2] Rossouw (1991) and McKenney (2002), among other sources, summarize other studies involving different lipid-modifying drugs and report similar associations between CHD and cholesterol.

These initial lipid-lowering studies helped to shape early medical practice parameters in the treatment of CHD. The first official cholesterol treatment guidelines were released by the NCEP in 1988 and focused on primary prevention of CHD. NCEP broadened its standards in 1993 to include secondary CHD prevention and specifically targeted LDL cholesterol for the first time. In the years to follow, benchmark clinical trials involving statins were the driving force behind a change in the NCEP's guidelines in 2001. The newest treatment criteria from NCEP's Adult Treatment Panel (ATP) III place a stronger emphasis on risk for CHD in patients without a history of coronary events and lower the recommended LDL threshold necessary to initiate drug therapy. As a result, it is expected that more than 36 million people are now eligible for pharmaceutical care for primary CHD prevention alone, more than twice as many as under the prior guidelines (Gotto and Kuller, 2002).

The decision to pursue aggressive drug therapy rather than only lifestyle adjustments is based on the evidence of CHD, CHD risk equivalents, 10-year CHD-risk, and CHD risk factors. Risk equivalents for CHD are defined as

Table 3.1 Drug therapy decision points as defined by the NCEP ATP III

CHD risk status	LDL goal	Level for drug therapy consideration
Confirmed CHD or CHD-risk equivalents	<100 mg/dl	>100 mg/dl
2 or more risk factors	<130 mg/dl	>130 mg/dl (10-year risk 10–20%) >160 mg/dl (10-year risk <10%)
<2 risk factors	<160 mg/dl	>190 mg/dl

non-coronary atherosclerosis, diabetes, or a greater than 20 percent 10-year risk for CHD. Patients satisfying one or more of these criteria without prior evidence of CHD should be treated as if they have CHD. Risk factors include a family history of CHD, high blood pressure (hypertension), current cigarette smoking, HDL levels below 40 mg/dl, greater than 45 years of age for men, and 55 years for women. Persons with two or more risk factors should be treated more aggressively than those with less than two. Risk for CHD is calculated using the Framingham Study criteria (see Grundy *et al.*, 1999; NCEP, 2001) and incorporates age, gender, total cholesterol, HDL, systolic blood pressure, hypertension treatment, and cigarette smoking. Table 3.1 summarizes risk status, LDL goals and the level of LDL at which drug therapy should be considered according to the NCEP ATP III.

Clinical efficacy of statins

Over the last decade, the statins have become the cornerstone of LDL lowering therapy for the long-term care of patients with or at high risk for CHD. Accumulated data from multiple clinical trials have convincingly demonstrated that early use of these lipid-lowering agents reduces morbidity and mortality from CHD (see Hunningkake, 2001 and Purcell *et al.*, 2001 for discussions of the major studies) with few side effects in those currently marketed. In fact, a medical researcher at Oxford University has declared statins the new aspirin in terms of treatment of vascular disease (Kmietowicz, 2001). Some statins are available without a prescription in the United Kingdom and there is increasing momentum for statins to be approved for over-the-counter use in the United States (CITE).

There is also strong evidence that statins improve non-lipid factors in CHD patients (Puddu *et al.*, 2001) as well as decreasing C-reactive proteins, a marker of myocardial infarction development (Strandberg *et al.*, 1999). Statins have played an instrumental role in cardiac risk reduction programs in health plans since 1988 when the Group Health Cooperative of Puget Sound developed successful guidelines for use of lipid-lowering drugs (Stuart *et al.*, 1991) and continue to be used to achieve NCEP guidelines on LDL reduction on an increasing basis (e.g., see Andrews *et al.*, 2001).

Statins effectively reduce risk for CHD

One of the first major clinical studies to investigate the impact of statin therapy on risk for CHD was the Scandinavian Simvastatin Survival Study (4S; 1994). In this trial of more than 4,000 patients 35–70 years old, simvastatin (Zocor) produced highly significant reductions in the risk of death (42% less likely in the drug treatment group) and morbidity in patients with CHD followed for a median of 5.4 years, relative to patients receiving standard care. In another study with over 6,500 patients 45–64 years old (Shepherd *et al.*, 1995), pravastatin (Pravachol) was determined to significantly reduce the risk of adverse cardiac events (such as nonfatal MI) in men with moderate hypercholesterolemia and no history of MI. For example, statin use reduced the risk for nonfatal myocardial infarction in the treatment group by 31 percent over the study period.

One of the first major studies of statin effectiveness for *average* LDL levels was the Cholesterol and Recurrent Events (CARE; Sacks *et al.*, 1996) trial which followed more than 4,000 patients 21–75 years old for an average of 5 years. Most persons with CHD, even after a MI in some cases, do not have overly elevated cholesterol levels but are still at risk for a major cardiac episode. CARE focused on the benefit achieved by lowering LDL levels in patients with a previous MI with pravastatin (Pravachol) for the typical patient with CHD—those with non-elevated LDL. The main finding was that patients treated with pravastatin were 24 percent less likely to experience a fatal coronary event or nonfatal myocardial infarction than persons treated with a placebo.

Another major clinical study focusing on pravastatin (Pravachol) treatment was the Long-term Intervention with Pravastatin in Ischemic[3] Disease (LIPID) Study (1998) which followed more than 9,000 patients aged 31–75 over an average of 6.1 years. Over the course of this study, drug therapy reduced risk of death from CHD by 24 percent and overall mortality risk by 22 percent as compared to treatment with a placebo in patients with a history of MI or unstable angina. The LIPID follow-up study (LIPID Study Group, 2002) further demonstrated that the benefits of Pravachol treatment continue to accumulate for two additional years. All-cause mortality, CHD mortality, myocardial infarction, and stroke risk remained significantly lower in the treatment cohort compared to the placebo group. Together, LIPID and CARE firmly cement treatment with Pravachol as an essential way to reduce a patient's risk of an unwanted coronary outcome.

Use of statins has also been associated with decreased incidence of cardiac events among elderly adults. In a study of nearly 2,000 patients aged 65–73 with a 7-year follow-up period, Lemaitre and colleagues (2002) observed a 56 percent lower risk and a 44 percent lower all-cause mortality associated with the use of statins (of unspecified type) compared to diet therapy (no drug use). The Prospective Study of Pravastatin in the Elderly at Risk (PROSPER) study also concluded that Pravachol treatment reduced the risk for coronary disease among elderly individuals (Shepherd *et al.*, 2002). PROSPER followed 5,804 patients aged 70–82 with a history of or risk factors for vascular disease over 3 years and found that mortality from coronary disease fell by 24 percent in the treatment group compared to the placebo cohort. This research extends the benefits of statin therapy to a portion of the population that is often at highest risk for fatal coronary events.

The Heart Protection Study (HPS) demonstrated that treatment with Zocor substantially benefits not only those with previous coronary disease but also those without diagnosed coronary disease who have cerebrovascular disease, peripheral disease, or diabetes (HPS Collaborative Group, 2002). Moreover, HPS also established that lowering LDL below 166–77 mg/dl reduces vascular disease risk by about 25 percent. Previously, it had been suggested that a LDL threshold existed under which CHD risk could not be reduced. In addition, HPS established that statin therapy also diminishes the risk of stroke, which was more than 30 percent lower in patients taking Zocor compared to those without drug therapy. These findings have recently spurred the US Food and Drug Administration to officially change Zocor labeling to reflect its effectiveness at reducing the risk for heart attack and strokes and the need for bypass surgery and angioplasty (P&T Community, 2003). Previously published results on the prevention of stroke (Schwartz *et al.*, 2001) with atorvastatin (Lipitor) were less conclusive among patients with previous hospitalization for a coronary event.

The use of statins is also mandated for primary prevention of CHD when the risk for CHD is sufficiently large.[4] Results from the West of Scotland Coronary Prevention Study (1996), which followed more than 6,500 men aged 45–64 years for an average of 4.9 years, confirmed that statin therapy for primary prevention was highly cost-effective. Treatment with pravastatin (Pravachol) was shown to significantly reduce the risk of MI and death (by 31%) from cardiovascular causes in men with moderately high cholesterol and no history of MI. The Air Force/Texas Coronary Atherosclerosis Prevention Study, which followed 6,500 men and women aged 45–73 years for an average of 5.2 years, demonstrated that lovastatin (Mevacor) reduces the risk for first acute major coronary event in persons with average LDL and triglyceride and below-average HDL levels by 37 percent (Downs *et al.*, 1998). These studies confirmed that statin therapy was useful for patients with risk for future CHD events as well as persons with previous diagnosis of CHD.

Statin therapy has been conclusively proven to reduce the risk for CHD and coronary events in many long-term clinical trials. However, the evidence for individual statins is mixed. For example, there is no documentation of the effectiveness of Lipitor on reducing CHD outcomes. While there may be some proprietary data, no published studies have established the CHD risk reduction power of Lipitor. On the other hand, as documented earlier, studies have shown that treatment with the other drugs in the class is able to effectively reduce risk for CHD death and coronary events. This is particularly true for Mevacor, Zocor and Pravachol and less so for Lescol. However, due to the possible connection between LDL cholesterol reduction and CHD risk, it is also important to consider the impact of individual statins on cholesterol levels. Moreover, its prominence in the NCEP's recent clinical standards make it an appropriate measure to consider.

Comparative efficacy of statins in modifying cholesterol

While different statins have been shown to be effective at reducing the incidence of cardiac events and LDL in comparison to placebo or diet therapy, only a handful of studies have compared the statins to one another. These investigations have found that atorvastatin (Lipitor) is most effective at reducing LDL and triglyceride levels compared to other statins over a short-term duration. The CURVES study (Jones *et al.*, 1998) compared statin effectiveness by dose on LDL, total cholesterol, triglycerides, and HDL in 518 patients aged 20–80 (mean age of 55) over an 8-week period. At 10, 20, and 40 mg doses, Lipitor produced greater reductions in LDL (38%, 46%, and 51%, respectively) than other statins. However, it is important to emphasize the study's very short duration, particularly when one considers that most CHD patients will expect to remain on drug therapy for a much longer period of time.

Ballantyne and colleagues (2001) employ data from the Atorvastatin Comparative Cholesterol Efficacy and Safety Study (ACCESS) to examine the effects of statins on lipids and apolipoprotein B levels. Apolipoprotein B is an indicator that reflects the level of LDL and triglyceride particles in a person's blood. A report from the Quebec Cardiovascular Study (Lamarche *et al.*, 1996) concluded that apolipoprotein B is a more powerful predictor of CHD than LDL. However, physicians have rarely tested for this marker in the past, leaving non-HDL, which includes LDL and triglycerides, results as the primary endpoint of consideration in most cases. ACCESS studied 3,916 patients over a 54-week period and separated them based on CHD risk factors and established CHD. In all patient categories, atorvastatin (Lipitor) reduced non-HDL more than other statins after 6 and 54 weeks, compared to baseline levels. In fact, atorvastatin dropped non-HDL by 6–13 percentage points more than any of the other statins.

Although Lipitor compares favorably to its competitor statins in terms of cholesterol reduction, there is no published evidence of its independent impact on the risk for CHD or an adverse coronary event. However, clinical research in the past has unequivocally established that "elevated cholesterol is one of the most important determinants, if not the most important" factor in the deterioration of arterial walls and "that its reduction significantly reduces risk for CHD" (Gotto and Grundy, 1999: p. 1). Furthermore, analysis of the data from 4S suggests that the beneficial impact of treatment with Zocor was determined mainly by the change in LDL (Pederson *et al.*, 1998).

At the same time, LDL reductions achieved with Pravachol during the CARE study were also associated with a decrease in coronary events at the threshold of 125 mg/dl. Patients with concentrations below 125 during treatment did not obtain additional benefit. Most importantly, however, "absolute or percentage reduction in LDL had little relationship to coronary events" (Sacks *et al.*, 1998: p. 1446). Thus, even though other research suggests that a 10 percent reduction in cholesterol is associated with a 25 percent drop in heart disease mortality (Law, 1999), there is little consensus on the usefulness of LDL targets suggesting that, on clinical grounds, there is much uncertainty involved in the choice of one statin over another. As a result, for patients with *average* LDL cholesterol, it appears that therapy with *any* statin would be adequate to reduce CHD risk, suggesting that the drugs are nearly perfect substitutes for most people in terms of clinical benefits.

On the other hand, patients in worse health status, such as those with diabetes or older patients with a previous coronary history, should receive more aggressive lipid-lowering treatment. This type of therapy is best pursued with Lipitor and Zocor since they have demonstrated to be most effective at lowering LDL levels over the short-term. Thus, clinically, the statins are near perfect substitutes for one another for many patients for whom drug treatment is recommended, but are less substitutable for persons in poor health status requiring an aggressive lipid-lowering regimen.

Side effect profiles of the statins

Only five percent of patients treated with statins generally discontinue use as a result of side effects (McKenney, 2002). The most common adverse reactions include gastrointestinal complaints, fatigue, headaches, or myalgias (achy muscles). They may also cause liver dysfunction but have not yet been associated with liver failure. The most serious side effect—muscle toxicity—is also rare, occurring in 2–4 patients per thousand treated with any statin. This rate was much higher with cerivastatin (Baycol), which was removed from the market in 2001. In the major clinical studies of other statins, little evidence of muscle toxicity is reported and side effects are normally negligible and equivalent to that of a placebo. However, there is some evidence suggesting a slightly increased risk of myotoxicity with higher doses of statins (Davidson *et al.*, 1997). A recent study also suggests that there is a minor risk of idiopathic polyneuropathy[5] associated with statin use (Gaist *et al.*, 2002); however, the sample size of the population studied in the research was small and not representative of the population of statin users in the United States.

Other research suggests that the statins are relatively similar in terms of adverse effects (Farmer and Torre-Amione, 2000). As a result, the prescribing of one agent over another is often not made on the basis of adverse consequences, suggesting that the statins are near perfect substitutes in terms of side effects. Consequently, it appears that both the comparative clinical benefits and costs of statins imply that the five drugs are near perfect substitutes for one another. In fact, current medical opinion suggests that the number of risk factors for CHD or CHD events should be the central focus of treatment with a statin. Persons with moderate risk for CHD can be treated with nearly any one of these agents and expect to benefit equally from any statin. The relative similarities among statins clinically make any potential economic differences important in terms of consumer choice behavior, as discussed in Chapter 4.

4 Economic differentiation among statins

Economic dissimilarities among statins in terms of price, advertising, and cost-effectiveness are factors that contribute to treatment choice. Statin prices differ at all levels of the pharmaceutical market: wholesale, retail, and insured copayments. At the same time, the manufacturers of these drugs spend considerable, but varied resource, promoting these drugs to physicians and patients in the form of detailing and direct-to-consumer (DTC) advertising. Coinciding with these first two economic dimensions is a vast literature that documents the cost-effectiveness of statin treatment. These estimates of cost-effectiveness are used primarily by insurers and other large drug purchasers to justify the use of one agent over another in the face of growing prescription drug costs. Together, these economic variables signal economic substitutability among statins and help determine utilization among treated individuals.

Pricing

In recent years, pharmaceutical pricing has become a controversial topic due in part to the magnitude of drug price inflation. Products in the statins class are not immune to public and private sector dismay over high average wholesale and retail prices. In fact, with a generic equivalents of Mevacor and Pravachol on the market, insurers and consumers alike have begun to substitute these versions for brand name statins (Winslow *et al.*, 2002).

The listed average wholesale prices (AWP) for statins provides one way to differentiate them from each other economically. Table 4.1 reports average AWPs (for a 30-day supply of pills) for statins as reported in MarketScan prescription drug claims during 1997 and 1998. These prices range from $36.93 for a 20 mg fill of Lescol to $122.87 for 40 mg of Mevacor. Of course, few large institutional purchasers actually pay average wholesale prices in the prescription drug market due to hidden rebates and discounts offered by pharmaceutical companies. These price breaks are offered to buyers to influence the utilization of one drug over another in any particular therapeutic class. In fact, pharmaceutical firms are mandated to report and charge the most favorable of these price discounts to the US government for purchases made by Medicaid but have come under scrutiny for alleged misreporting (Adams, 2003). Given the size of the market for

Table 4.1 Average statin wholesale prices by dosage (1997–1998) (Market Scan)

Statin	5 mg$	10 mg$	20 mg$	40 mg$	80 mg$
Lescol	n/a	n/a	36.93	40.50	n/a
Lipitor	n/a	54.43	82.25	101.16	n/a
Mevacor	n/a	39.21	68.25	122.87	n/a
Pravachol	n/a	57.77	62.62	103.56	n/a
Zocor	89.25	61.86	107.83	n/a	107.91

Table 4.2 Average statin retail prices by dosage (1997–1998)

Statin	5 mg$	10 mg$	20 mg$	40 mg$	80 mg$
Lescol	n/a	n/a	35.62	39.08	n/a
Lipitor	n/a	50.22	65.25	58.93	n/a
Mevacor	n/a	40.69	54.66	101.77	n/a
Pravachol	n/a	48.37	56.46	86.63	n/a
Zocor	68.35	58.56	90.41	58.05	n/a

Source: Medical Expenditure Panel Survey's (MEPS) 1997 and 1998 publicly available prescribed Medicine files.

cardiovascular drugs and competition between statins, it is probably safe to assume that many large purchasers receive discounts from AWP when buying a statin.

The most useful way to compare statin prices is to consider the most commonly prescribed dosages. The usual starting dose for all statins but Lipitor is 20 mg; Lipitor's initial dose is normally 10 mg (Pasternak *et al.*, 2002). This is also representative for the data used in this study. The majority of prescriptions for Mevacor (70%), Pravachol (67%), and Lescol (68.4%) were for the 20 mg version, while most Lipitor fills (65.3%) were at 10 mg. The only contrasting evidence in the data was for Zocor; it had roughly the same percentage of filled prescriptions (40%) for both the 10 and 20 mg version. AWPs for the most prescribed doses ranged in 1997 and 1998 from a high of $107.83 for a 30-pill, 20 mg Zocor prescription to a low of $36.93 for 20 mg of Lescol. The 10 mg fill of Lipitor was priced nearly half as much as Zocor's 20 mg version at $54.43, and was moderately lower than the prices for Pravachol ($62.62) and Mevacor ($68.25). This type of variation among commonly used doses suggests that large purchasers have a nontrivial degree of discretion when choosing one agent over another in this drug class.

Retail prices for statins also vary from one to another and by dose; average cash prices in 1997 and 1998 (for a 30-pill prescription) reported in Table 4.2 range from $35.62 for 20 mg of Lescol to $101.77 for a 40 mg fill of Mevacor. The data in this table were collected from the Medical Expenditures Panel Survey's (MEPS) prescribed medicines files. These prices represent the average amount paid for statins out of pocket by persons without insurance in 1997 and 1998 as reported in MEPS.[6] Average cash prices for frequently used statin dosages ranged from $35.62 for a 20 mg fill of Lescol to $90.41 for a 20 mg fill of Zocor. This spread is similar to the range for average wholesale prices, except that the highest average cash price is lower by nearly $20. As in the AWP case, 10 mg of Lipitor costs much less than the 20 mg cash price of Zocor.

One representation of potential bias that exists with using MEPS data to find average retail payments for statins is evident in Table 4.2 as dosages of Lipitor and Zocor increase from 20 to 40 mg. The reported average retail price for the 40 mg dosages of Lipitor and Zocor are actually lower than the prices for the 20 mg prescription. The sample sizes for the 40 mg dosages of Lipitor and Zocor are much smaller than those for the 20 mg strength (particularly for Zocor), suggesting that there may not be enough data to estimate this figure. However, this is counteracted by the fact that the median and mean retail prices as reported in MEPS for these dosages are similar to one another. Moreover, while it is possible that these data are misrepresentative of real world retail prices (as one might expect, prices rise with dosage level), the 40 mg dosage is not the most highly prescribed strength for these statins in the marketplace (Pasternak *et al.*, 2002).

Although the datasets are different, a comparison of average wholesale and cash prices for statins can provide some insight into this pharmaceutical market. First, note that cash prices are lower than AWPs for nearly every drug and dose. This suggests that even uninsured patients may not be paying AWP, on average. It is possible that any discounts that are offered to pharmacies are also passed on to cash customers in the form of cash prices that are lower than stated AWP. The largest differences between cash price and AWP are for Lipitor, particularly the 40 mg fill where the discrepancy is over $40. Of course, it is possible that a comparison of these data is biased since they are derived from two different sources; however, both databases are relatively representative snapshots of US drug consumption behavior.

Much like large purchasers, such as a managed care organization, patients with health insurance rarely face cash or average wholesale prices when they buy a prescription drug. Most insured persons pay nominal copayments that mask the true cost of the prescription. Table 4.3 reports copayment statistics in the 1997–1998 MarketScan data for the five statins across health plans in the dataset. These data are not partitioned by dosage because insurers do not typically fix copayments or coinsurance levels by the strength of a prescription drug. Thus, a 10 and 20 mg fill of Lipitor normally costs the same to an insured patient facing a copayment. This pricing structure has led many patients, with physician approval,

Table 4.3 Statin copayment statistics (1997–1998) (Market Scan)

Statin	Mean	Std dev	Median	Low	High
Lescol	7.86	3.07	7.82	0.44	13.80
Lipitor	8.80	3.55	8.72	0.44	14.63
Mevacor	8.25	3.89	8.11	0.40	18.11
Pravachol	8.55	3.87	8.76	0.41	17.64
Zocor	8.66	4.34	8.16	0.45	19.49

to split higher dose pills when possible to save money (Stafford and Radley, 2002). The average copayments range from $7.86 for Lescol to $8.80 for Lipitor. In general, there is little variation in the data from the MarketScan claims in 1997 and 1998, but this is representative of benefit plans during this time period as insurers developed prescription drug benefit packages with greater differentiation between copayments after this period.

During this period insurers also moved towards more restrictive benefit packages for prescription drugs that required patients to use preferred agents prior to non-preferred drugs or receive prior authorization for some pharmaceutical agents, and limited the options available to some patients by refusing to reimburse for certain agents. In Health Maintenance Organizations (HMOs) alone, from 1998 to 2000, the percentage of covered lives in these plans affected by three-tier benefits rose from 5 to 40 percent (Scott-Levin, 2001). Interestingly, according to a 2000 report by Scott-Levin, HMO pharmacy executives reported that three-tier copayment plans would have the biggest impact on drugs within the statins class. Nearly 80 percent of HMOs and three-quarters of PBMs that used a three-tier system put one or more statins on the third tier, normally requiring the highest copayment. Benefit managers suggest that this therapeutic class is susceptible to a three-tier system because the drugs are seen to have little difference in efficacy and safety, are multi-source brands, and treat chronic conditions. In other research, the Emron Formulary Study reviewed the benefit packages of 425 plans and found that coverage of drugs within the statins class varied from one to another as reported in Table 4.4 (Sax and Emigh, 1999).

According to these data, each statin was not listed on health plan formularies at least 35 percent of the time. Mevacor has the highest rate of rejection at 57 percent of plans. Pravachol and Zocor were approved or preferred for use most often at 62 and 58 percent, respectively. Strikingly, in 1998, Lipitor was either not listed or restricted from use in more than half of plans. Since 1998, Lipitor has risen to capture the largest share of the statins market, suggesting that the data in this table are not representative of today's market environment.

Advertising

In today's prescription drug marketplace, pharmaceutical manufacturers spend a considerable amount of money on promotion to physicians and patients. The

Table 4.4 Statin formulary status (1998)

Status	Percentage of plans with coverage type				
	Lescol	*Lipitor*	*Mevacor*	*Pravachol*	*Zocor*
Preferred or approved	44	46	26	62	58
Restricted or prior authorization	4	9	11	3	3
No reimbursement	16	0	5	1	2
Not listed	35	45	57	35	37

Source: Sax and Emigh, 1999.

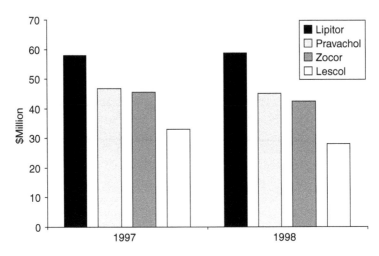

Figure 4.1 Detailing expenditures per statin (1997–1998).

producers of the statins are no different, having spent $134 million as a group in 2000 alone (Liebman, 2001). As shown in Figure 4.1, spending on detailing (promotion to physicians by pharmaceutical company agents) in 1997 and 1998 varied substantially among statins. In 1997, annual expenditures on drug detailing for statins reached nearly $60 million for Lipitor and $30 million for Lescol. Data for Mevacor is excluded from this chart as it was trivial (less than $5 million in 1997).

An additional form of drug promotion employed by pharmaceutical companies in recent times is DTC advertising, usually in the form of television or radio commercials and magazine or newspaper ads. Figure 4.2 reports this form of advertising for Lipitor, Pravachol, and Zocor on annual basis from 1997 to 1999;[7] data for Mevacor were unavailable and DTC expenditures for Lescol were trivial during this period.

Pfizer introduced Lipitor in early 1997 and did not begin DTC advertising until late 1998 but vastly outspent other competitors in 1999. Bristol-Myers Squibb spent $60 million or more in 1997 and 1998 to promote Pravachol, but nothing in 1999. Merck's DTC spending on Zocor declined steadily from 1997 to 1999. This variation in expenditure among statins creates the possibility that consumers are influenced by different advertising at different times.

Cost-effectiveness

Treatment of the symptoms and consequences of coronary heart disease (CHD) can be costly; the average cost per episode of care in 2000 has been estimated at more than $22,000 (Managed Care Measures, 2001). Inpatient care accounts for

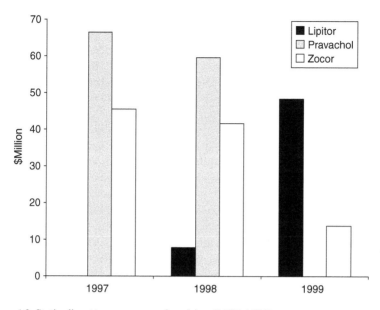

Figure 4.2 Statin direct-to-consumer advertising (1997–1999).
Source: Comptetitive Medical Research.

nearly 75 percent of the cost of a CHD episode while outpatient care, emergency room services and pharmacy expenditures make up the remaining portion at 20, 2, and 4 percent, respectively. Thus, there is much opportunity to temper the cost of CHD by reducing the incidence of costly inpatient utilization. In addition to being safe and effective at treating CHD, under average conditions the statins have been shown to be a cost-effective alternative for many people with and without evidence of CHD (Reckless, 2000).

Cost-effectiveness analysis is a formal method of comparing the benefits and costs of a medical intervention in terms of standard clinical outcomes such as mortality rates, years of life added, or quality-adjusted life years (Gold *et al.*, 1996; Sloan, 1995). The central measure used in cost-effectiveness analysis is the cost-effectiveness ratio. This proportion represents the incremental price of obtaining a unit of health (e.g. an additional year of life added) from another unit of intervention (such as additional treatment with a statin). This type of research can have an impact on an insurers' formulary decisions and, in turn, the out-of-pocket cost of one statin versus another faced by patients (Grabowski, 1998). Cost-effectiveness analyses can directly influence demand of large institutional purchasers by demonstrating that one agent will produce greater cost savings to the payer than other drugs for a fixed level of benefit. As a result, pharmaceuticals with the most favorable cost-effectiveness profiles may be given more desirable formulary or benefit status by insurers. This action then may indirectly sway demand by patients since the out-of-pocket costs to consumers of insurers' preferred medications are normally lower than the costs for non-preferred agents.

Most pharmaco-economic analyses employ characteristics of a theoretical cohort or data from a previous clinical study to examine the cost of drug therapy over time through a Markov analysis (Sonnenberg and Beck, 1993). Markov models assume that patients are in one of a number of finite health states and move across these states via some predetermined transition probabilities. These studies help to distinguish one pharmaceutical agent over another when clinical research can accurately differentiate them such as in the case of the statins. Since clinical trials are normally performed on only one drug and placebo-controlled trials across statins do not study similar patient populations, cost-effectiveness analyses have become a "useful way to evaluate comparative cost effectiveness of multiple agents" (Russell *et al.*, 2001). However, since most studies assume that costs are equivalent to average wholesale prices of statins and most purchasers do not pay this price, informational content may be somewhat limited. At the least, cost-effectiveness estimates provide an upper bound on cost-saving for insurers. The following will review some of the major cost-effectiveness studies that evaluate the financial benefits of statins.

Comparing statins in terms of cost-effectiveness helps to distinguish one agent from another and other treatments for CHD and CHD-related complications. In general, medical interventions that cost $50,000 or less per life year (or quality-adjusted life year) saved are considered cost efficient and preferred for care for a medical condition (Stinnett *et al.*, 1996). For example, Zocor has consistently been shown to cost less than the $50,000 threshold per life year saved for secondary prevention of CHD (Grover *et al.*, 1999; Grover *et al.*, 2001; Prosser *et al.*, 2000). In one study, Zocor therapy cost less than $10,000 per life year saved for high risk (hypertensive smokers) patients with an LDL-to-HDL ratio of five or greater (Grover *et al.*, 1999). In a recent study, van Hout and Simoons (2001) argue that when a cost-effectiveness threshold of €18,000 (roughly $22,300 on July 14, 2004) deemed acceptable, statin therapy should be considered for patients with established CHD (secondary prevention) and persons with a 10-year CHD risk exceeding 20.2 percent (primary).

Treatment with Zocor has also been demonstrated to be as "cost-effective for diabetics as non-diabetics" (Grover *et al.*, 2001). As displayed in Table 4.5, when patient profiles match those from the 4S study, the cost per life year saved with Zocor is almost always lower for men and women with diabetes but no evidence of CHD compared to patients with cardiovascular disease, with the exception of women aged 70. Jonsson and colleagues also confirmed the cost-effectiveness of Zocor in diabetics (1999); substantial hospital cost savings offset 67–76 percent of drug costs in that study. These results are meaningful because excess annual costs to insurers due to diabetes have been estimated at nearly $3,500 per person (Selby *et al.*, 1997) and nearly 40 percent of this expenditure was due to long-term diabetes complications such as CHD.

Other research has also demonstrated that the direct and indirect medical costs of cardiovascular disease are higher for diabetics than non-diabetics

Table 4.5 Mean, estimated cost-effectiveness of Zocor in US patients with diabetes or cardiovascular disease in secondary prevention

	Cost per life year saved			
Men (age)	40	50	60	70
Diabetes	$6,017	$5,063	$5,740	$14,156
Cardiovascular disease	$12,111	$9,513	$8,799	$14,996
Women (age)	40	50	60	70
Diabetes	$19,019	$14,481	$13,121	$23,792
Cardiovascular disease	$20,494	$16,020	$14,164	$21,628

Source: Grower *et al.*, 2001.

(see Chaiyakunapruk *et al.*, 2000). However, there is little evidence for the cost-effectiveness of Zocor in primary prevention of CHD. In one study (Prosser *et al.*, 2000), Zocor was consistently less cost-effective than diet therapy; primarily because diet therapy was assumed to cost only one-tenth as much as statin therapy.

Pravachol therapy has also been shown to be cost-effective in secondary prevention of CHD compared to placebo therapy, other cardiac medications, and diet or exercise therapy (usual care) for CHD (Ashraf *et al.*, 1996; Ganz *et al.*, 2000; Tsevat *et al.*, 2001) and primary prevention of CHD events for patients with an annual CHD risk as low as 1.5 percent (Caro *et al.*, 1999; Lim *et al.*, 2001; Shepherd, 2001). Ashraf and colleagues (1996) calculated the cost per life year saved with Pravachol to range from $7,124 to $12,665 for patients with similar characteristics to those in the PLAC I (Pravastatin Limitation of Arteriosclerosis in the Coronary Arteries) (Pitt *et al.*, 1995) and PLAC II (Crouse *et al.*, 1995) trials. However, a study employing data from the Cholesterol and recurring events (CARE) trial (Tsevat *et al.*, 2001) was slightly less favorable for Pravachol; the incremental cost per quality adjusted life year gained to range from $16,000 to $32,000. Other research employing CARE data demonstrates that Pravachol is most cost-effective for patients older than 60 ($9,000 to $12,000 per quality-adjusted life year saved) and for patients with LDL greater 125 ($16,000 to $18,000). However, for older patients (75–84 years) with previous myocardial infarction, Pravachol therapy cost $5,400 to $97,800 (Ganz *et al.*, 2000) with a 75 percent probability of it costing less than $39,800 per quality-adjusted life year saved. These conflicting results demonstrate that cost-effectiveness analyses can often be influenced by initial analytical assumptions used to calculate the incremental benefit of prescription drug utilization.

For persons without evidence of CHD and an annual risk for a cardiac event as low as 1.5 percent, treatment with Pravachol has been demonstrated to be cost-effective. Table 4.6 reports the cost per life year saved for West of Scotland Coronary Prevention Study (WOSCOPS) patients, demonstrating that intervention

Table 4.6 Pravachol cost-effectiveness for primary prevention of CHD by annual CHD risk

Annual CHD risk	Cost per life year saved
1.5%	$31,800
2–3%	$21,855
>3	$15,116

Source: Shepherd, 2001.

Table 4.7 Cost per life year saved with a 40 mg dose of Mevacor

	Age range				
	35–44	*45–54*	*55–64*	*65–74*	*75–84*
Men	$14,000	$8,600	$17,000	$27,000	$38,000
Women	$49,000	$30,000	$29,000	$30,000	$29,000

Source: Goldman *et al.*, 1991.

with Pravachol "achieves clinical benefit at a reasonable cost" (Shepherd, 2001). These data indicate therapy with Pravachol is increasingly cost-effective as the annual risk for CHD rises. Another study based on Australian data (Lim *et al.*, 2001) calculated the cost of Pravachol therapy per year of life saved to range from $27,000 to $40,000, in Australian dollars, in men and $33,000 to $53,000 in women for primary prevention among patients with a 2.5 percent 15-year risk of CHD mortality. A more thorough analysis of WOSCOPS data for other countries has found that cost-effectiveness remained below $25,000 per life year gained over a broad range of inputs (Caro *et al.*, 1999).

Mevacor has also been demonstrated to be cost-effective in primary and secondary prevention of CHD (Goldman *et al.*, 1991; Goldman *et al.*, 1993; Hay *et al.*, 1991). Hay and colleagues (1991) calculated that the cost of Mevacor in primary prevention of CHD ranged from $6,000 to $53,000 in high risk men and $19,000 to $160,000 in high risk women aged 35–55 per life year saved. For men with one or more risk factors and women with two or more risk factors, Mevacor was demonstrated to cost less than $45,000, on average, per life year saved (Goldman *et al.*, 1993). Thus, studies have not shown conclusively that Mevacor is always cost-efficient (cost less than the $50,000 per life year threshold).

In secondary prevention, Mevacor therapy cost less than $50,000 in men and women with pretreatment cholesterol levels greater than 250 (Goldman *et al.*, 1991); Table 4.7 reports cost-effectiveness data for a 40 mg fill of Mevacor. Mevacor, like other statins, is often more cost-effective for men than women because men tend to have greater risk for CHD than women at all ages. Interestingly, Mevacor's cost-effectiveness profile for men bottoms between ages

Table 4.8 Lipitor cost-effectiveness in primary prevention of CHD

	Age group, cost per life year saved		
Low-risk (age)	40s	50s	60s
Men	$11,816	$7,885	$5,365
Women	$19,866	$10,747	$4,275
High-risk (age)	40s	50s	60s
Men	$5,124	$4,161	$3,846
Women	$7,580	$4,982	$3,756

Source: Grower *et al.*, 2003.

Table 4.9 Statin therapy cost-effectiveness by risk category (Age = 55)

	Lipitor	*Zocor*	*Pravachol*	*Mevacor*	*Lescol*
Primary prevention (with 3 risk factors), cost per life year saved					
Men	$7,276	$9,417	$11,988	$15,823	$10,928
Women	$25,570	$31,170	$37,495	$46,693	$33,207
Secondary prevention (with no risk factors), cost per life year saved					
Men	$11,940	$14,536	$17,693	$22,084	$16,351
Women	$22,681	$27,229	$32,735	$40,861	$30,505
Secondary prevention with diabetes, cost per life year saved					
Men	$9,311	$11,384	$13,908	$17,414	$12,849
Women	$11,142	$13,523	$16,409	$20,661	$15,264

Source: Huse *et al.*, 1998.

45–54 and climbs thereafter, suggesting that it is less preferable for older men. On the other hand, the curve for women is relatively flat for ages 45 and up.

The most recent entrant in the statin market, Lipitor, has been shown to cost less than $20,000 per year of life saved in the primary prevention of CHD (Grover *et al.*, 2003). In both men and women with high and low risk of CHD, the direct costs of treatment with Lipitor were well within the subscribed threshold, as displayed in Table 4.8. Moreover, these cost-effectiveness data display a declining trend as age rises, suggesting that Lipitor is a preferable lipid-lowering agent for the elderly. As with the other statins, this level of cost-effectiveness for Lipitor is comparable to other treatments for CHD (Kuntz *et al.*, 1996; Mark *et al.*, 1995; Pitt *et al.*, 1999; Tsevat *et al.*, 1991) such as thromboltyic therapy (drug therapy that breaks up or dissolves blood clots) and angioplasty procedures.

A number of studies have compared the cost-effectiveness of one statin to another in an attempt to more accurately differentiate them (Attanasio *et al.*, 2001; Barry and Heerey, 2002; Cobos *et al.*, 1999; Huse *et al.*, 1998; Maclaine *et al.*, 2001; Russell *et al.*, 1998; Spearman *et al.*, 1997). In studies where all five statins are considered, Lipitor is the most cost-effective in primary and secondary prevention of CHD. Huse and colleagues (1998) find that Lipitor was more cost-effective, on average, than the next cost-effective alternative (Zocor) for primary prevention of CHD. The mean cost per life year saved of Lipitor therapy for men with CHD and diabetes cost nearly $2,500 less than Zocor therapy. Complete results from this study appear in Table 4.9; the cost-effectiveness magnitudes and ordering of statins are generally in accordance with other studies (Barry and Heerey, 2002; Maclaine *et al.*, 2001; Russell *et al.*, 1998). These data suggest that, among the statins, Lipitor should be preferable to managed care organizations hoping to decrease drug expenditures for CHD but also to maintain a high level of care for their enrollees.

5 The structure of demand for prescription drugs

Consumer demand for prescription drugs is different from demand for many other goods in the economy. Normally, the consumer is not the person who decides which, if any, pharmaceutical agent to use and/or purchase. This judgement is left to a physician or other healthcare professional licensed to write a prescription. Moreover, oftentimes, the insured consumer does not pay the full price for the prescribed medicine. Instead, that person's insurer normally requires only a nominal copayment at the time of purchase that is usually a fraction of the drug's true cost. These aspects of the demand for prescription drugs raise interesting agency and information issues that are missing in many other consumer goods markets.

The doctor–patient relationship

Any time one individual delegates authority to another person to take actions on his behalf, an agency relationship arises. The doctor–patient relationship in medical care is no different. To obtain a prescription drug, a patient must consult with a physician or other health care professional capable of providing a prescription. The doctor evaluates the patient's health status and makes a decision to prescribe or not. In a perfect world, the doctor will choose a drug based not only on therapeutic value but also on the basis of cost to the patient. However, in the past, researchers have found evidence that physicians' information about relative prices of drugs is limited (Steele, 1962; Temin, 1980; Walker, 1971).

Yet, there are also some indications that doctors are becoming more aware of relative prices (Boston Consulting Group, 1993; DeVries, 2001; Hellerstein, 1998). These findings suggest that physicians contacted by drug companies or affiliated with Health Maintenance Organizations (HMOs) and other managed care organizations have a greater awareness of patients' out-of-pocket costs. Moreover, even insurers who are primarily indemnity-based use pharmacy benefit managers to manage their drug benefit programs on an increasing basis (Cook *et al.*, 2000; Lipton *et al.*, 1999). Prescription drug marketing aimed at physicians has also become increasingly price- and cost-effectiveness-based, bringing prices closer to the forefront of physicians' prescribing decisions.

Agency problems hinge on informational asymmetries where monitoring of agents' behavior and assigning enforceable contracts is costly. This is evident in the decision to prescribe drugs when the physician often has multiple choices for pharmaceutical therapy. Not only must doctors be able to assess patients' physical conditions, but they also need to be aware of the different alternatives available.

For many medical conditions, treatment with prescription drugs can be accomplished with a brand name or generic version. Interestingly, prices faced by insured consumers for generic drugs are almost always lower than that of a branded drug. Yet, prescribing of brand name drugs when generic substitutes exist still occurs on a regular basis. In addition to the Hellerstein (1998) study mentioned in the literature review, other research has focused on this issue as well.

In a study on physicians' prescribing behavior in markets where a brand name drug faces a generic alternative (Lundin, 2000) employing data on prescriptions dispensed in pharmacies across Sweden, the probability of prescribing a generic rose after initiation of a price control on brand name products. In another investigation with panel data from the Italian National Institute, Coscelli (2000) finds significant persistence in doctors' prescribing behavior in the anti-ulcer market which, the author concludes, can translate into significant persistent market shares for branded drugs at the aggregate level, despite higher prices.

To help physicians choose the appropriate drug therapy, pharmaceutical companies provide copious advertising materials, both promotional and educational in nature. According to IMS Health and Competitive Media Reporting, in the United States alone, total promotional expenditures by pharmaceutical companies surpassed $19 billion in 2001. More than half (55%) of this amount was spent on the free samples which pharmaceutical "detailmen" offer to doctors.[8] One study found that drug samples provided to doctors does influence subsequent prescribing behavior, despite prior preferences (Chew et al., 2000). Gifts to physicians, ranging from pens and notepads to dinners at fancy restaurants, account for another sizeable portion of this expenditure ($5 billion in 2000). Not surprisingly, various studies have demonstrated a positive association between pharmaceutical gifts and physician prescribing behavior as well as negative patient perceptions of doctors who accept drug firm contributions (Steinman, 2000).

Other research has found that patients with high expectations for a prescription are more likely to receive one from a doctor (Steinke et al., 1999). Much of this behavior can likely be explained by the $2.7 billion of total advertising spending in 2001 directed towards direct-to-consumer (DTC) promotional campaigns designed to empower the patient. Recent research (Zachry et al., 2002) suggests that the number of prescriptions written for antihyperlipidemics between 1992 and 1997 was positively correlated to advertising expenditure for these drugs. Moreover, the same study demonstrates that prescriptions of Zocor (simvastatin) are significantly associated with DTC promotion. Results of an ongoing Federal Drug Administration (FDA) study on DTC advertising suggest that approximately 60 percent of patients ask for a particular brand name drug and that 57 percent of those patients receive a prescription for that drug during a typical office visit (Aikin, 2003). However, the same FDA study also suggests that, when done correctly, DTC advertising can serve positive public health consequences by increasing consumer awareness of diseases and expediting discussions with physicians that may result in treatment for previously undiagnosed conditions.

Wosinska (2001) found that DTC advertising for statins raises the likelihood of choosing one statin over another only for drugs that have preferred formulary status within a managed care organization. She also concludes that DTC spending affects the choice of a statin much less than detailing promotion to doctors. However, her research is limited by data that covers only one West Coast PPOs (Preferred Provider Organization) drug claims and aggregate US estimates of statin advertising expenditures.

Additional actors who contact doctors include representatives of managed care organizations and pharmacy benefit managers. These officials inform physicians of their groups' preferred pharmaceutical agents and the reasons for the preference. Many of these organizations rely on incentive-based systems to control doctors' prescribing behavior, and have created new opportunities to monitor the principal–agent relationship existing between doctor and patient (Dranove and White, 1987). Despite the fact that drug costs make up less than 10 percent of total health plan expenses, insurers activities to influence prescribing behavior demonstrates a tendency towards a high level of responsiveness to drug prices, particularly when agents compete with generic or therapeutic substitutes. Moreover, with the rapid increase of pharmaceutical prices and utilization in recent years, these groups have a strong impetus to play a growing role in physicians' prescribing behavior.

The agency relationship that arises between doctor and patient in the prescribing decision is an imperfect one. Actors outside of, but with interest in, the partnership help to inform both parties. Pharmaceutical company agents act in the interest of the firms to promote their products while also educating physicians and consumers on the benefits and costs of particular drugs. Insurance representatives contribute to the prescribing decision by alerting doctors of different benefit schemes that their patients may fall under and encouraging physicians to utilize preferred alternatives. The growing use of incentives by managed care insurers may make it more difficult for physicians to have a strong knowledge of their patients' pharmacy benefit packages. However, although forces from the drug and insurance industry can appear to counter one another, the prevailing evidence highly suggests that prescribers are becoming better informed as to patients' options both clinically and financially.

The structure of managed insurance drug benefits

The advancement of pharmaceutical technology in the last half century has been phenomenal. Individuals can lead longer and healthier lives while drugs relieve them of pain, control their bodies' glucose or cholesterol levels, and delay the onset of degenerative disease. Not surprisingly, a growing number of people are demanding such treatments, among others, to prolong their lives as well as improve their quality of life. As a result, one of the services that managed care and other health insurers have increasingly provided to their enrollees is a prescription drug benefit. From 1990 to 2000, payments for drugs at retail pharmacies by third parties rose from 26 percent to over 70 percent of all payments for drugs, according to data compiled by IMS Health.

However, great medical breakthroughs are usually accompanied by a large price tag. In fact, Lu and Comanor (1998) find that the most important factor affecting the price of new pharmaceuticals is the extent of the therapeutic advance. As the use and cost of drugs have escalated, insurers have devised a number of strategies to minimize the impact of potentially large drug bills, including generic and therapeutic substitution, tiered copayment structures, cost-sharing provisions, drug formularies, maximum allowable cost programs, drug utilization review, prior authorization, step-care protocols, disease management programs, academic detailing, and capitation.

Generic and therapeutic drug substitution programs require the use of less expensive products when available. When a generic substitution program is in place, consumers receive a bioequivalent version of the brand name while providers pay a lower cost. Generic substitution has become increasingly popular in the United States. A 2001 study found that nearly 40 percent of all prescriptions dispensed by retail pharmacies were for generic drugs (Takeda-Lilly, 2001). More recent data from IMS Health suggest that almost half of all retail prescriptions are for generics, suggesting an upward trend in generic drug utilization and prescription.

Therapeutic interchange occurs when different pharmaceutical formulations in the same therapeutic drug class, such as one statin for another in the class of antihyperlipidemics, are substituted for each other. One example of a therapeutic interchange program for statins where cost-effectiveness plays a predominant role can be found in Grace *et al.* (2002). This study describes a Department of Defense program which switched existing statin users to preferred agents—cervistatin (Baycol) and simvastatin (Zocor)—within a specified time period. In the first year, this therapeutic interchange program saved $115 per patient in a population of more than 1,300 studied. The program subsequently removed Baycol from its preferred list when its serious adverse side effects were discovered.

Another option employed by health plans to elicit consumers to use preferred drugs is the tiered copayment structure. In this system, generic drugs are available to the enrollee at a negligible price, usually zero to ten dollars, but brand name or non-preferred drugs have a larger copayment. Most health plans employ two or three tiers, but increasingly insurers are moving to a four-tier approach (Perlstein, 2001). Oftentimes, the copayment faced by the consumer reflects to some extent the cost to the insurer, though this relationship is tenuous. Thus, a tiered copayment system, as a market-based approach, embodies the need for health plans to alert patients of the true cost of prescription drugs while allowing choice to patients (Kessler, 1999). In lieu of a fixed-dollar copayment, insurers may instead require enrollees to pay for a fixed percentage of a prescription's cost. This is an additional, and increasingly popular (Mays *et al.*, 2001) way in which health plans inform consumers of prescription drugs' true costs.

Another method used to educate consumers of a drug's cost is for an insurer not to reimburse for its use. This is accomplished by establishing a list of covered or reimbursable drugs, normally referred to as a formulary. This roster of drugs will differ from one health plan to another and range in generosity from "open" (all drugs covered) to "closed" (only selected drugs reimbursed). Formulary decisions are often made by a committee of physicians, pharmacists, and administrators both internal and external to a health plan. Inclusion in a formulary is based on a variety of factors such as therapeutic value, safety, and cost-effectiveness. Only drugs listed in the formulary are available for reimbursement after the patient fulfills the copayment. Increasingly, formulary committees are relying on pharmaco-economic data and assessments of pharmacy benefit managers, information from drug manufacturers, consensus statements from experts, opinions of other managed care organizations, and peer-reviewed medical literature to make informed decisions on which products to cover (Kessler, 1999; Lyles *et al.*, 1997). Active formulary management within the statins class in one health plan (Petitta *et al.*, 1997) decreased annual drug costs by $345,000 (16%) and increased life-years saved by 154 years (7.4%) when the managed care plan switched some patients to Zocor. However, most plans have begun to abandon closed formularies due to lack of physician compliance, consumer dissatisfaction, and regulatory restrictions (Mays *et al.*, 2001).

Costs are not the only factor that influence the choice of an insurer to cover a particular drug. A patient's physician may also have the option to prescribe non-preferred drugs to specific patients with an extraordinary condition or need. This usually requires the doctor to receive prior authorization before the consumer can be reimbursed for the pharmaceutical product. Through this route, the patient can access drugs off the formulary but it requires additional, and sometimes burdensome, effort on the part of the physician.

Other programs sponsored by health plans to monitor and manage prescription drug costs are primarily aimed at doctors and pharmacists. Maximum allowable cost programs mandate that pharmacists receive a specified reimbursement per drug, regardless of the cost to them. When faced with this option, many pharmacists would rather dispense a generic over a brand name since the former is much less costly to have in stock and carries a larger gross retail profit margin (Steiner, 1993). Moreover, pharmacists will often receive a higher dispensing fee for a generic equivalent of a brand name drug. In the past, some health plans have also contracted with specific pharmacies or chains to provide drugs exclusively to enrollees (Jones, 1996).

Drug utilization reviews are undertaken to evaluate drug use by health plan enrollees. Insurers use the information accumulated by these studies to monitor physicians' prescribing behavior in an effort to ensure that the lowest cost and highest quality pharmaceutical products are made available to patients. The review may also be able to identify situations where prescriptions were deemed to be unnecessary or inappropriate.

While the drug utilization review is retrospective in nature, step-care protocols are designed to be proactive. These programs are designed to treat chronic clinical conditions in a systematic fashion. Stepped protocols that focus on particular diseases are known as disease management programs. Oftentimes, these regimens call for initiation of treatment with basic, low-cost care and progress to more complicated and expensive therapies. For example, patients with low to moderate risk for CHD may be started on a diet and exercise routine. If symptoms were to persist or new risk factors to develop, primary prevention of cardiac events might be initiated with low-dose statin therapy. McAlister and colleagues (2001) find compelling evidence that disease management programs for CHD reduce hospital admissions and enhance the quality of life of patients with CHD.

An additional prospective strategy employed by insurers, and to an even greater extent by drug firms, is academic detailing. This normally entails a health professional meeting with an individual or group of physicians to discuss pharmaceutical options open to health plan enrollees. The insurance representative is usually a specially-trained pharmacist with clinical and financial knowledge of the products preferred by the health plan. Meetings occur at the doctor's convenience in her office or another meeting place if there is a larger group. Another strategy used to monitor physicians' prescribing behavior with a similar name, counterdetailing, primarily targets doctors who prescribe high-cost options through reminders placed in charts and letters sent to inform them of the prescription of non-preferred agents (Mays *et al.*, 2001). Soumerai and Avorn (1986) conclude that these types of academic detailing can be a highly cost-effective method for improving drug therapy decisions and reduce prescription drug expenditures significantly for a health care organization.

Insurers have also attempted to influence the behavior of individual doctors and physician groups by imposing capitation schemes. These programs attempt to distribute the risks inherent in drug usage among payers and providers while providing these organizations with incentives to control drug costs (Levy, 1999). Fixed price schemes call for payers to reimburse providers for all drug usage on a per person, per month, or per prescription basis. On the other hand, a percentage-based setup requires that payers and providers negotiate reimbursement limits on the basis of some percentage of health insurance premiums. The capitation schemes also provide doctors an additional glimpse at the true cost of some pharmaceutical products which they prescribe.

Interestingly, the actual cost of prescription drugs to insurers is often unknown to everyone but a privileged handful of people. Listed drug prices are, in essence, simply reference prices and the true price at any given time will depend on the identities of the buyers and sellers. Normally, list prices (average wholesale prices) of brand name drugs are higher than those of their generic equivalents. As a result, it may be reasonable to believe that an insurer would always encourage its enrollees to use lower-priced generics when available. However, there is little or no evidence to demonstrate that the *actual* prices paid for brand name drugs by insurers are significantly higher than generic prices. Moreover, there is little literature concerning the reality that wholesale prices are meaningless since drug firms and their customers enter into numerous dealings surrounding the price and quantity of drugs sold (United States Department of Health and Human Services, 2000). Furthermore, contracts between drug firms and insurers often involve complex schemes designed to maximize market exposure of the drug firm's product line by use of bundling tactics. These negotiations with drug firms allow health plans to lower their overall drug bill and still provide high quality products to their enrollees.

Patient selection into plans with favorable drug coverage

With the multitude of drug management options available at many different health plans, one may suspect that a patient could choose to enroll in a plan with benefits favorable to him. For example, it is possible that an insured patient using a statin to manage high cholesterol may choose a health plan where his drug copayment would be lower. As a result, it is possible that a person's copayment may not be exogenous but endogenous to the patient. Even in the sample of patients available to this study, any given patient may have an incentive to examine the choice of plans offered by his employer and choose that plan with the most beneficial drug benefit structure.

While, in general, the incentive to move from one insurance plan to another because of differential cost-sharing requirements may exist, to believe that a consumer would do so solely, or mostly, on the basis of drug coverage is unreasonable. Health insurers normally reimburse for a large variety of services within which prescription drugs make up a small, albeit increasing, subset. Moreover, transaction costs involved with switching plans may be large for some people. For example, many patients may be loathe to leave one insurer for another if they cannot continue to visit a preferred primary care physician. It is also unclear as to whether or not enrollees are completely aware of all the drug benefit options available to them (Momani *et al.*, 2000).

At the same time, the data employed to investigate the economic questions of interest do not exhibit signs of this type of selection bias. Within the data, there is only a handful of patients who enroll in multiple health plans and these persons are not included in multivariate analyses. Also, the basic benefit structure of many of the plans represented in the sample are relatively similar, leaving persons in the study group little incentive to switch.

An additional argument against potential bias would be whether or not it is reasonable to believe that selection into and out of plans would occur due to treatment with one particular class of drugs. Given that the drugs in the class of interest are relatively similar and the possibility that patients are likely to be treated with multiple drugs for different conditions, it seems unlikely that a patient will switch plans due only to the out-of-pocket costs of one product.[9] As a result, it is reasonable to presume that drug benefit structures are exogenous to the consumer choice problem.

6 The economics of prescription drug demand

Prescription drug demand, like many empirically important economic decisions, involves a choice between discrete alternatives. Initially, the decision whether or not to begin a regimen of pharmaceutical treatment is a binary one. The choices are to treat a patient's condition with prescription drugs or monitor it without them. While the decision to prescribe a drug is normally made by a physician, the agency relationship that exists between doctor and patient can be an imperfect one (as discussed in Chapter 5). Informational asymmetries that exist between the principal and agent can have ramifications on not only a doctor's choice of treatment but also a patient's health. When the decision to initiate pharmaceutical care is affirmative, the physician and patient will often encounter a complex set of alternatives with multiple drugs from which to choose in a therapeutic class. Moreover, the choice between products, like *any* economic choice, involves the evaluation of available options in terms of cost or price.

For individuals with insurance, the price of prescription drugs is often expressed as a copayment or a coinsurance rate. Insurers often set copayment schedules to influence patient purchasing behavior when there are multiple agents in any one therapeutic class. Although they are set by distinct mechanisms, copayments are no different from actual market prices in consumers' budget sets.

Market prices for goods are set by firms who maximize profits, while copayments are fixed by insurers seeking to influence patient behavior and may be indirectly determined by the cost of the drug to the insurer. But, the relationship between copayments and the price paid by an insurer to the drug manufacturer is often a tenuous one. There is no direct evidence to suggest that these two distinct prices are linked causally and that insurers behave in this manner to maximize wealth in the prescription drug purchasing decision.

Although not set by a traditional market mechanism, copayments—like prices for any other market good—are simply the out of pocket costs paid by patients. When faced with differing costs for substitute goods, consumers will assess the utility to be gained from purchasing one good over another (whether or not the capability of buying a fixed quantity of both goods exists) and choose the good (or combination of goods) that maximizes utility. The choice of one prescription drug within a set of alternatives by consumers is made in much the same way as the choice of any other market good except that the choice of a pharmaceutical is always a discrete one made by an agent (the doctor). As a result, particularly when informational asymmetries are minimized,[10] one should not expect demand behavior to differ because consumers face a copayment fixed by an insurer rather than a price determined by a profit-maximizing firm.

To treat an illness or disease state such as CHD or hyperlipidemia, patients normally utilize only one drug option from a distinct therapeutic group *at any given time*. While it is possible that patients take more than one drug in any one class over the course of time, it is not likely for medical reasons that more than one product in that class is chosen at *any one point in time*. As a result, analysis of this type of discrete choice behavior using conventional marginalist consumer theory is "quite awkward" (McFadden, 1981: p. 199).

To illustrate why this is the case, consider the choice of using one statin among existing options. Assume that the number of patients is fixed in order to concentrate on the proportion of persons using one of the drugs. An empirical approach to forecasting the impact of differential copayments on statin usage within the class would be to fit a demand function to aggregate data on prescription drug usage. Thus, the dependent variable in an econometric specification would be the percent of patients using a particular statin in the set of alternatives. This aggregation could be done for each drug and health plan in the sample. Since this decision variable is continuous, conventional marginalist analysis would apply. Market demand is then the aggregate of a population of identical representative consumers. While this model may appear appropriate, "it provides a poor description of individual behavior" (McFadden, 1981). The effect of different copayments is felt primarily on the extensive margin of consumers, where some individuals choose one drug or another; information as to how consumers choose drugs in the face of differential copayments is lost in the aggregation. Or, in other words, traditional consumer theory places structural restrictions on mean behavior, but the distribution of responses about the mean is not tied to the theory (McFadden, 2001).

To solve this problem, tastes must be explicitly allowed to vary in a population of consumers. For instance, consider a group of patients with specific utility functions who are distributed according to some probability distribution. Then, the proportion of persons choosing Lipitor, for example, over other statins can be expressed as the probability that an individual drawn at random will have characteristics and face prices (copayments) such that the utility derived from Lipitor exceeds that received from other statins. The parameters of the underlying probability distribution of price and characteristic coefficients are then interpreted as parameters of a demand function for the population of statin users. In this way, the discrete choice problem can be transformed into a model that allows for predictions at the market level.

Probabilistic consumer theory

This type of analysis is best approached by developing a theory of probabilistic consumer choice and applying a random utility model to agents who maximize over a given set of pharmaceutical alternatives. The development of this population demand behavior parallels exactly the conventional treatment of the individual consumer. Distributions of observed demands and preferences in the discrete choice setting replace a single demand system and preference ordering in the traditional setting where consumption of goods is measured over a continuum. This section will describe the components needed to study choice behavior in a probabilistic context.

A study of choice behavior is described by three major elements. First, the objects of choice and sets of alternatives available to decision-makers, along with the objects' attributes must be defined. In this study, the alternatives are the drugs in the statins class and there is one choice set—all five statins.[11] A model of consumer choice must also include the observed characteristics of decisionmakers. Relevant patient characteristics include age, gender, health status, type of health insurance, and US region of residence. Here, consumers (patients) are assumed to be the decision-makers and their agency relationship with prescribing physicians is assumed to be a perfect one. However, other studies have viewed the problem from the perspective of the doctor (see Hellerstein, 1998), and this approach is a potential extension of this work discussed in Chapter 12.

Moreover, the empirical results of this study can be interpreted as a test of this proposition. If physicians are not acting in the best financial interest of patients, then multivariate results should suggest that the choice of a statin is not influenced by differences in relative copayments since the prescription was presumably filled by doctor reference. However, if relative copayments are associated with the choice of a statin, then this may provide some evidence that doctors are acting as informed agents.[12]

Lastly, it is necessary to explicitly state the model of individual choice and behavior and the distribution of behavior patterns in the population. Individual behavior is normally defined by a rule which maps decisionmakers' characteristics and possible alternatives into a chosen member of the alternative set. A *model* of behavior is a set of rules distributed throughout the population by a specified probability measure. Here, demand behavior for statins is modeled among decisionmakers in a population with diverse demand functions that result from random variations in a specific utility function.

These elements of choice behavior can be formally defined as a vector (K, Z, ξ, B, S, P) where K is the set of alternatives (drugs in the statins class), Z is the universe of vectors of measured attributes of the alternatives (copayments and other attributes that may be measured[13]), and $\xi : K \rightarrow Z$ is a mapping specifying the observed attributes of alternatives. A family of finite, nonempty choice sets from K is represented by B, S is the universe of vectors of measured characteristics of individuals, and $P : K \times \xi \times S \rightarrow [0,1]$ is a choice probability for any given alternative in a choice set $\mathbf{B} \in B$.

The index set is the set of drugs available to consumers and is assumed to be external to the actual choice process. The choice probability $P(k | \mathbf{B}, \mathbf{s})$ specifies the probability of choosing any option $k \in K$, given that a selection must be made from a choice set $\mathbf{B} \in B$ and the decisionmaker has characteristics $\mathbf{s} \in S$. Note that B is any family of finite subsets of the five drug alternatives, including all five drugs, while **B** is one choice set contained in the family of sets *B*. Choice probabilities are assumed to be non-negative, sum to one over all options in the choice set, and to depend only on the measured attributes of alternatives and individual characteristics[14] (McFadden, 1981).

The probability choice system serves as the foundation on which a model of utility maximization is built in a discrete choice setting. The next section discusses the random utility maximization hypothesis (RUM) and its implications for the problem as outlined by McFadden (1981).

The random utility maximization hypothesis

RUM postulates that the distribution of demands in a population is the result of individual preference maximization, and is defined by a vector (K, Z, ξ, S, μ) where (K, Z, ξ, S) are defined as before, and μ is a probability measure depending on $s \in S$ on the space of utility functions on K. Most importantly, the probability μ represents the distribution of tastes in the population of individuals with characteristics $s \in S$, so that persons' tastes vary explicitly.

For $B = \{k_1, \ldots, k_m\} \in B$, μ^B is a probability measure that represents the manner in which the demand for statins is distributed throughout the population among decisionmakers when faced with the choice set **B**. In other words, μ specifies individual variation that exists between the choice of one statin over another. In the traditional model, this type of variation would be disregarded as optimization error and unexplained variation in demand. The probability measure, μ, is assumed to depend only on the measured attributes of alternatives, to not allow for "ties" between options, and to assure that the choice of an alternative in the family of sets **B** is determined by utility maximization.[15]

When preferences satisfy these assumptions they are said to be RUM-consistent. As explained later, the random utility hypothesis allows for aggregation to the population demand function among many individual demanders. The next section discusses how choices are made on the individual level and aggregated to the population level.

Aggregation of preferences

Individual preference maximization is crucial to the discrete choice problem, but the objective is to aggregate individual decision-making behavior throughout the population to represent a population demand function, where the use of one alternative or another is represented by choice probabilities. When individual preferences have sufficient structure to aggregate to a social (indirect) utility function yielding an aggregate demand function, this structure can be considered an analogue of the simple sufficient (integrability) conditions of individual utility theory.[16] In this case, the traditional representative consumer with fractional consumption rates can be assigned the social utility function, justifying this approach as an analytic shortcut consistent with some underlying population of utility maximizers who make discrete choices (McFadden, 1981). Without this structure on preferences, underlying choice probabilities for options in the choice set will not be an accurate representation of demand and it would not be possible to have predictive models of aggregate market level behavior.

Let an individual's total consumption be represented by a vector **x** of divisible commodities and the choice of a discrete alternative k (a drug in the statins class) which has a vector of measured attributes **w**. The individual has a utility function $\tilde{U} : \tilde{X} \times W \times K \to [0,1]$, where $\tilde{X} \times W$ is the space of pairs of vectors (**x**, **w**). So, an individual's utility is dependent on drug characteristics **w** and the set of divisible goods **x**. The utility function is assumed to be continuous, twice continuously differentiable, and strictly differentially quasi-concave for each $\mathbf{w} \in W$ and $k \in K$ (McFadden, 1981).[17]

Suppose the individual has income y and faces a vector of prices $\mathbf{h} > 0$ for divisible commodities and a cost q associated with the discrete alternative; for insured individuals, q is the copayment for the prescription drug and, like the alternative set, is exogenous to decisionmakers. For a specified discrete alternative k with measured attributes **w**, the individual chooses **x** to maximize utility subject to the budget constraint $\mathbf{h} \cdot \mathbf{x} + q = y$. The result is a conditional indirect utility function $V(y - q, \mathbf{h}, \mathbf{w}, k; \tilde{U})$ defined for $y - q > 0$, $\mathbf{h} > 0$, $\mathbf{w} \in W$, $k \in K$ and $\tilde{U}$ satisfying

$$V(y - q, \mathbf{h}, \mathbf{w}, k; \tilde{U}) = \max_{\mathbf{x}} \{ \tilde{U}(\mathbf{x}, \mathbf{w}, k) | \mathbf{h} \cdot \mathbf{x} \le y - q \}. \tag{6.1}$$

The decisionmaker evaluates the value of (6.1) for each vector of attributes **w** set of divisible goods **x**, and alternative k for a given choice set and chooses the k thoption that maximizes total conditional indirect utility. Specifically, (6.1) reports the maximum utility achievable at given prices and income for an individual consumer choosing alternative k. This function in (6.1) is assumed to be continuous, twice continuously differentiable and homogeneous of degree zero in $(y - q, \mathbf{h})$, strictly differentiably quasi-convex in **h**, and to satisfy Roy's Identity.[18]

When $\mathbf{h} > 0$ and $y - q > 0$ are confined to a compact set, there exists a monotone transformation of $\tilde{U}$ which implies the corresponding transformation of V is convex in **h**. Thus, for most applications, V can be assumed without further loss of generality to be convex in **h** (McFadden, 1981). This convexity and the continuity of the indirect utility function allows the individual decision process to be aggregated to the population level.

Prior to demonstrating that preferences can be aggregated, a representation of any individual's demand function is needed. Suppose the consumer faces a finite set of discrete alternatives $\mathbf{B} \in B$. A vector of measured attributes, $z_i = (q_i, \mathbf{h}, \mathbf{w}_i) = \xi(k)$, consistent with earlier terminology is associated with alternative $k \in \mathbf{B}$, and income y is a component of the vector **S** of consumer characteristics. The unconditional indirect utility function of the consumer is then

$$V^*(y - \mathbf{q_B}, \mathbf{h}, \mathbf{w_B}, \mathbf{B}; \tilde{U}) = \max_{k \in B} V(y - q_k, \mathbf{h}, \mathbf{w}_k, k; \tilde{U}),$$

where $y - \mathbf{q_B}$ denotes a vector with component $y - q_j$, and $\mathbf{w_B}$ a vector with component w_j, for each $j \in \mathbf{B}$. This unconditional indirect utility function V^* and the assumptions made about it allow for the depiction of consumer utility for discrete goods via a typical set of indifference curves. For almost all $y - \mathbf{q_B}$, *consumer demand* for the discrete alternatives is given by,

$$\delta_j = D(j \mid \mathbf{B}, \mathbf{s}; \tilde{U}) \equiv \frac{\partial V^* / \partial q_j}{\partial V^* / \partial y}$$

$$\equiv 1 \quad \text{if } j \in \mathbf{B} \text{ and } v_j \geq v_l \text{ for } l \in \mathbf{B}$$

$$0 \quad \text{otherwise,}$$

where $v_l = V(y - q_l, \mathbf{h}, \mathbf{w}_l, l; \tilde{U})$. Thus, an individual decision-maker chooses alternative j in set $\mathbf{B} \in B$ given attributes $\mathbf{s}$ when the unconditional indirect utility derived from that alternative is larger than utility derived from any other option.

Aggregation to the population choice probabilities follows from the individual choice decision and occurs in the following manner (McFadden, 1981):

$$P(k \mid \mathbf{B}, \mathbf{s}) = E_{U|s} D(k \mid \mathbf{B}, \mathbf{s}; \tilde{U})$$

$$= \int D(k \mid \mathbf{B}, \mathbf{s}; \tilde{U}) \mu(d\tilde{U}, \mathbf{s})$$

$$= \mu(\{\tilde{U} \in R^K \mid V(y - q_k, \mathbf{h}, \mathbf{w}_j, k; \tilde{U}) \geq V(y - q_j, \mathbf{h}, \mathbf{w}_j, j; \tilde{U})$$

$$\text{for } j \in \mathbf{B}\}, \mathbf{s}).$$

First, note that population choice probabilities for alternatives in the choice set are equivalent to the expected value of consumer demands over all individuals in the population. However, the expected value of these demands are, by design, a function of the probability measure μ that determines taste variation among consumers. So, the expected value of consumer demands is dependent on the assumption that individual choices are made via utility maximization as specified by μ and the indirect utility function. Because of the continuity of individual indirect utility functions and, consequently, consumer demands, individual choices are aggregated to represent population choice probabilities. In this way, the parameters of the underlying probability distribution of price and characteristic coefficients are interpreted as parameters of a demand function for the population of consumers.

McFadden (1981) outlines sufficient conditions on preferences such that a social utility function can be defined with fractional consumption rates for the discrete alternatives, yielding the earlier expression. This is done by demonstrating that a social utility function exists if the choice probabilities satisfy Roy's identity. When this conclusion holds, the demand distribution can be interpreted as if it were generated by a population where each (representative) consumer has fractional consumption rates for the discrete alternatives. Thus, the aggregation of choices of many individual consumers with varying tastes allow for an interpretation on the market level that mirrors the classical marginalist perspective. The practical question of how to construct a parametric probabilistic choice system suitable for econometric and policy analysis is handled in Chapter 7.

7 Econometric specification of prescription drug choice

The economic question of interest lends itself well to estimation with the conditional multinomial logit (MNL) model, developed by McFadden (1973), since the choice of a prescription drug in a class with multiple alternatives is a discrete one. Utility derived by the ith patient in the jth plan from choosing the kth drug, U_{ijk}, is latent and only the choice is observed. If Y_{ijk} represents the choice of the *kth* alternative we have

$$Y_{ijk} = 1 \quad \text{if } U_{ijk} = \text{Max } (U_{ij1}, U_{ij2},...,U_{ijk})$$
$$Y_{ijk} = 0 \quad \text{otherwise}$$

The MNL estimates the impact of exogenous variables on the probabilities[19] of using different drug alternatives. If X represents the set of measured attributes of agents with an individual drawn at random from the sample population having some attribute vector x_{ij} with m elements, then the conditional probability that the ith consumer in the jth plan chooses the kth drug can be written as

$$P_{ijk} = \text{Pr}(U_{ijk} > U_{ijg} \ \forall g \in Y, g \neq k | x_{ij})$$

where Y represents the universe of drugs from which the consumer may choose a particular alternative.

Consistent with the traditional application of MNL regression, utility is modeled within a random utility framework which can be expressed in the form

$$U_{ijk} = v(x_{ij}) + w(x_{kj}) + \varepsilon_{ijk}$$

where x_{ij} is a vector of attributes for the ith patient in the jth plan, x_{kj} is a vector of kth drug characteristics in plan j, and ε_{ijk} is a residual that captures unobserved variations in consumer tastes, health plan, and drug attributes as well as errors in individual optimization behavior (Maddala, 1983). To estimate the MNL, the residuals are assumed to be independently and identically distributed as specified by the type I extreme-value distribution where the cumulative distribution function is $F(\varepsilon_{ijk} < \varepsilon) = \exp(-e^{-\varepsilon})$.

Given this distributional assumption, the probability of choosing the kth drug can be expressed as

$$P_{ijk} = \frac{\exp(\beta'_{k1}x_{ij} + \beta'_{k2}x_{kj})}{\sum_{k=1}^{k} \exp(\beta'_{k1}x_{ij} + \beta'_{k2}x_{kj})}, \quad \text{for } k = 1, \dots, K$$

where β'_{k1} is the vector of coefficients for the kth drug corresponding to the elements of x_{ij} and β'_{k2} is the vector of coefficients for the kth drug corresponding to the elements of x_{kj}.

To identify the model, one set of the coefficient vectors for one drug option must be set to zero. Letting this happen arbitrarily for the lth drug, we have

$$P_{ijl} = \frac{1}{1 + \sum_{k \neq 1} \exp(\beta'_{k1}x_{ij} + \beta'_{k2}x_{kj})}.$$

Parameter estimates for each exogenous variable for each option can be shown to correspond to changes in the log odds ratio (of the kth drug to the lth drug) by noting that

$$\frac{P_{ijk}}{P_{ijl}} = \exp(\beta'_{k1}x_{ij} + \beta'_{k2}x_{kj})$$

and

$$\ln\left(\frac{P_{ijk}}{P_{ijl}}\right) = \beta'_{k1}x_{ij} + \beta'_{k2}x_{kj}. \tag{7.1}$$

A well-known concern with using the MNL model is that it can produce misleading inferences when a subset of the alternatives in question are close substitutes. This arises because the MNL specification imposes the restriction that the ratio of the probabilities of choosing one alternative over a second depend only on the characteristics of those two options. The attributes of other alternatives in the choice set have no influence on the odds ratio between the two choices. This property is commonly referred to as the independence from irrelevant alternatives (IIA) because the ratio is independent from other options or "irrelevant" alternatives (Horowitz and Savin, 2001; Train, 1986).[20]

McFadden's classic example of commuting to work by car or bus is a simple illustration of the problem introduced by the IIA property. Suppose that one's initial mode of transportation was either an automobile or blue bus. Assume that half of the population prefers automobiles and the other half commute to work by the blue bus. This implies that the odds of taking the blue bus over driving are 1 to 1. Now, suppose another company introduces a red bus which is exactly the same as the blue one except for color. It would then be reasonable to suspect that bus commuters simply split their time evenly between the blue and red buses while the automobile drivers continue to commute in the same fashion.

However, when IIA holds the odds of taking the blue bus to driving would still be 1 to 1 while the odds of taking one bus option to the other is also 1 to 1. Since the probabilities of the three options must sum to 1, IIA implies that the probabilities of driving, taking the red bus, or taking the blue bus must all equal one-third. Thus, the MNL provides the counterintuitive prediction that some of the drivers will switch to commuting by bus even though the new option is no different from the original in terms of mode of transportation.

For the purposes of this study, the IIA property should not pose a problem in estimation of choice probabilities for statins. Although the statins are similar to one another by nature, they are differentiated in their effectiveness at reducing low density lipoprotein (LDL) cholesterol. Moreover, it is not clear if the IIA property poses the same problem when all alternatives of a choice set are relatively close substitutes for one another. Nonetheless, estimation of the problem with a simulated multinomial probit model or semiparametric methods (as discussed in Horowitz and Savin, 2001) are options to be explored in future work. A test of the IIA property is presented in Chapter 11.

Equation (7.1) can be estimated easily by maximum likelihood techniques. First, for simplicity, classify the N individuals regardless of their health plan affiliation and index them by n. Using consistent notation, define

$$Y_{nk} = \begin{array}{ll} 1 & \text{if the } n\text{th individual chooses option } k \\ 0 & \text{otherwise} \end{array}$$

Then the likelihood function for the MNL can be expressed as

$$L = \prod_{n=1}^{N}\prod_{k\in Y}(P_{nk})^{Y_{nk}}.$$

And by substituting with (7.1) and taking logarithms,

$$L' = \sum_{n=1}^{N}\sum_{k\in Y}Y_{nk}\left(\beta_k' x_n - \ln\sum_{k\in Y}\exp(\beta_k' x_n)\right)$$

where x_n represents the vector of drug and patient attributes.

Maximization of the likelihood function yields the coefficient estimates of the MNL which represent the marginal impact of selected regressors on the log of the odds ratio for choice k relative to a reference option. However, the economic question of interest is the impact of the regressors on the probability of choosing one drug over another. To estimate this marginal impact, Crawford *et al.* (1998) have demonstrated that for any regressor (element of x_{ij})

$$\frac{\partial \hat{P}_k}{\partial x_{ijm}} = \hat{P}_k\left[\hat{\beta}_{km} - \sum_{l=1}^{K}\hat{P}_l\hat{\beta}_{lm}\right] \qquad (7.2)$$

Table 7.1 Initial statin usage distribution (example)

Statin	Percent of population
Lescol	10
Lipitor	35
Mevacor	10
Pravachol	20
Zocor	25

Table 7.2 Marginal effect of Lipitor to Pravachol relative copayment (example)

Statin	Marginal effect[a]
Lescol	0.05
Lipitor	−0.50
Mevacor	0.06
Pravachol	0.14
Zocor	0.25

a Note that the marginal effects add up to zero as required.

where $\hat{P}_k$ is the estimated probability of choosing option k, x_{ij} is the vector of exogenous variables and $\hat{\beta}_k$ is the vector of coefficients for the kth drug.[21] This is the marginal effect of the mth exogenous variable on the probability of choosing the kth drug. Note that (7.2) is a function of the estimated coefficient for the mth variable and the kth drug choice, $\hat{\beta}_{km}$, and the predicted probability of choosing the kth option, $\hat{P}_k$. Intuitively, (7.2) represents the deviation of the estimated log odds ratio coefficient for option k and explanatory variable m ($\hat{\beta}_{km}$) from a weighted sum of all of the statin choice coefficients ($\sum_{l=1}^{k} \hat{P}_l \hat{\beta}_{lm}$). This, in turn, is weighted by the estimated probability of choosing option k. The nature of probabilities insures that at least one of the marginal effects will be negative and at least one will be positive (Crawford *et al.*, 1998). So, if one drug alternative (k) is improved so that its probability of being chosen rises, then the other probability (or probabilities) must be drawn from other drug options (Train, 1986). Moreover, the change in probability of any alternative is proportional to the value of the choice probability prior to the change (Train, 1986).

Intuitively, marginal effects calculated by the MNL impact the probability distribution of drug usage among alternatives available in the choice set. Suppose the initial distribution of use among the five statins is as in Table 7.1. Moreover, let the marginal effects of a change in the relative copayment of Lipitor to Pravachol be estimated as in Table 7.2.

Table 7.3 New statin usage distribution (example)

Statin	Percent of population
Lescol	10.5
Lipitor	30
Mevacor	10.6
Pravachol	21.4
Zocor	27.5

That is, the figures in Table 7.2 represent the assumed estimated marginal impacts of a change in the relative copayment of Lipitor to Pravachol on the probability of using the statin in the left-hand column.

For example, if the relative copayment of Lipitor to Pravachol changes by 10 percent, then the probability distribution of statin usage changes in the following manner, if the values of all other variables are held constant.

As an exercise, consider the case of Zocor. The marginal impact of a 1 percent change in the relative copayment of Lipitor to Pravachol on the choice of Zocor is 0.25. As illustrated in Tables 7.1 and 7.3, when the relative copayment of Lipitor to Pravachol increases by 10 percent, the percent of the population using Zocor increases by 2.5 percent from 25 to 27.5 percent. Thus, the marginal effects calculated in the MNL regression represent the manner in which the probabilities of usage change for particular explanatory variables, holding other characteristics constant.

8   Data

This study's primary data source is medical and pharmacy claims from the 1997 and 1998 MarketScan Commercial Claims and Encounters (CCE) database. This database contains the healthcare experience and insurance plan enrollment information of several million privately insured individuals who work for one of several large US Fortune 500 companies.

For many of the patients in the database, medical claims (inpatient and outpatient) can be linked to outpatient pharmaceutical claims data. Individuals' healthcare is provided under a variety of fee-for-service (FFS), fully capitated,[22] and partially capitated health plans, including exclusive provider organizations, preferred provider organizations, point of service plans, indemnity plans, and health maintenance organizations (HMO). Given the question of interest, this research was based on the subset of patients with available drug data.

Final sample of patients

Patients selected for inclusion in the final sample were required to meet criteria on statin use, continuous health plan enrollment, and enrollment in a single health plan with available benefit plan design data during 1997 or 1998. A little more than 1.6 million patients have some enrollment evidence and drug data available for both 1997 and 1998 in the dataset. Table 8.1 details the selection steps used to include or exclude patients into the final sample. Patients in the final sample may or may not have evidence of coronary heart disease (CHD) as represented by International Classification of Diseases, 9th revision, Clinical Modification (ICD-9-CM) diagnosis codes corresponding to hyperlipidemia and coronary heart disease.[23] A total of 208,389 patients had evidence of at least one of the selected diagnosis codes in their medical claims during 1997 and 1998. Regression analyses include an indicator variable for secondary prevention of CHD and sensitivity analyses explore any differences that might exist when only patients with or without CHD are considered in the model.

When creating the final sample, patients were first required to have used at least one statin during 1997 or 1998. Each pharmacy claim includes the National Drug Code (NDC) number corresponding to the purchased drug; statin prescriptions were identified by NDC numbers (Appendix A). Of all the patients in the dataset,

Table 8.1 Sample selection from claims data

	No.	%
Patients with at least one statin prescription	86,414	
Patients enrolled in health plans with benefit plan design data available	69,600	80.5
Patients meeting continuous enrollment criteria	56,524	65.4
Patients with statin monotherapy	45,362	52.5
Final sample (due to missing data)	44,642	51.7

86,414 had at least one prescription for a statin. Note that this figure is much smaller than the 208,389 persons with evidence of CHD, suggesting that many patients, for whom statins are recommended, are not prescribed statins. This result is consistent with much research that has found undertreatment, mistreatment, and inequity in the treatment of CHD with statins (Feely *et al.*, 2000; Frolkis *et al.*, 1998; Hoerger *et al.*, 1998; Marcelino and Feingold, 1996; Pearson, 2000; Pearson *et al.*, 2000; Reid *et al.*, 2002). Moreover, this is also in line with utilization data reported for 1998–2000 (Managed Care Measures, 2001).

Patients were included in the final sample only if their health plan information was available in the MarketScan database. A total of 69,600 patients were eligible for inclusion in the final sample after this step.

Continuous enrollment criteria were contingent upon the first date of statin use in the dataset. Patients with a first statin prescription in 1997 were required to be continuously enrolled within one health plan during all of 1997, while patients with an initial prescription in 1998 were required to be continuously enrolled within a health plan during the 365-day period prior to that date. Requiring an entire year of continuous enrollment data ensures the complete availability of medical data used to identify health status information for each patient. In addition, to ensure that there would be at least two months of follow-up data available for analysis, patients were dropped from analysis if their first statin prescription date occurred after November 1, 1998. Throughout 1997 and 1998, 56,524 of the patients considered were continuously enrolled in one health plan.

The last steps restricted the final statin monotherapy sample to patients who used only one statin, eliminated those patients with missing data, and dropped patients younger than 18 years old. A total of 44,642 patients remained after implementation of these criteria. These patients make up the final analysis sample.

Concerns with retrospective data

The use of retrospective medical claims data to examine trends in health care utilization requires some caution. Although claims data contain patients' diagnoses, these diagnoses may not always be reliable or coded properly, adding some uncertainty to calculations where these codes are used. Also, there are few convincing methods of determining a patient's progression of CHD simply by analyzing claims data. In particular, these data do not contain laboratory results for cholesterol and other blood tests. One patient may receive a statin due to high levels of low density lipoprotein (LDL) cholesterol while another is treated for preventative reasons. Nonetheless, the level of detail in the medical claims database allows for an approximation of patient health status using existing indexes and identifying primary CHD diagnoses, ICD-9 codes for other comorbid conditions of CHD such as diabetes, and evidence of other lipid-lowering drugs used concurrently with a statin.

Benefit plan data are also limited on a drug-to-drug basis. These data only capture the purchase of one particular statin by a patient at a point in time. The prices this person would have paid for the other drugs, had he made a different choice, are not recorded. One must rely upon the accuracy of the average copayment across all other patients using these other drugs during a specified time period to approximate the cost of other statins to the patient of interest. This procedure is discussed in more detail later in the analytical variables section.

An additional concern with this type of data is selection bias. Medical claims databases are excellent recording tools for persons who use medical services but cannot capture decisions made by patients not using these services. For example, it is possible that persons who use statins differ in some fundamental manner from those who do not use them. While some of the bias may be eliminated by employing well-known econometric techniques, the unobserved differences may still be quite substantial and critical to the decision to use a statin.

Patients who do not use a statin to treat CHD may be more sensitive to their cost in comparison to other available therapies. More importantly, persons with evidence of CHD but no statin utilization may simply be in better health than other patients. Consequently, one might expect these persons to be more sensitive to relative copayment differences if their health status is not as dire as others. This implies that multivariate results may be slightly biased upwards and observations from the sample of choice may suggest more responsiveness to copayments than exists in the population of CHD patients. Moreover, persons in moderate health may be less likely to choose the more potent lipid-lowering statins and opt for treatment with a lower dosage of another alternative. This also suggests that the estimated probability of statin utilization based on health status characteristics may be skewed towards those agents that are used to treat more complex cases of CHD.

Analytical variables

Statin of choice

Statin treatment is defined by the specific statin used by the patient during the study period. To examine the impact of primary prevention, an indicator variable taking the value 1 if the patient had no evidence of a CHD diagnosis or other cardiac procedure, such as a percutaneous angioplasty (PCTA), was formed. This variable can help to determine if statin choice is influenced by a patient's overall health status. It is expected that patients without previous CHD diagnoses are less likely to use the most potent drugs, Lipitor and Zocor, and more likely to utilize the other drugs.

Statin copayment

The copayment variable is constructed to correspond to the economic and econometric theory underlying the investigation of statin choice. For each patient, five average copayment values are imputed from the data, allowing four relative copayment ratios to be formed, in the following manner. First, for each statin prescription record in every health plan represented in the final sample, the copayment field for each observed prescription purchased is standardized to represent a 30-pill fill. Next, using these values, an average plan-level copayment statistic is constructed for each statin on every service date in the dataset. That is, for every represented health plan, five average copayment statistics corresponding to each statin are imputed from prescription records for every purchase date. Thus, for any health plan, if its enrollees purchased statins on every day of 1997 and 1998, then 730 average copayments are calculated for each statin (for that plan).

For any particular date and plan, the copayment statistic for a statin is formed by taking the mean of all recorded copays for that plan available during a specified time window. The time window is dependent on the number of available claims per health plan in the dataset and varies from 13 to 29 days. The idea is to impute average plan-level copayment values from prescription drug records available in the vicinity of any service date in the data. The length of the time window (similar to a bandwidth in non-parametric smoothing procedures) was determined for each individual plan with the thought that an average of 30–100 claims would be available around each service date for analysis. In reality, the mean number of claims around each date in the data was approximately 60. These records allow for reasonable approximation of copayments that any patient would have made for statins since only claims within any one health plan around the time of purchase are considered.

The final copayment values for each person are then determined by the actual dates that any one patient purchased a statin. For example, suppose that a patient has four different fill dates for Lipitor: June 31, July 30, August 31, and September 30, 1997. Copayment statistics calculated from the earlier procedure are combined in a weighted average to produce plan-level copayments for this individual. This procedure is duplicated for all people in the sample. Last, Pravachol is chosen as the statin of reference (arbitrarily) and its copayment value is divided into each other statin copay to form four relative copayment ratios to be used in multivariate analysis.

Sensitivity analyses consider different copayment specifications to ensure that this analysis is not *ad hoc*. One alternative method of calculation is to calculate copayment averages per plan per month rather than a window surrounding any one service date. The second formulation is to attempt to use actual copays as coded in the data by visually inspecting the data. However, this last procedure has its own problems since the data often report differing copays for patients in the same plan at the same time. Nonetheless, employing these different specifications is an important activity to ensure the robustness of results.

Insurance type

Insurance plan type consisted of four different values for this sample: indemnity, point of service plan, HMO, and PPO. These variables are coded directly into the MarketScan database for each patient. Only persons with evidence of enrollment in only one insurance plan are included in regression analysis. It is expected that the patterns of statin utilization will differ significantly between indemnity and managed care insurers. Moreover, statin choice should also vary for patients across managed care insurer type. Since various managed care organizations have disparate degrees of control over health care utilization it is reasonable to suspect a differing influence on statin utilization accordingly.

Demographic variables

Demographic variables of interest include a patient's gender, age, US geographic region (Northeast, Midwest, South, West), employee relationship (employee, spouse, or dependent), and employment status. Age was calculated as of the date of each patient's first observable statin prescription and can be found on each observation in the claim-level dataset.

There are nine different potential employment categories coded in the MarketScan databases. For the purposes of this study, patients in the final sample were aggregated into three distinct categories: active employees, retirees, and other classifications. Patients in the active employees group were full- or part-time employees or COBRA (Consolidated Omnibus Budget Reconciliation Act) continuees. Those in the retiree group were early retirees, Medicare eligible retirees,[24] or retirees of unknown origin. Persons in the other category were on long-term disability, surviving spouses or dependents, or of unknown employment status.

Geographic region was determined primarily by the region variable in the MarketScan database. In some cases, this variable was coded as unknown. When this occurred, the patient's MSA (Metropolitan Statistical Area) or geographic location variable was used to determine the region. This variable is important since some researchers have found regional differences in prescribing behavior and drug treatment choice after an inpatient cardiac episode.[25]

Patient health status

Patients with CHD are also likely to have other major medical conditions that may contribute to the choice of a statin. Three of the major comorbid conditions evaluated in this study are diabetes, essential hypertension, and other respiratory symptoms. Other medical conditions that may be related to CHD are also measured in this study and include cardiac dysrhythmias, cardiovascular symptoms excluding heart failure, congestive heart failure, hypertensive heart and renal disease, obesity, hypothyroidism, and renal failure. To find evidence of these conditions, each patient's inpatient and outpatient records are searched for the appropriate ICD-9-CM codes. In addition to searching for evidence of individual medical conditions, the Charlson comorbidity index (Charlson *et al.*, 1987) is calculated to assess patients' overall health status. The index contains 19 categories of comorbidity, which are primarily defined using ICD-9-CM diagnoses codes. Each category has an associated weight which is based on the adjusted risk of one-year mortality. The overall comorbidity score reflects the cumulative increased likelihood of one-year mortality; the higher the score, the more severe the burden of comorbidity. A description of the index calculation can be found in Appendix B.

Medical utilization

Medical utilization is measured by a patient's number of outpatient visits and incidence of a hospital visit (inpatient admission or ER visit for CHD) in the year prior to the patient's first statin prescription.[26] Records with Current Procedure Terminology version 4 (CPT-4) codes of 99201-99215 and 99241-99245 were selected as evidence of an outpatient visit. In addition, records where the place of service was an outpatient hospital or doctor's office and the coded procedure group was an office visit were also counted as an outpatient visit.

Outpatient table records with CPT-4 codes 90870-90871 were selected as evidence of an ER visit, and a record was counted as an ER visit if the place of service was an ER hospital, the type of service was an emergency service, or the procedure group was an ER or emergency office visit. Measuring the incidence of an inpatient admission or ER visit for CHD conditions and the total number of outpatient visits per patient provides a gauge of patients' healthcare utilization behavior. Differences between statin treatment groups in these variables may suggest significant differences between healthcare seeking behavior among patients in the sample.

Concurrent lipid-lowering medication

In addition to statins, there are other drugs that are commonly prescribed alone and in conjunction with statins for unhealthy levels of cholesterol in some patients. The major classes of drugs included are fibric acid derivatives, niacin, and bile acid resins. Drugs in the first two classes are used primarily to decrease triglyceride levels and increase high density lipoprotein (HDL) cholesterol, while bile acid resins reduce low density lipoprotein (LDL) levels. Since statins have become a first-line therapy in the treatment of CHD, it is expected that there will be little use of these drugs in the final sample. Moreover, utilization of these drugs can also be viewed as an indicator of poor patient health status; physicians are probably attempting different drug interventions as a means to control a patient with serious cardiovascular disease. Patients using at least one drug from any one of these classes is identified with an indicator variable.[27]

9 Descriptive statistics

This section provides descriptive statistics for the analytical variables discussed earlier for the 44,642 patients in the research sample and by each statin. Database analysis was performed with SAS version 8; descriptive tables are provided for guidance.

Statin treatment

Table 9.1 reports the aggregate distribution of specific statin use in the final sample as well as statistics for the proxy indicator variable of primary prevention of coronary heart disease (CHD). This latter variable takes the value 1 if the individual had no evidence of diagnosis of a myocardial infarction, hyperlipidemia, or other cardiac procedure performed in 1997 or 1998. Statin use in the final sample is highly skewed towards Lipitor (35.9%) and Zocor (35.4%) while the remaining three drugs make up less than 30 percent of the sample. These data are representative of statin usage among patients in the United States in 1997 and 1998 but in recent years Lipitor has had a larger share of the market.

The proxy for primary CHD prevention is suggestive of Lipitor being chosen for treatment of patients with previous coronary symptoms. Although 22.5 percent of the entire sample has no evidence of cardiac diagnoses, only 18.7 percent of patient's with Lipitor treatment are captured within this group, suggesting that patients with previous cardiac events may be more likely to receive Lipitor as statin treatment. This is in contrast to persons treated with Lescol where the proportion of users without a CHD diagnosis is 30.8 percent.

Statin utilization by dosage level is reported in Table 9.2. Most prescriptions for four out of the five statins are filled for recommended dosage levels. Approximately 70 percent of Lescol, Lipitor, Mevacor, and Pravachol observations are for the 20 mg or 10 mg (Lipitor) strengths. Prescriptions of Zocor demonstrate a more even spread in the data as the 5, 10, and 20 mg doses are observed 18.9, 40.4, and 40.6 percent of the time. A negligible number of Zocor prescriptions were filled for the 80 mg strength.

The average therapy period length among all patients in the final sample is 10.2 months (median is 10.4). This begins from the time of statin initiation and ends on the last day of available supply. Within drugs, mean therapy length ranges

Table 9.1 Statin monotherapy and primary prevention indicator (%)

	Lescol	Lipitor	Mevacor	Pravachol	Zocor	Total
Total sample	6.1	35.9	5.8	16.8	35.4	100.0
Primary prevention	30.8	18.7	26.9	21.5	24.6	22.5

Table 9.2 Distribution of dosage levels among sample (%)

	Percent of prescriptions filled				
	Lescol	Lipitor	Mevacor	Pravachol	Zocor
5 mg	n/a	n/a	n/a	n/a	11.9
10 mg	n/a	70.7	2.7	11.5	40.4
20 mg	70.4	25.0	71.6	68.7	40.6
40 mg	29.7	4.3	25.7	19.9	n/a

Note
n/a = not applicable

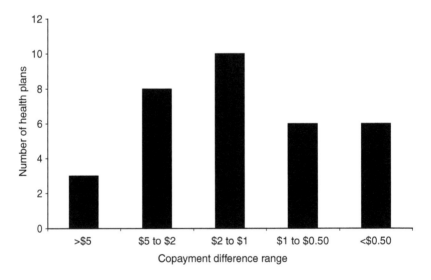

Figure 9.1 Magnitude of within-plan copayment differences.

from 13.8 months for Mevacor to 8.4 months for Lipitor, on average. Note that some therapy periods may be truncated since the data ends in 1998.

Statin copayments

Copayments in the final sample range from $0 to $40 with considerable variation among statins and across health plans. Figure 9.1 demonstrates the differences

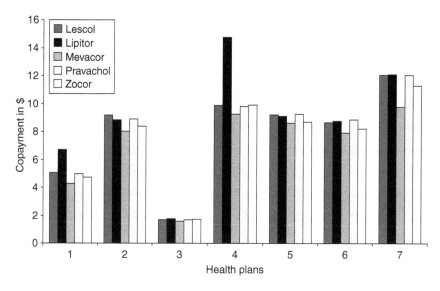

Figure 9.2 Copayment comparison in best represented health plans.

that exist among statin copayments within insurance plans. Each column in Figure 9.1 represents the number of plans where the copayment difference between the highest and lowest statin copayments are within the range specified on the horizontal axis. Although most differences are small (less than \$2), there is significant variation across all health plans and at least a \$5 difference in 15 percent of them. Unfortunately, these plans account for only 8 percent of all of the patients in the final sample. However, even a one dollar difference can imply that the difference between the highest and lowest copayments is 20 percent, for example, if the smallest average copayment is five dollars and the largest is six.

An additional copayment comparison of interest is to consider the average copayment by statin in the best represented health plans in the final sample. Each groups of bars in Figure 9.2 reports the average copayment for each statin in one of the seven health plans with more than 1,000 enrollees. Except for two of the health plans where Lipitor has the largest copayments, copayments across these insurers for the five statins are relatively similar, suggesting that variation in the largest plans is small. The health plan with the lowest copayments represented on this chart is an indemnity plan.

The average copayment for statins also varies substantially across insurance type in the sample as demonstrated in Table 9.3. Health maintenance organizations (HMOs) have the largest average copayments for statins followed closely by Paint of survive POS plans, while indemnity insurance plans have the lowest average statin copayments. There is also interesting variation across statins within insurance types. For example, statin copayments in HMOs range from \$11.48 for

Table 9.3 Average statin copayments by insurance type (in $)

	Lescol	Lipitor	Mevacor	Pravachol	Zocor	Average
HMO	8.96	11.48	9.51	9.97	8.97	9.91
PPO	5.40	6.67	5.33	4.99	6.13	5.99
POS	9.12	9.06	8.76	9.27	8.80	8.97
Indemnity	4.81	5.21	3.68	4.58	4.46	4.71

Table 9.4 Average statin copayments—pharmacy versus mail order (in $)

	Lescol	Lipitor	Mevacor	Pravachol	Zocor	Average
Average pharmacy and mail order copayments						
Pharmacy	6.77	7.22	5.85	6.13	6.70	6.73
Mail order	4.34	4.68	3.85	3.82	4.29	4.28
Average pharmacy copayments by insurer type						
HMO	8.96	11.50	10.39	9.97	8.79	9.90
PPO	5.88	7.09	6.13	5.34	6.82	6.53
POS	9.40	9.50	9.04	9.45	8.65	9.13
Indemnity	5.00	5.28	3.86	4.68	4.52	4.81
Average mail order copayments by insurer type						
HMO	8.99	10.97	8.04	9.96	13.41	10.02
PPO	3.26	4.04	3.17	2.90	3.53	3.51
POS	6.53	5.56	5.00	5.50	5.04	5.31
Indemnity	3.33	4.37	2.80	3.39	3.96	3.77

Lipitor and $8.96 for Lescol, a difference of $2.52 or 22 percent. POS plans have the smallest average copay variation among statins at $0.51.

Beyond these data, there is little direct evidence comparing drug copayments across insurer type. However, descriptive data from other studies (Escarce *et al.*, 2001; Gianfrancesco *et al.*, 2002) report lower mean copayments at HMOs compared to the out-of-pocket costs at indemnity plans or Preferred provider organizations (PPOs). At the same time, the insurance claims database used for this study is much more representative of the overall US population than the data employed in other research. Although it is possible that these drug copayment differences are isolated to the statins class, these data probably provide an accurate portrayal of prescription drug copayments across insurer type for other drug classes as well.

Copayments for drugs normally differ for patients if they are purchased from a mail order provider rather than a pharmacy. A 30-pill fill bought via a mail service is usually less expensive than one purchased from a pharmacy. There is some evidence that this is true in the MarketScan database as well. Although not explicitly coded, it is possible to impute the place of purchase (pharmacy or mail order) in the insurance claims data. Approximately 15 percent of all claims in the dataset were for fills made by mail service providers. The data in Table 9.4 report copayments for statins by pharmacy and mail order and also by insurer type.

The first two rows of Table 9.4 demonstrate, as expected, that copayments for a 30-day fill of a statin purchased from mail order houses are lower than pharmacy copayments, on average. The average difference is $2.45 and ranges from $2 to $2.54. The last eight rows of the table compare copayments by insurer type for pharmacy and mail order providers. Again, mean mail order copayments are always lower with the exception of purchases made by HMO enrollees where they are surprisingly higher. This discrepancy may be due primarily to the small amount of data available for HMO mail order copayments. In addition, the difference is negligible at only $0.12.

Insurance type

Table 9.5 reports the distribution of patients in the final sample by insurance type. By far, the largest type of insurer in this sample is indemnity (37.4%) while the least represented is the HMO, covering only 8.7 percent of the sample. Across statin treatment there is considerable variation in insurance coverage. For example, persons insured by POS plans are more likely to use Zocor (31.8%) than Mevacor (16.8%). At the same time, patients covered by PPOs are treated with Mevacor more often than Lipitor (37.0–24.4%). Patients in managed care plans appear more likely to be treated with Zocor and use Pravachol the least.

Overall, the sample drawn from the MarketScan databases is not nationally representative for the time period studied in terms of insurance enrollment. According to the Kaiser Family Foundation (2001), from 1996 to 1998, the market share for conventional health plans (indemnity) dropped from 27 to 14 percent, HMO share from 31 to 27 percent, PPOs from 28 to 35 percent, and POS plans from 14 to 24 percent. As Table 9.5 demonstrates, indemnity and POS plans in this sample are clearly overrepresented, while HMOs and PPOs are underrepresented.

Demographic variables

The final sample of patients is primarily male (58.9 %) with little variation among the users of different statins (Table 9.6). There are more females in the Lescol group than other statins while a larger proportion of men use Lipitor, Pravachol, and Zocor. The predominantly male influence most likely reflects the fact that men are at higher risk for cardiac events than women at the same age.

Table 9.5 Statin utilization by insurance type (%)

	Lescol	*Lipitor*	*Mevacor*	*Pravachol*	*Zocor*	*Total*
Patient count	2,734	12,924	1,958	5,887	12,503	44,642
Indemnity	35.6	40.9	39.6	43.8	30.8	37.4
HMO	10.9	7.2	6.6	8.7	10.2	8.7
PPO	23.7	24.4	37.0	26.6	27.3	26.5
POS	29.8	27.5	16.8	21.0	31.8	27.4

Table 9.6 Statin utilization by gender (%)

	Lescol	Lipitor	Mevacor	Pravachol	Zocor	Total
Patient count	2,734	12,924	1,958	5,887	12,503	44,642
Male	54.5	59.1	56.8	59.1	59.8	58.9

Table 9.7 Statin utilization by age group (%)

Age range	Lescol	Lipitor	Mevacor	Pravachol	Zocor	Total
	2,734	12,924	1,958	5,887	12,503	44,642
18–45	13.2	12.9	7.0	12.7	9.8	11.4
45–55	35.4	37.1	27.5	36.0	33.9	35.2
55–60	25.5	24.8	26.6	23.6	26.7	25.4
>60	25.9	25.2	39.0	27.7	29.7	28.0

Table 9.7 reports the distribution of statin usage by age in four pre-specified ranges: 18–45, 45–55, 55–60, and greater than 60. Age is an important factor because CHD severity, in particular greater plaque burden, tends to rise with age (Grundy, 1999). The largest group of statin users in this sample fall in the 45–55-year-old range. Of these patients, Mevacor is least favored among all statins. However, persons older than 60 tend to prefer Mevacor and not utilize Lescol or Lipitor as much as other statins. The smallest spread in utilization exists among persons aged 55–60-years old.

Other demographic variables include employment status and the patient's relationship to the insured. There are very few dependents in the sample as most patients are employees (the insured enrollee) or spouses (Table 9.8). In addition, most patients in all drug treatment groups are represented by either active employees or retirees; only a small percent of the sample falls into the "other" employment status category. There is little variation or difference across statins, so these variables are not of interest for multivariate regressions. Moreover, while interesting descriptive statistics, these variables may not play a direct role in the choice of one statin over another.

Regionally, the entire sample is skewed toward the northeast (26.2%) and midwest (43.2%) portions of the United States (Table 9.9). Across statins, there appears to be regional differences in the distribution of statin choice. For example, patients in northeastern states are more likely to use Zocor, while Pravachol and Mevacor are used more often in the midwest United States. In the southern states, there is slight bias for Zocor and Lescol. Patients in the West receive Lescol most often. In terms of national variation and representation, these data closely resemble other research (Managed Care Measures, 2001) that reports the highest utilization of statins in the Northeast and Midwest portions of the United States. In that data, the West has the lowest reported proportion of statin users among CHD patients. So, the small group of statin users in this sample may be representative.

Table 9.8 Employment status and relationship to insured (%)

	Lescol	Lipitor	Mevacor	Pravachol	Zocor	Total
Patient count	2,734	12,924	1,958	5,887	12,503	44,642
Employee status						
Active	67.0	66.1	58.2	67.4	63.1	64.8
Retiree	32.7	33.6	41.3	32.2	36.4	36.4
Other	0.3	0.4	0.6	0.4	0.5	0.4
Relationship						
Employee	65.8	66.2	66.6	64.5	67.3	66.3
Spouse	30.8	33.2	33.3	34.4	32.3	32.9
Dependent	3.4	0.6	0.2	1.1	0.4	0.8

Table 9.9 Region of United States (%)

	Lescol	Lipitor	Mevacor	Pravachol	Zocor	Total
Patient count	2,734	12,924	1,958	5,887	12,503	44,642
Northeast	23.0	26.0	24.6	22.7	28.8	26.2
Midwest	40.5	43.8	49.9	50.3	38.5	43.2
South	28.2	22.5	18.4	19.5	26.8	23.6
West	8.3	7.7	7.2	7.6	5.9	7.1

While the literature on regional patterns of statin use is sparse, Hellerstein (1998) finds a significant regional variation in the propensity of physicians to prescribe generic drugs instead of brand name ones. Thus, it is likely that this propensity also exists among physicians for similar drugs in one therapeutic class. It is possible that these regional variations are also correlated to insurance type since managed care organizations tend to be more cost conscious and concentrated in the western United States. Moreover, O'Connor *et al.* (1999) have previously found geographic differences in the treatment of acute myocardial infarction with ace inhibitors and beta-blockers. Given these results, it would not be unfathomable that there were regional differences in the prescription of statins across the United States.

Patient health status

The most common clinical comorbidities for CHD patients in this sample are essential hypertension (31.5%), symptoms of the respiratory system (22.5%), and diabetes (13.1%) (Table 9.10a). Moreover, there are differences across statin treatment patterns for these three conditions. For example, there are more patients with diabetes treated with Lipitor compared to other statins. This finding is not surprising since patients with CHD and diabetes are at extremely high risk for a future cardiac event (AHA, 2002; NCEP, 2001) and Lipitor is considered one of the most effective statins at reducing low density lipoprotein (LDL) cholesterol.

Table 9.10a Patient health status: most common comorbidities (%)

	Lescol	Lipitor	Mevacor	Pravachol	Zocor	Total
Patient count	2,734	12,924	1,958	5,887	12,503	44,642
Diabetes[a]	10.6	15.7	12.6	12.5	11.5	13.1
Essential hypertension[b]	31.6	28.4	36.5	31.8	33.7	31.5
Respiratory symptoms[c]	22.9	19.9	28.4	22.6	24.0	22.5

Notes
a Diabetes: ICD-9-CM codes of 250.xx, 362.0, 366.41, and 648.0.
b Essential hypertension: ICD-9-CM codes of 401.xx.
c Respiratory symptoms: ICD-9-CM codes 786.xx.

Table 9.10b Patient health status: other comorbidities

	Lescol	Lipitor	Mevacor	Pravachol	Zocor	Total
Patient count	2,734	12,924	1,958	5,887	12,503	44,642
Cardiac dysrhythmias[a]	6.1	4.9	11.1	7.4	5.3	5.9
CVD ex HF[b]	4.6	3.9	8.5	5.7	4.1	4.6
CHF[c]	1.4	2.5	1.7	2.3	2.0	2.1
HHRD[d]	1.9	3.0	2.5	3.0	2.7	2.8
Hypthyrd[e]	5.9	7.0	5.0	6.9	5.4	6.2
Obesity[f]	1.4	1.1	2.3	1.6	1.0	1.3
Renal failure[g]	0.5	0.7	1.1	0.8	0.6	0.7
CCI (mean)	0.48	0.58	0.63	0.57	0.57	0.57
Standard deviation	0.93	0.99	1.10	1.02	1.02	1.01

Notes
a Cardiac dysrythmias: ICD-9-CM codes 427.xx.
b Cardiovascular symptoms excluding heart failure: ICD-9-CM codes 785.xx.
c Congestive heart failure: ICD-9-CM codes 428.xx, 402.01, 402.11, 402.91, 404.01, 404.03, 404.11, 404.13, 404.91, and 404.93.
d Hypertensive heart and renal disease: ICD-9-CM codes 402.xx, 403.xx, and 404.xx.
e Hypothyroidism: ICD-9-CM codes 243.xx and 244.xx.
f Obesity: ICD-9-CM codes 278.xx.
g Renal failure: ICD-9-CM codes 584.xx, 585.xx, and 586.xx.

Other measured medical conditions do not appear in more than 10 percent of the full sample of statin users (Table 9.10b). However, there is a wide range of patients within each statin group with evidence of cardiac dysrythmias.[28] While only 4.9 percent of Lipitor patients show signs of this condition, 11.1 percent of persons on Mevacor therapy have this comorbidity suggesting that this may be an informative variable.

Patients using Mevacor tend to be less healthy than other patients in the sample. Mevacor patients have the highest incidence in six out of the ten measured clinical comorbidities. This is also evident in the mean value of the Charlson Comorbidity index (CCI) in the sample. Mevacor patients have the highest CCI, on average, compared to other statin users. Interestingly, Lipitor users have the

Table 9.11 Healthcare utilization

	Lescol	Lipitor	Mevacor	Pravachol	Zocor	Total
Patient count	2,734	12,924	1,958	5,887	12,503	44,642
IP or ER admission (%)	5.8	4.7	10.3	7.1	5.1	5.6
OP visit (mean)	4.6	4.7	4.8	4.8	5.0	4.8
Standard deviation	5.2	5.2	5.0	5.3	5.3	5.2

Table 9.12 Concurrent use of other lipid-lowering drugs (%)

	Lescol	Lipitor	Mevacor	Pravachol	Zocor	Total
Patient count	2,734	12,924	1,958	5,887	12,503	44,642
Number	2.1	2.6	3.6	2.7	2.0	2.4

second largest CCI and the highest incidence of comorbidities in 40 percent of measured health status variables.

Medical utilization

Patients in the full sample average less than five outpatient visits in the period prior to statin utilization (Table 9.11). Across statin groups, this figure ranges from 4.6 to 5.0 visits per patient. Lescol and Zocor patients tend to visit their physicians the least and most, on average, respectively. There does not appear to be enough variation between groups to include this variable in a multivariate analysis.

Only a small percentage (5.6 percent) of the final sample has evidence of a previous inpatient admission or emergency room visit. Patients using Mevacor are most likely, in this sample, to have had a hospital visit while those taking Lipitor are least likely. This variable may be an informative one in multivariate analysis and can be interpreted as another proxy for health status.

Concurrent lipid-lowering medication

Other lipid-modifying agents, fibric acid derivatives and bile acid resins, are taken by only 2.4 percent of the total sample concurrently with statins (Table 9.12). This suggests that CHD progression among patients may be relatively similar in the overall sample since patients with complex forms of CHD are sometimes recommended to seek combination drug treatment of statins with one of these two compounds (NCEP, 2001). There is slight variation among statin groups with Mevacor patients more likely to use these drugs, on average. This is an indication that Mevacor patients may have relatively more complex forms of CHD than others. For example, these agents are often used to increase high density lipoprotein (HDL) cholesterol since stations are not as effective at this as they are at decreasing LDL.

10 Multivariate regression results

Multinomial logit (MNL) regressions are employed to estimate the likelihood of using one statin over another. Tables with complete results with coefficient estimates, robust standard errors, z-statistics, and confidence intervals appear in Appendix C along with tables for marginal effects calculations. Specific results for explanatory variables of interest are also displayed and interpreted in this section. Sensitivity analyses to test the robustness of the copayment variables, in particular, are included and examined in the following section. MNL regression and marginal effect results were performed using STATA 7. The discussion here will focus primarily on the interpretation of marginal effects estimates.

Relative copayments influence choice of a statin

Results suggest that a patient's relative copayment level is associated with the choice at a statin. An increase in the plan-level copayment of the patient's drug of choice relative to the Pravachol copayment, over the patient's therapy period, decreases the likelihood of using that statin in all cases. According to the marginal effects results, calculated at the mean of each variable, if a patient's relative copayment increases by 10 percent, the probability of receiving the drug of choice falls by as much as 3.9 percent (Lipitor) and as little as 0.4 percent (Lescol). This suggests that, at the grand mean, a *one dollar* Lipitor copayment change from $5 to $6, holding the Pravachol copay and other factors constant, implies that patients are about 8 percent less likely to choose Lipitor. Marginal effect results for own relative copayment for the four statins other than Pravachol, since it is the base category, are displayed in Table 10.1; all estimates are significant at the 1 percent level.

The magnitude of coefficient estimates warrant further discussion. First, note that the marginal effects estimates for Lescol and Mevacor are much smaller than those for Lipitor and Zocor. In particular, Lipitor's coefficient is nine times as large as the one for Lescol. This pattern is partially explained by the larger shares of Lipitor and Zocor usage in this sample. The marginal effects formula itself directly accounts for a large estimated probability of utilization. To recall, the

Table 10.1 Own-copay ratio coefficient estimates

Statin	Marginal effect	Standard error	90% confidence interval	
Lescol	−0.041	0.0129	−0.063	−0.020
Lipitor	−0.388	0.0290	−0.435	−0.340
Mevacor	−0.048	0.0217	−0.084	−0.013
Zocor	−0.249	0.0536	−0.337	−0.161

Table 10.2 Ratio of own relative copayment marginal effect to estimated choice probability of the statin

Statin	Marginal effect	Choice probability	Ratio
Lescol	−0.041	0.061	−0.67
Lipitor	−0.388	0.356	−1.09
Mevacor	−0.048	0.051	−0.94
Zocor	−0.249	0.359	−0.69

marginal effects formulas is

$$\frac{\partial \hat{P}_k}{\partial x_{ijm}} = \hat{P}_k \left[\hat{\beta}_{km} - \sum_{l=1}^{K} \hat{P}_l \hat{\beta}_{lm} \right] \tag{10.1}$$

The estimated choice probability, $\hat{P}_k$, plays a prominent role in the equation. As a result, alternatives with large estimated choice probabilities, like Lipitor (36%) and Zocor (36%), will have much larger estimated marginal effects, on average.

One informative way to consider the own copayment marginal effects is to interpret them proportional to the estimated choice probabilities (Table 10.2).

While the marginal effects measure the change in the likelihood of using a statin, the ratios of marginal effects to estimated choice probabilities provide a measure of scale. For instance, given an equal change in relative copayments for all statins, Lescol and Zocor users are least responsive, while Lipitor users appear most responsive. In other words, a change in copayments is least likely to impact aggregate utilization of Zocor or Lescol because relative to the overall choice probability, the marginal effect of an own copayment change for Zocor or Lescol is small compared to other statins. Although the Lescol and Zocor ratios are not statistically different from one another, the ratios for Lipitor and Mevacor are significantly different from the former two. In addition, the Liptior and Mevacor ratios are statistically different from each other.[29] Consequently, it appears that patients respond to relative copayment changes differently across statins.

The quantitative differences in marginal effect estimates and responsiveness ratios are also possibly due to efficacy differences across drugs. Lipitor and Zocor tend to be more effective at low density lipoprotein cholesterol (LDL) reduction than Lescol and Mevacor. Yet, consumer sensitivity to Zocor copayment differences compared to Lipitor is much smaller. In fact, own-copayment elasticity of demand is largest for Lipitor compared to other statins. Thus, although elevated cholesterol is an important determinant of coronary heart disease (CHD) progression (Gotto and Grundy, 1999) and Lipitor has been demonstrated on a dose-by-dose basis to reduce LDL cholesterol more than other alternatives (Ballantyne et al., 2001; Jones et al., 1998), the absence of definitive proof of Lipitor's ability to reduce coronary events may cause many people to be more sensitive to its price differences compared to other statins. At the same time, the relative inelasticity of demand for Zocor may be a response to the vast literature suggesting the clinical benefits of this statin. Thus, the independent therapeutic effects of these agents appears associated to some extent with patients' price sensitivity. This result seems reasonable since patients should be less responsive to out-of-pocket cost differentials for drugs that are evidenced to produce positive health status outcomes. Intuitively, the relative utility gained from use of one agent over another results in behavioral differences among patients that correspond to these disparities in relative copayment sensitivity.

Cross-price marginal effects estimates also tell an interesting story. Since the statins are technically substitutes for one another, one should expect that cross-price effects are positive. That is, a rise in the relative copayment of a substitute increases the probability of initiating therapy with the statin of choice. In general, the results confirm this conclusion as displayed in Table 10.3.

In 11 of 16 cases, the cross-price marginal effects are positive. For instance, a 10 percent rise in the Lipitor-to-Pravachol copay ratio increases the probability of using Zocor by 2.8 percent. In fact, all Lipitor cross-price effects are positive and the one for Zocor, its closest substitute in terms of LDL cholesterol reduction and cost-effectiveness, is largest. In contrast, however, the Zocor-to-Pravachol copayment ratio cross-price marginal effect with Lipitor is negative, implying that an increase in the Zocor-to-Pravachol copay ratio decreases the probability of using Lipitor.

This apparently counterintuitive result is likely to be a result of the actual marginal effect calculation itself. A necessary aspect of marginal effects on choice probabilities is that the changes in choice probabilities must sum to zero since the probabilities must sum to one. Thus, marginal effect directions may be intuitively misleading but mathematically correct (Crawford et al., 1998). For the case of the statins, note that the Zocor-to-Pravachol own price ratio effect

Table 10.3 Cross-price marginal effects on statin choice

	Lescol	Lipitor	Mevacor	Pravachol	Zocor
Lescol/Pr copay	—	0.108*	0.007	0.034	−0.107*
Lipitor/Pr copay	−0.007	—	0.023*	0.097*	0.276*
Mevacor/Pr copay	0.060*	−0.050	—	−0.073*	0.111*
Zocor/Pr copay	0.066*	−0.246*	0.094*	0.336*	—

Note
* Significant at the 1 percent level (Pr=Pravachol).

(−0.249, Table 10.2) and the Lipitor cross marginal (−0.246, Table 10.3) sum to −0.496 while the cross-copayment marginal effects for Mevacor (0.094), Pravachol (0.336), and Lescol (0.066) sum to 0.496 (see Table 10.3). So, the positive marginal effects on the choice probability of Zocor balance out the negative ones. Ultimately, the estimated marginal effect's sign will depend on the size of the parameter estimate, $\hat{\beta}_{km}$, relative to the sum $\sum_{l=1}^{k}\hat{P}_{l}\hat{\beta}_{lm}$ as seen in equation 10.1 earlier. As a result, it is possible to obtain a marginal effect estimate on the choice probability that is counterintuitive.

Insurers affect choice via non-price methods

Patients' insurance type also appears to influence the choice of a statin. For instance, relative to persons with indemnity insurance, patients enrolled in Health maintenance organizations (HMOs) tend to be less likely to receive Mevacor, Pravachol, or Lipitor, but more likely to use Lescol or Zocor. This suggests that HMOs (compared to indemnity plans) may influence enrollee behavior toward these alternatives with non-price steering methods. Interestingly, other managed plans (PPOs and POS plans) also tend to treat patients with Lipitor less often compared to indemnity plans. Complete insurance type results are presented in Table 10.4.

Results on the influence of insurance type on drug choice is not convincing, however, unless an interaction term between insurer type and copayment levels is also included in the regression specification. This explanatory variable indicates the association of insurer type at differing copayment levels, holding copayments constant within insurers as well as across them (as is accomplished with the relative copayment variables). The marginal effects results for these variables are reported in Table 10.5. Interestingly, as copayment levels rise across managed care plans, the likelihood of using Lipitor increases. This is in opposition to the direct effect reported in Table 10.4 but does not overpower it. Likewise, while the probability of using Zocor falls as copayment levels rise across managed care plans, it does not do so enough to counterbalance the direct impact of managed health plan enrollment.

The probability of treatment with Mevacor appears to be lower in HMOs but higher in preferred provider organizations (PPOs) and point-of-service (POS)

Table 10.4 Insurance type effects on statin choice

	HMO	PPO	POS
Lescol	0.020	0.041*	−0.083
Lipitor	−0.420*	−0.225*	−0.653*
Mevacor	−0.029*	0.103*	0.275
Pravachol	−0.054*	0.000	−0.248*
Zocor	0.484*	0.080*	0.709*

Note
* Significant at the 1 percent level.

Table 10.5 Marginal effects of insurance type interaction with copayment level on statin choice

	HMO	PPO	POS
Lescol	0.006*	0.008*	0.034*
Lipitor	0.084*	0.035*	0.237*
Mevacor	−0.003*	−0.011*	−0.057*
Pravachol	−0.011*	−0.006	0.094*
Zocor	−0.065*	−0.010*	−0.308*

Note
* Significant at the 1 percent level.

plans compared to indemnity plans. Although Mevacor is the oldest statin, some managed insurers are still more likely to treat patients with this statin. At the same time, the probability of using Pravachol is less for patients in any of the managed plans as well (although PPO results are not statistically significant). A study of generic Pravachol and Mevacor usage by these types of plans would be interesting since these formulations are likely to be more cost-effective than their brand name equivalents because their prices will be significantly lower.

These results should also be viewed with some caution given the under-representation of HMO patients in the sample in relation to the US HMO market share at the same time. In addition, the number of health plans, particularly HMOs, represented in these data relative to the total number of health plans in the United States is small. Yet, there is some precedence for these type of non-price effects to influence use of drugs. DeVries (2001) supports the contention that health plans can actively work to manage care through means beyond benefit design, contracting, and pharmacy intervention. Pharmacist visits to physicians and the number of managed care contracts per doctor were demonstrated to increase prescribing towards preferred agents, suggesting that non-pecuniary pharmacy interventions influence prescribing behavior.

Age, gender, and region

Compared to patients aged 18–45, older patients are more likely to be treated with Mevacor or Zocor. Moreover, this general trend increases as patients age. For example, the probability of treatment with Zocor rises by 5, 7.6, and 8.1 percent for persons aged 45–55, 55–60, and greater than 60, respectively. The opposite trend exists for Lipitor as older patients are less likely to be treated with it compared to persons aged 18–45. Older patients also appear less likely to receive Pravachol compared to other statins.

While it appears surprising that some older patients are less likely to use one statin over another, recall that given the nature of marginal effects on the *probability* of using a drug some patients will have to be less likely to use a drug and others will be more likely. Thus, while older patients are more likely to use a statin than younger patients on average, among a selected group of older patients the mix of

Table 10.6 Influence of age on statin choice

Statin	45–55	55–60	>60
Lescol	−0.004	−0.002	−0.005
Lipitor	−0.045*	−0.075	−0.100*
Mevacor	0.012*	0.029*	0.044*
Pravachol	−0.014#	−0.027*	−0.019*
Zocor	0.050*	0.076*	0.081*

Note
* (#) Significant at the 1 percent (5%) level.

Table 10.7 Influence of gender on statin choice (male = 1)

Lescol	−0.011*
Lipitor	−0.005
Mevacor	−0.000
Pravachol	0.000
Zocor	0.016*

Note
* Significant at the 1 percent level.

statin utilization will dictate that specific drugs are used more often than others. In this sample, the oldest patients appear most likely to be treated with Zocor and Mevacor while they are least likely to use Lipitor and Pravachol (see Table 10.6).

Gender appears to play a rather limited role in these data. Men were less likely to receive Lescol or Lipitor for treatment relative to women but almost two percent more likely to begin treatment with Zocor. One might expect men would be more likely, on average, to be treated with Zocor since they are often more likely to suffer complications of CHD compared to women and Zocor is highly effective at reducing LDL levels compared to most other statins (see Table 10.7). Moreover, Zocor advertising appealing to men may affect decisionmaking as well (Burton, 2002).

Regional differences in the data are abundant. Living in the Northeastern or Midwest United States decreases the probability of being treated with Lescol and Zocor, but increases one's chances of using Lipitor, Pravachol, and Mevacor relative to persons in the South. Patients in the West, relative to the South, have a lower likelihood of being treated with Zocor but are more likely to use the other statins (see Table 10.8). These regional differences in usage may be attributable to a number of factors such as differences in prescribing behavior and statin advertising across the country.

Strong association between choice and health status

Patients' health status parameters also help explain considerable variation in statin treatment. Four variables representing evidence of comorbid conditions

Table 10.8 Influence of region on statin choice

Statin	Northeast	Midwest	West
Lescol	−0.016*	−0.011*	0.006
Lipitor	0.011	0.038*	0.029*
Mevacor	0.022*	0.001	0.010[#]
Pravachol	0.012	0.034*	0.046*
Zocor	−0.029*	−0.061*	−0.092*

Note
* (#) significant at the 1 percent (5%) level.

Table 10.9 Influence of comorbid conditions on statin choice

Statin	Diabetes	Hypertension	Respiratory symptoms	Cardiac dysrythmias
Lescol	−0.013*	−0.010*	0.026*	−0.000
Lipitor	0.080*	−0.085*	0.031*	0.102*
Mevacor	−0.007*	0.007[#]	−0.014*	0.007
Pravachol	−0.014*	0.004	0.004	0.000
Zocor	−0.046*	0.083*	−0.047	−0.109*

Note
* (#) significant at the 1 percent (5%) level.

and two other indicator variables are used to approximate patients' health status: utilization of other cholesterol monitoring drugs, an indicator for primary prevention of CHD and evidence of diabetes, hypertension, respiratory symptoms, and cardiac dsyrhythmias. In all cases, persons with a particular medical condition, or those with use of other agents, are compared to those without that comorbidity, or who are not treated with other drugs. The presence of diabetes, cardiac dysrythmias, or other cholesterol drug utilization are serious CHD risk factors, in general. In fact, diabetes is considered a CHD risk equivalent by the National Cholesterol Education Program (NCEP) (2001) and because of its various vascular complications, it should be treated as a cardiovascular disease (Grundy *et al.*, 1999). As a result, it is not surprising that marginal effects estimates suggest that patients with diabetes have a higher probability of treatment with Lipitor (Table 10.9).

Patients with previous cardiac dsyrhythmias (abnormal heart rhythms) are more likely to be treated with Lipitor and less likely to receive Zocor. The contrast between these two drugs for this one condition is quite large. These data suggest that Lipitor is considered a first-line treatment for patients in poor cardiovascular health status since the probability of using Lipitor is higher for patients with diabetes, cardiac dysrhythmias, and respiratory symptoms compared to persons without these conditions.

Persons with hypertension have a higher probability of initiating with Mevacor, Pravachol, or Zocor and a lesser chance of using other statins. The presence of

Table 10.10 Influence of other health status indicators on statin choice

Statin	Concurrent lipid-modifying drug use	Primary prevention indicator
Lescol	−0.007	0.027*
Lipitor	0.048*	−0.073*
Mevacor	0.017*	0.026*
Pravachol	0.018	0.006
Zocor	−0.077*	0.014*

Note
* Significant at the 1 percent level.

respiratory symptoms is associated with a greater likelihood of using Lescol or Lipitor. Although, in general, retrospective claims data measures are poor proxies for health status, these variables appear to capture significant variation in demand patterns for statins.

Two other variables that account for some health status differences among patients include indicators that signal the concurrent utilization of other lipid-modifying drugs and primary CHD prevention (Table 10.10). Using other lipid-modifying agents is an indication that a patient's health is poor; it also may be a signal that high density lipoprotein (HDL) cholesterol levels are low. These patients appear more likely to utilize Lipitor and Mevacor and less likely to receive Zocor. Again, Lipitor and Zocor appear to be competing with one another for persons in poor health status. Moreover, there is a large disparity of patients enrolled in indemnity plans using Zocor compared to Lipitor. If patients in poorer health are attracted more often to these plans, then it is likely that this interaction is also a factor in the use of Lipitor by persons in worse health status. Of course, this logic counters the result that older patients, who tend to be in worse health status, have a lower likelihood of using Lipitor.

The indicator of primary CHD prevention also accounts for some variation in choice behavior. Patients without evidence of CHD are less likely to use Lipitor and more likely to utilize Lescol, Mevacor, and Zocor. Since Lescol and Mevacor are not as cost-effective as other statins, it is not surprising to find that these drugs are utilized by those persons with the best health status of statin users. While the positive association of Zocor use with primary prevention is interesting, note that the magnitudes of the marginal effect coefficients are roughly equal for Zocor, Pravachol, and Mevacor. The measure of scale (ratio) comparing the marginal effect to the choice probability would suggest that the result here is much more vital to the choice of Lescol and Mevacor and not so important to the distribution of Zocor.

The probability of using Lescol or Mevacor increases by nearly 3 percent when primary prevention patients are considered, but the total utilization of each is only about 6 percent overall. Thus, the addition of more primary therapy patients to the drug-utilization pool would greatly increase the number of Mevacor and Lescol users in the total population of statin users. Interestingly, the largest group of patients most likely to initiate statin therapy in the next few years, due to the newest NCEP drug treatment guidelines, are patients without previous evidence of CHD.

Summary of main multivariate results

Among all of the multivariate regression results, the most important are those related to relative copayments and insurance type. Statin relative copayments apportion utilization of these drugs in the same way that market prices allocate goods in the marketplace. As a consequence, one should expect that insurers can direct patients to one drug substitute over another successfully by differentiating copayments. At the same time, this research also confirms that insurers also influence drug choice through non-pecuniary methods. Both independently and controlling for the level of copayments, managed care insurers appear to steer patients towards some statins, like Zocor, and away from others, such as Lipitor and Pravachol. Consequently, this study supports the notion that drug choice is impacted by both financial and non-financial mechanisms in pharmaceutical markets where multiple substitutable alternatives exist and compete for market share with one another.

11 Multivariate sensitivity analyses

This section will describe and present results from multiple regression specifications that were estimated to test the robustness of the study's main findings. First, the hypotheses are tested for patients identified with and without evidence of coronary heart disease (CHD) diagnoses. Marginal effects calculations for the variables of interest are presented and compared across these two distinct sub-populations of the data. Second, the impact of copayments is tested more rigorously by employing two different copayment calculation methods across health plans. These procedures are contrasted to the one proposed in this study and pertinent multivariate results are presented for comparison. Last, a test of the multinomial logit property of independence from irrelevant alternatives is put forth. The results of this test are examined and interpreted for the case of the statins.

Patient's CHD status

Since the final sample of 44,642 statin users includes persons identified as having or not having evidence of CHD, it is natural to consider whether or not each distinct sub-population reacts differently to copayment differentiation among statins. Patients without evidence of CHD (primary prevention therapy) are likely to be in better health, in general, than their counterparts. As a result, it is possible that these patients are less influenced by copayment differences among statins since the five drugs in the class are near perfect substitutes for persons in fair health.

Table 11.1 compares health status indicators used in the multivariate regressions among patients with and without CHD. Interestingly, patients treated for primary prevention of CHD have a similar incidence of hypertension, respiratory symptoms, and other cholesterol-modifying drug utilization compared to patients with CHD evidence (secondary prevention therapy). However, patients with prior CHD diagnoses are more likely to have diabetes and cardiac dysrhythmias. In addition, patients treated for secondary prevention of CHD are also more apt to have congestive heart failure, hypertensive heart and renal disease, hypothyroidism, and to be obese.[30] These data suggest that, on average, persons without CHD evidence are in better health status than other patients in the sample.

Table 11.1 Health status across patients with and without CHD

	Percent of patients with condition	
	Evidence of CHD	*No CHD evidence*
Total patients	34,607	10,035
Diabetes	14	10.3
Hypertension	31.4	31.9
Cardiac dysrythmias	6.7	3.2
Respiratory symptoms	22.9	20.9
Oth. chol. drug use	2.6	2.0

Table 11.2 Own-copayment marginal effects by CHD status

Statin	*Evidence of CHD diagnosis*			*No CHD diagnosis evidence*		
	Estimate	*90% confidence interval*		*Estimate*	*90% confidence interval*	
Lescol	−0.032[#]	−0.056	−0.007	−0.071[#]	−0.12	−0.02
Lipitor	−0.358*	−0.465	−0.250	−0.44*	−0.53	−0.35
Mevacor	−0.080*	−0.104	−0.054	0.031	−0.058	0.119
Zocor	−0.190*	−0.289	−0.092	−0.442*	−0.635	−0.249

Note
* (#, +) denotes significance denoted at 1 percent (5%, 10%) level.

Table 11.2 reports marginal effects estimates for the impact of a change in own copayment ratios for statins across evidence of CHD. For all statins, patients without evidence of CHD are more responsive to changes in relative copayments than persons with prior diagnoses of CHD with the exception of Mevacor. This suggests that patients undergoing primary prevention therapy are more apt to substitute one statin for another than patients treated for secondary prevention of CHD. This conclusion seems reasonable since patients under watch for primary prevention are normally in better health status and can more easily substitute one statin for another. On average, persons with previous CHD evidence will have less flexibility in choosing a statin, especially if the need to decrease low density lipoprotein (LDL) cholesterol is great. Complete multivariate regression results, including standard errors, for these sub-populations of the final sample appear in Appendix E.

Estimated own-copayment demand elasticities for these two groups of patients, as reported in Table 11.3, also demonstrate that persons without prior evidence of CHD are more responsive to copayment differentials. Demand for Lescol, Lipitor, and Zocor is more elastic among patients treated for primary prevention of CHD. The estimate for Mevacor is not statistically significant and, hence, is in the wrong intuitive direction.

Table 11.3 Own-copayment demand elasticities by CHD status

	Patients with CHD	*Patients without CHD*
Lescol	−0.57	−0.84
Lipitor	−1.01	−1.53
Mevacor	−1.55	0.46
Zocor	−0.53	−1.09

Table 11.4 Marginal effects of insurer type by CHD status

Statin	*Evidence of CHD diagnosis*			*No evidence of CHD diagnosis*		
	HMO	*PPO*	*POS*	*HMO*	*PPO*	*POS*
Lescol	0.028^{+}	0.030*	−0.106*	0.016	0.087*	−0.066*
Lipitor	−0.454*	−0.258*	−0.642*	−0.326*	−0.160*	−0.634*
Mevacor	−0.021$^{\#}$	0.109*	0.804*	−0.051*	0.099*	0.016
Pravachol	−0.024	0.006	−0.230*	−0.109*	−0.023	−0.295*
Zocor	0.472*	0.113*	0.174^{+}	0.471*	−0.003	0.978*

Note
* (#, +) denotes significance denoted at 1 percent (5%, 10%) level.

Estimated cross-copayment marginal effects for patients with evidence of CHD were similar to those in the main multivariate results in both direction and magnitude. The size of cross-price marginal effects for patients treated for primary therapy are, in general, greater than those for patients with a CHD history. As discussed earlier, this signals a greater responsiveness on the part of patients with no CHD evidence to copayment differentials in the statins class. The most striking exception to this rule occurs with the relative copayment of Zocor to Pravachol. In some instances, patients without previous CHD history appear *less* responsive to Zocor copayment differentials when choosing to consume Lescol, Mevacor, or Pravachol. That is, copayment differentials appear to not influence choice as much for these drugs relative to Zocor. This suggests that patients under treatment for primary prevention of CHD appear less likely to choose one of these statins over Zocor compared to persons with prior CHD evidence.

The direct influence of insurer type on statin choice also differs among patients with and without CHD. Table 11.4 reports marginal effects estimates of the impact of insurer type on drug choice. All patients, regardless of CHD status, appear influenced by managed care steering methods when choosing statin treatment. However, there are some noticeable differences between the two distinct sub-populations. Patients undergoing treatment for primary prevention of CHD and enrolled in a managed health care plan are less likely to use Mevacor or Pravachol than the same patients with prior CHD evidence.

Managed care enrollees without evidence of CHD are also more likely to choose treatment with Lescol while those enrolled in point-of-service (POS) plans have a higher likelihood of using Zocor. All patients enrolled in managed care plans are less apt to use Lipitor compared to indemnity plan enrollees. However, it appears that managed care plans have less influence on the choice of Lipitor for patients without evidence of CHD, although the marginal effects estimates are still rather large.

In general, managed care health plans appear to steer patients without CHD evidence as much as they influence the choice of a statin among patients with prior CHD evidence. Moreover, the direction of steering does not vary much based on patient CHD status. Thus, it does not appear that non-pecuniary incentives imposed by managed care insurers are directed toward different patient sub-populations for the primary and secondary treatment of CHD. This result differs from the conclusion on the impact of relative copayments where some patients were more sensitive to price differentials than others. However, it is not counter to common prescription drug benefit design practice. While step-care protocols and disease management programs for CHD at some managed care insurers might explain some of the variation in parameter estimate magnitudes, the vast majority of insurers have a single set of benefits to which all patients are entitled, regardless of health status. Thus, it is not surprising to see few disparities among these sub-populations based on the direct impact of insurer type alone.

The indirect impact of managed care enrollment as measured by the interaction of insurer type and copayment level is more similar than different across patient sub-populations. Marginal effects estimates for this variable are reported in Table 11.5. In half of the cases, the impact of insurer type holding copayments constant is similar for patients with and without CHD. In these circumstances, differential copayment levels within insurance type do not influence statin choice disparately across patient sub-populations. This interaction is most evident among preferred provider organizations (PPO) enrollees and with the utilization of Lescol and Pravachol. This second-order result contradicts the idea that patients treated for primary prevention of CHD are less responsive to out-of-pocket costs than their counterparts. Moreover, it suggests that within some managed care plans it is not possible to distinguish statin choice behavior across patient sub-populations with different copayment levels.

When the impact is dissimilar, patients without prior evidence of CHD are less influenced by higher copayment levels compared to persons with CHD. This

Table 11.5 Marginal effects of insurer type–copayment interaction by CHD status

Statin	Evidence of CHD diagnosis			No evidence of CHD diagnosis		
	HMO	PPO	POS	HMO	PPO	POS
Lescol	−0.007[+]	−0.006*	0.041*	−0.006[#]	−0.016*	0.036*
Lipitor	0.101*	0.041*	0.258*	0.051*	0.021*	0.196*
Mevacor	−0.004*	0.012*	−0.072*	0.001	−0.011*	−0.030
Pravachol	−0.018*	−0.008*	0.094*	0.004	−0.001	0.098*
Zocor	−0.072*	−0.016*	−0.321*	−0.050*	0.007	−0.300*

Note
* (#, +) Denotes significance denoted at 1 percent (5%, 10%) level.

result further solidifies the conclusion that persons treated with statins for primary prevention of CHD are not as likely to be influenced by differential copayments. This is particularly evident in the case of Lipitor. Across managed care insurer type, Lipitor utilization increases as absolute copayment levels rise compared to use of other statins. However, patients with prior evidence of CHD are more likely to be impacted by higher copayment levels than those without CHD.

Marginal effects estimates for demographic and health status variables are similar qualitatively and quantitatively for persons with and without CHD with notable exceptions. For example, in terms of demographic factors, patients aged 45–55 or those older than 60 with previous CHD are more likely to use Zocor than the same persons without CHD. This result may be related to the higher incidence of poor CHD health status in the elderly and the relative effectiveness of Zocor to reduce cholesterol levels.

Statin utilization occasionally differs regionally for these two sub-populations as well. Patients without CHD in the Northeast are more likely to use Lipitor than persons treated for secondary prevention. Mevacor treatment also differs regionally among the two groups. Patients without CHD in the West are less likely to choose Mevacor but the same persons in the Northeast are more apt to use Mevacor than patients with evidence of CHD. There are also quantitative differences across all regions for Zocor utilization, but all marginal effects estimates are qualitatively similar. These regional differences highlight the small area variation problem in the utilization of health care services, and point out that this variability exists across patient sub-populations where health status differs rather dramatically.

There are also limited differences in estimated marginal effects among health status variables between patients with and without CHD. Patients without evidence of CHD but prior diagnosis of cardiac dysrhythmias are nearly twice as likely to use Lipitor and almost half as likely to choose Zocor than patients with CHD. So, the presence of this serious comorbidity appears to increase the use of Lipitor among patients treated for primary prevention of CHD while decreasing the likelihood of Zocor utilization. This further entrenches Lipitor as an apparently favorable option for patients in poor health status as the main findings demonstrated. Compared to persons with evidence of CHD, hypertensive primary therapy patients are more likely to choose Mevacor. At the same time, persons without CHD evidence but respiratory symptoms choose Lescol much more often than patients with CHD and respiratory symptoms. Lastly, the utilization of other cholesterol-modifying agents appears to be a stronger signal of Lipitor use among patients with CHD than patients treated for primary prevention of CHD. This again suggests a tendency for patients in poor health status to choose Lipitor.

In general, multivariate results for patients with and without CHD suggest that copayment responsiveness and insurance type effects are dependent on coronary disease history. Patients without CHD are, on average, in better health than their counterparts and are more responsive to copayment differentials. That is, patients attempting to prevent the onset of CHD treat the statins as closer substitutes than patients with a prior diagnosis of CHD. At the same time, any differences in the marginal effects of other patients in poorer health will choose the more potent and cost-effective cholesterol-lowering statins.

Copayment estimation

Since this insurance claims database does not explicitly report the structure of prescription drug benefits for represented health plans, copayments for the studied class of drugs are imputed from the claims data. For each patient, five average copayment values are formed by finding an average copayment value for each statin on each prescription service date in the dataset. For any particular date and health plan, the copayment statistic is formed by taking the mean of all recorded copays for that plan available during a specified time window. The time window is dependent on the number of available claims per health plan in the dataset and varies from 13 to 29 days. The idea is to impute average plan-level copayment values from prescription drug records available in the vicinity of any service date in the data. These records allow for reasonable approximation of copayments that any patient would have made for statins since only claims within any one health plan around the time of purchase are considered.

One concern with employing such a method to calculating copayments is that the procedure may provide an inaccurate picture of actual copayments in the dataset. In order to justify the use of this method and test the results against alternative measures, two different modes of estimating copayments are explored in this section. The first alternative procedure is to calculate copayment averages per plan on a monthly basis rather than during a window surrounding any one service date. The second method will be to visually inspect copayments among plans in the data and attempt to discover their actual levels. However, this second procedure has its own problems since the data often report differing copays for patients in the same plan at the same time due to data entry issues primarily. Nonetheless, employing these different specifications is an important activity to ensure the robustness of results. Complete multivariate results for the copayment sensitivity analyses are available in Appendix F.

Averaging copayments on a monthly basis

The first alternative mode of calculating statin copayments is to collect all relevant drug claims per represented health plan per month and find the average copayment for each statin during that month. For each prescription during any given month, these statistics then serve as mean copayment values. This procedure is advantageous because health plans do not normally change prescription drug benefits in the middle of a month. Moreover, unlike the original method described earlier, it is not possible to calculate average copayments with data from more than one calendar month. However, this newer method may suffer from data limitations if there are too few insurance claims during any calendar month for a health plan to calculate average copayments for all statins.

Table 11.6 Average statin copayments by insurance type (in $) monthly copayment
estimation method

	Lescol	Lipitor	Mevacor	Pravachol	Zocor
Monthly copayment estimation method					
HMO	10.69	12.44	11.15	10.15	11.17
PPO	6.83	7.20	6.74	6.98	6.60
POS	9.39	9.27	9.07	9.39	8.86
Indemnity	6.08	6.36	5.76	6.28	6.08
Initial copayment estimation method					
HMO	8.96	11.48	9.51	9.97	8.97
PPO	5.40	6.67	5.33	4.99	6.13
POS	9.12	9.06	8.76	9.27	8.80
Indemnity	4.81	5.21	3.68	4.58	4.46

Table 11.7 Comparison of own relative copayment marginal effects estimates across
copayment specification

Statin	Original specification		Copayments calculated on a monthly basis	
	Estimate	Standard error	Estimate	Standard error
Lescol	−0.041*	0.013	−0.031[+]	0.018
Lipitor	−0.388*	0.029	−0.057	0.043
Mevacor	−0.048*	0.022	−0.056*	0.021
Zocor	−0.249*	0.054	−0.208*	0.074

Note
* (#, +) denotes significance denoted at 1 percent (5%, 10%) level.

Table 11.6 reports descriptive statistics for average statin copayments across
insurer type. These data differ slightly from those for the original copayment
formulation in Chapter 9; but, the comparison of average copayments across
insurers and statins is similar to the initial calculation method. In particular, mean
statin copayments are highest among health maintenance organizations (HMO)
enrollees and lowest for patients with indemnity insurance. Within plans,
copayments for Lipitor are largest while the lowest out-of-pocket costs are most
often associated with use of Mevacor. Multinomial regressions and marginal
effects were estimated for the full sample of patients with this monthly copayment
specification. Complete parameter estimates, standard errors and confidence
intervals appear in Appendix F in Tables F1–F9.

The marginal impact of own relative copayment differences when the new
copayment definition was used are similar to estimated effects from the original
copayment specification as suggested by data in Table 11.7. In three of four cases,
marginal effects estimates from regression using copayments calculated on a
monthly basis are smaller than initial computations. The only incidence of a larger

own copayment marginal effect is for Mevacor; however, these estimates differ by less than one percentage point.

The largest disparity for own copayment marginal effects exists for Lipitor where the newest estimate is 33 percentage points smaller than the original one, suggesting that the own-copayment demand elasticity for Lipitor is much more inelastic than originally estimated. Moreover, the marginal effect estimate for Lipitor, employing copayments calculated on a monthly basis, is not statistically significant. The large difference is surprising since copayment disparities between Lipitor and other statins are not different when the two types of calculations are compared to one another. Marginal effect estimates of cross copayments for the choice of a statin are qualitatively similar across specifications and any quantitative differences are negligible.

Most other marginal effects estimates for explanatory variables included in the multivariate regression employing copayments calculated on a monthly basis are qualitatively similar to original regression results. In fact, many of the parameter estimates are exactly equal to one another across specifications. There is only one major exception to this rule among 76 marginal effects estimates for the five drugs. Patients enrolled with an HMO are initially less likely to choose Pravachol for therapy, but become more likely to use it when the new copayment specification is employed. An explanation for these contrasting estimates may be found in an analysis of the copayment data. Average copayments made by HMO enrollees for Pravachol, according to the new specification, are smallest among the statins. However, average Pravachol copayments using the original calculation method ranked second largest for HMO patients. These ranking disparities among statin copayments appear to influence the marginal impact of Pravachol utilization among HMO enrollees. Interestingly, in terms of average copayment rankings among HMO patients, mean copayments for Zocor also vary across calculation methods. As a result, the likelihood of choosing Zocor by HMO enrollees drops nearly 35 percent when the monthly copayment definition was used compared to the original technique.

Visual inspection of copayments

The second alternative procedure for calculating copayments is through a visual inspection of the claims data. All statin copayment data for all health plans in the sample are first separated by pharmacy or mail order purchase. Then, for each plan, copayments are inspected over time for pharmacy and mail order fills to attempt to determine the actual copayments for each statin. While this should provide a highly reliable measure of actual copayment levels in each health plan, in reality, even this method suffers from some drawbacks. In particular, there is no precise method of separating pharmacy and mail order claims. Moreover, most plans still report different copayments for different purchasers at roughly the same point in time. Also, in this dataset, this method will display the least sample variance among statin copayments because many plans appear to have not differentiated copayments to a great extent in 1997 and 1998. As a result, the

Table 11.8 Health plan comparisons of visually inspected copayments

Characteristic	No. of health plans	% of Patients
Health plans without mail order claims	14	21.4
Health plans where mail order and pharmacy copayments appear the same	17	73.0
Health plans where mail order and pharmacy copayments appear different	4	4.2
Health plans where statin copayments appear the same throughout 1997–1998	27	88.9

Table 11.9 Comparison of own relative copayment marginal effects estimates across copayment specification

Statin	Original specification		Copayments calculated through visual inspection	
	Estimate	Standard error	Estimate	Standard error
Lescol	−0.041*	0.013	−0.073#	0.031
Lipitor	−0.388*	0.029	−0.281*	0.045
Mevacor	−0.048*	0.022	0.178*	0.063
Zocor	−0.249*	0.054	−0.026	0.060

Note
* (#, +) denotes significance denoted at 1 percent (5%, 10%) level.

relative copayment variables used in the multivariate regressions may have little variance as well.

Table 11.8 describes the relationship of copayments among health plans in the dataset. Less than a quarter of the 35 health plans in the dataset appear to have evidence of mail order pharmacy claims. As expected from 1997–1998 data, through a visual inspection, it appears that many patients in the sample did not face highly differentiated copayments. Almost 90 percent of patients, represented by 27 different health plans appear to have faced the same copayment for all statins. However, without this information explicitly reported, it is not clear if these data are accurate. Moreover, regardless of the situation in 1997–1998, the study's results are still relevant for the prescription benefit climate of 2003, where copayments for drugs in any one therapeutic class are differentiated.

Multivariate results for multinomial regressions utilizing copayments visually inspected from the database are reported in Appendix F in Tables F10–F18. Table 11.9 compares marginal effects estimates from the original copayment specification and the visual inspection method for own relative copayments. Estimates obtained using this alternative method are quantitatively different from original estimates. In particular, the own relative copayment of Mevacor is estimated to be positive rather than negative. This counterintuitive result is also highly statistically significant, suggesting a positive association between the relative copayment of Mevacor to Pravachol and the probability of using

Mevacor. In this case, it appears that copayments may not be allocating Mevacor across patients as market prices allocate other goods. However, other own copayment marginal effects are qualitatively similar to the original estimates. Interestingly, the new estimate for Zocor is one-tenth as large as the original estimate, suggesting that the own copayment elasticity of demand for Zocor is much more highly inelastic when copayments from this alternative methodology are used. Cross copayments for statins are qualitatively similar to those calculated originally.

Many of the marginal effects for the other explanatory variables included in the regression specifications are qualitatively similar across the two types of copayment calculation methods. The most notable differences exist with the marginal effects estimates for the direct impact of insurer type. Contrary to the main results in Chapter 10, patients enrolled in any managed care plan (HMO, PPO, or POS plan) appear more likely to choose Pravachol, on average, relative to persons with indemnity insurance. In addition, marginal effects estimates for the regression utilizing visually inspected copayment suggest that patients enrolled in PPOs or POS plans are less likely to choose Zocor among other statins. These results are also contrary to those presented earlier. One explanation for these conclusions is that there is much less variation in copayments across insurer type when the copayment measure is taken from a visual inspection of the data. However, given that copayments are controlled for in the regression, the results are still somewhat surprising and suggest that the issue of insurer type steering behavior within a drug class deserves more study.

Estimating marginal effects of copayments with differing copayment specifications does not shed much doubt on the general conclusion that copayments appear to effectively allocate drugs within the statins class. While there are some counterintuitive results, most marginal effects estimates suggest that the choice of a statin is influenced by relative copayments. Moreover, the fact that most other marginal effects estimates are not influenced by different copayment specifications also seems to suggest that the main results are robust.

Independence from irrelevant alternatives

As discussed earlier, a well-known concern with using the multinomial logit (MNL) model is that it can produce misleading inferences when a *subset* of the alternatives in question are close substitutes. This arises because the MNL specification imposes the restriction that the ratio of the probabilities of choosing one alternative over a second depends only on the characteristics of those two options. The attributes of other alternatives in the choice set have no influence on the odds ratio between the two choices. This property is commonly referred to as the independence from irrelevant alternatives (IIA) property because the ratio is independent from other options or "irrelevant" alternatives (Horowitz and Savin, 2001; Train, 1986).

As discussed in Chapter 7, for the purposes of this study, the IIA property should not pose a problem in estimation of choice probabilities for statins.

Although the statins are similar to one another by nature, they are differentiated in their effectiveness at reducing LDL cholesterol. Moreover, it is not clear if the IIA property poses the same problem when all alternatives of a choice set are relatively close substitutes for one another. Nonetheless, this section describes and provides results from a test of the IIA restriction to ensure that it is not violated in this examination of pharmaceutical demand in the statins class. To test this property, at least one of the alternatives in the initial choice set, $\mathbf{B}^u$, are eliminated to form a smaller set of options, $\mathbf{B}^r$. Then, a new regression is performed for the smaller sample $\mathbf{B}^r$ and parameter estimates from the constrained regression, β_r are compared to those from the full multivariate analysis, β_u.

If IIA holds, the two sets of estimates should not be statistically different. But, if the choices in $\mathbf{B}^r$ correspond to a nest of similar alternatives, then there will be sharper discrimination within $\mathbf{B}^r$ and coefficient estimates will be statistically and economically dissimilar (McFadden, 2001). Hausman and McFadden (1984) demonstrated that the quadratic form $(\beta_u - \beta_r)'\,(\Omega_r - \Omega_u)^{-1}(\beta_u - \beta_r)$ has an asymptotic chi-square distribution when IIA is true, where Ω_r and Ω_u denote the estimated covariance matrices for the two sets of regressions.

For this study, the constrained regression excluded Lipitor as a member of the choice set. Conventional prescribing and utilization patterns in the United States suggest that physicians and patients may consider Lipitor to be different from other statins. If this is true, then a regression excluding Lipitor should produce statistically different estimates from the main results in Chapter 10 and the IIA property would not hold and the MNL would not be the proper model for these data. However, if in reality Lipitor is not different from other statins, then parameter estimates should not be statistically different from one another.

The calculated statistic $(\beta_u - \beta_r)'\,(\Omega_r - \Omega_u)^{-1}(\beta_u - \beta_r)$ for 72 parameter estimates in three equations is roughly 49 and smaller than the 95 percent chi-square critical value of 91.67. Thus, since the estimated test statistic is smaller than the critical value, one cannot reject the null hypothesis that the two sets of parameter estimates are different from each other. This test confirms that the MNL model is an appropriate estimation tool for these data and economic problem. However, future work should also consider alternative econometric specifications such as the multinomial probit or a semiparametric model that do not impose potentially restrictive properties.

12 Extensions

While there are numerous potential direct and indirect extensions to this line of research, this section will mention three of them. The first is to consider the drug utilization decision from the point-of-view of physicians. The second is to contemplate the impact of copayments and other factors, particularly health status, on switching from one statin to another. The last is to reflect on the possibility of maximizing the power of claims data in a panel data framework to eliminate the variation that exists due to unobservable variables.

A physician's point-of-view

Some studies, notably Hellerstein (1998), have been able to explicitly model the drug utilization decision from the perspective of the doctor. This type of research is helpful because it eliminates the imperfect nature of the physician–patient agency relationship. This study did not pursue this direction because the data do not explicitly record physicians' prescribing behavior. Pharmacy claims data do not normally include the prescribing physician for each reported claim.

However, physician and independent practise association identifiers are listed on some outpatient services claims. As a result, it is possible to match specific physician office visits to particular pharmacy claims and presume, within reason, that a prescribing decision occurred. But, this process is imperfect at best, and must be undertaken with extreme care to ensure the minimization of bias since the data do not directly observe physician behavior.

Additionally, to examine physician prescribing behavior, it is necessary to have a reasonable number of observations. In this case, to have a sizeable cohort of physicians identified on multiple claims and who treated multiple patients in the dataset. One challenge to overcome in obtaining physician data are that many doctor identifiers are reported as missing. In addition, reliability of the field itself is uncertain. Tables 12.1 and 12.2 display some information on physician identifiers; these data were captured from the outpatient files of statin users in the 1997 and 1998 MarketScan database.

More than 60 percent of identifiable doctors in nearly 2.5 million outpatient claims, have less than ten reported records in the database. Moreover, it is unclear as to how many of these records can be matched to a distinct drug purchase in the

Table 12.1 Number of physicians with multiple records in database

Number of records	Number of physicians	Percent
<10	50,181	62.5
10–29	17,054	21.3
30–49	4,902	6.1
50–100	4,285	5.3
100–1000	3,643	4.5
>1000	226	0.3
Total	80,291	100

Table 12.2 Number of patients per identifiable physician

Number of patients	Number of physicians	Percent
<10	74,008	92.2
10–29	4,600	5.7
30–49	755	0.9
>50	928	1.2
Total	80,291	100

drug claims dataset. The vast majority of identifiable doctors are reported on less than 100 records.

A similar pattern of identification appears when one considers the number of unique patients per identifiable physician (Table 12.2). The vast majority of identifiable physicians can be matched to less than ten unique patients on outpatient claims. In fact, more than 50 percent of doctors can only be paired with one patient. However, the critical number of patients needed to pursue with such a line of research is unknown and subject to debate. If the crucial figure was ten or more, then there are potentially more than 6,000 doctors in the dataset that may provide the basis for a sample of statin prescribers. Even if each doctor could only be connected to ten prescribing decisions, the sample size would be 60,000 claims. At the same time, the data in Table 12.2 does not account for the type of outpatient service rendered. Some of the outpatient claims may not be for office visits, rather they may be for outpatient surgeries or medical testing. Moreover, there has been no attempt at matching these physicians and patients to dates on which the patients purchased a statin. Thus, it is likely that a sample of physicians indirectly derived from the data may be small.

Nonetheless, an attempt should be made to extract these data from the claims. The advantage of such a database would help to alleviate the problem of imperfect agency between physician and patient. An analysis of physician prescribing behavior using this information could also account for persistence in statin prescribing over time and help explain why some patients switch between agents and others do not. It is possible that some doctors prescribe only one statin all the time, rather than recommending different agents for distinct patients. This type of information would be beneficial to policy research that focuses on modifying behavior of physicians.

To switch or not to switch?

Since this research only considers patients with statin monotherapy, a natural extension is to consider the factors that influence patients to switch from one statin to another over the course of time. The role of copayments in the decision to alter treatment are, clearly, of particular importance. However, an additional factor of interest would be a patient's health status. If coronary heart disease progresses rapidly while the person is taking one statin, then it is likely that he will switch to another. Although imperfect, claims data can provide some marker of changing health status by examination of diagnosis codes, for instance. In some cases, an increase in the dosage of a statin is also a sign of worsening health status. Since higher doses of statins tend to have a greater impact on cholesterol reduction, it may be safe to presume that a change to a higher dose is due to worsening health. In the MarketScan database, there is some evidence of patients who switch statins over the course of therapy as displayed in Table 12.3.

Nearly 6,700 patients display evidence of a distinct switch from one statin or another in the dataset. These patients are treated with their first statin for at least three months and, after demonstrating evidence of a change of therapy to a second statin, do not return to the original drug. Interestingly, the majority of these persons switch from Pravachol or Zocor to Lipitor (53%). In addition, there are many patients who substitute Lescol or Mevacor for Lipitor as well (19%). A sizeable group of patients also switch to Zocor from other statins (20%). The factors involved with this type of behavior would certainly be informative for policy makers hoping to influence drug purchasing behavior and attempting to understand the reasons underlying the decision to switch.

Table 12.3 Patients that switch statins

First drug	Second drug					Total
	Lescol	Lipitor	Mevacor	Pravachol	Zocor	
Lescol	—	520	6	76	152	754
Lipitor	27	—	14	134	332	507
Mevacor	11	721	—	79	371	1,182
Pravachol	19	1417	8	—	454	1,898
Zocor	49	2105	19	185	—	2,358
Total	106	4763	47	474	1,309	6,699

Panel data approach to prescription drug demand

One drawback in using insurance claims data to estimate consumer demand for prescription drugs is that many variables that may influence the choice decision are unobservable. For instance, one might reasonably expect that a patient's income plays a role in choosing one drug over another. Consumers without income restrictions may not be influenced by differential copayments and simply purchase the most expensive alternative. However, this data element is not available on most claims data. A second challenge to examining demand patterns with this data is that intertemporal decisionmaking may be lost with aggregation to the individual patient. As discussed earlier, interesting and policy-relevant choices may occur when patient characteristics and/or drug attributes change over time.

To minimize the biases inherent with the omission of pertinent explanatory variables and lost intertemporal variation in choice behavior, a discrete choice panel data model could be applied to this type of data and choice problem. The challenges to such a method would be in the actual formation of a panel of consumers and determining the design of the panel. Recall that a panel dataset combines elements of cross-sectional and time series data. While insurance claims data have both of the crucial elements, the data are not designed to be collected in a panel format and any artificial panel formed will certainly be biased to some extent. Moreover, there is a problem of synchronicity across patients. Since different persons will fill prescriptions at different times during any given month, there is no one date at any given time at which everyone has an observation of interest.

One design option that could alleviate these problems would be to define a time period to equal two or three months of observed patient data for continuously enrolled persons. By setting time periods in this manner and applying panel data estimation methods, unobserved time-invariant explanatory variables can be differenced out of the data. Moreover, over any one time window, specific individual characteristics, such as health status variables, can be measured and compared across time periods accordingly. It is likely that differences in health status (or other variables of interest) over time impact the choice of a statin. In addition, a panel setting could help to account for changes to a person's insurance coverage over time and its influence on statin choice.

With the current dataset, the feasibility of a demand study within a panel data framework is uncertain. Two years of claims data would probably not provide a long enough time period with which to find accurate estimates; more data would most likely be necessary. This issue becomes more clear when considering the data in Table 12.4. This table reports the median number of potential time periods available per statin using patient in the 1997 and 1998 MarketScan databases by statin if 60 days were considered equal to one time window. The median number of periods overall, across statins, is 5.4. The total number of patients with at least 6 periods (180 days) of continuous therapy is 16,893.

The advantages of such a panel data approach is that it is likely to control for unobserved time-invariant individual characteristics, avoiding any potential

Table 12.4 Median potential time periods per statin

	No. of periods	No. of patients	No. of patients with six or more periods
Lescol	5.6	4,171	1,441
Lipitor	4.4	18,029	2,858
Mevacor	6.0	4,583	2,193
Pravachol	5.6	10,901	3,862
Zocor	5.6	20,258	6,539
Median/Total	5.4	57,942	1,6893

specification bias. Moreover, this estimation procedure could be applied to not only the consumer demand problem but also the physician prescribing and switching issues described in the earlier two sections. By controlling for unobserved variables, the biases inherent in claims data may dissipate when considering the causes underlying the decision to switch from one drug to another or the choice to prescribe different drugs or the same drug over time.

13 Discussion of policy implications and conclusions

The results of this study have direct relevance for decisions made by large institutional drug purchasers in the public and private sectors of the US economy. In particular, a purchaser's ability to influence consumer demand implies that it may sway the market share of a pharmaceutical product. As a result, that purchaser may be able to negotiate for a lower price from a drug firm. The implications for this type of market behavior will be discussed in general and also for the specific case of the Medicare prescription drug benefit. This will be followed by some concluding remarks regarding this research.

Bargaining in the prescription drug market

As noted earlier, prescription drug prices and utilization in the United States have increased considerably over the course of the last decade. At the same time, the rate of therapeutic advance for prescription drugs has also climbed steadily. Thus, although costly, Americans have access to quality-of-life-enhancing medicines.

In order to remain profitable and still provide these drugs to enrollees, insurers must choose between higher premium rates or larger, more complex prescription drug plan designs. In almost all cases, insurers actually decide to raise premiums as well as increase out-of-pocket costs and/or place restrictions on prescription drug utilization. These restrictions may not be universal for all drugs and therapeutic classes but targeted to specific pharmaceuticals. The results of this research suggest that financial differentiation from the point-of-view of the consumer among alternatives in a therapeutic class impacts the choice of one drug over another. In other words, differing copayments instituted by an insurer or drug benefit manager will allocate drugs the same way prices will assign goods in a marketplace.

An insurer's ability to influence consumer behavior is especially important in a market where therapeutically equivalent drugs compete with one another. In these pharmaceutical markets, the battle for industry-wide market share can be intense and characterized by a great amount of advertising in an attempt to differentiate one drug from the others. In this monopolistically competitive environment, it is highly likely that firms will provide price breaks to large institutional purchasers who may favor their product over another and offer them the ability to increase their market share at the expense of competitors.

The usual form of price reductions in the pharmaceutical industry are discounts and rebates, many of which are hidden and unknown to the general public (Levy, 1999). A drug firm will also engage in bundling tactics to sell multiple products to health plans from its cache of drugs to ensure that its key profit-driving pharmaceuticals are on plan formularies (Kessler, 1999). In return, the insurer or prescription benefit manager gives preferred status to the drug firm's product by setting a lower copayment (consumer out-of-pocket cost) for it compared to therapeutically equivalent substitutes. Thus, to some extent, the cost faced by the consumer is reflective of the price paid by the insurer, though the full price reduction is probably not passed on to consumers.

This process occurs only if the insurer demonstrates the ability to influence consumer purchasing behavior (or physician prescribing behavior) and shift drug market share. Clearly, insurers with smaller populations of enrollees will find it much more difficult to demand discounts from drug manufacturers than companies with many covered lives. This economies of scale argument has manifested itself in the United States with the formation of large prescription benefit managers (PBMs) that aggregate the buying power of numerous insurers to extract price breaks from pharmaceutical firms. The largest four PBMs in the United States are purported to control the drug benefits for 210 million people or 70 percent of the nation's population, suggesting they have much individual negotiating power (Martinez, 2003). An interesting extension of this issue would be to examine if drug manufacturers, in turn, raise cash prices to the uninsured population. If the elasticities of demand in each market are different enough and goods are not transferable, one might expect that this type of price discrimination does occur.

The market for statins is one in which monopolistically competitive market behavior is evident. The five drugs are manufactured by four firms that actively compete for market share through advertising and, presumably, price breaks. Moreover, these drugs have become increasingly important and costly components of insurers' drug benefit plans. In fact, increased utilization of statins was the single largest contributor to total drug expenditures in 2001 in the AdvancePCS managed care system, one of the nation's largest PBMs (NewEdge, 2002). Moreover, in 2000, Lipitor and Zocor ranked second and sixth, respectively, in terms of annual managed care costs per member enrolled in managed care firms (Novartis, 2001). As detailed earlier, different health plans have diverse benefit arrangements for statins that then influence consumer behavior.

In the near future, this market will become even more competitive. Two of the agents have already lost patent protection, Mevacor and Pravachol. Moreover, additional competitors are set to market new agents that promise to improve upon the beneficial effects of the current generation of statins. In addition, an influx of new statin users is expected to nearly triple the market's size as a result of recent updates to the National Cholesterol Education Program's (NCEP) guidelines for CHD treatment (Liebman, 2001). These developments may cause the manufacturers of existing statins to compete more aggressively to retain market share.

The medicare prescription drug benefit

In December 2003, the United States government passed into law the Medicare Modernization Act, authorizing for the first time in United States history sweeping prescription drug coverage for the elderly under Medicare. As a part of the legislation, Medicare will approve private insurance companies and other organizations to serve as prescription drug plans (PDPs) all over the country. The cohort of more than 40 million Medicare beneficiaries represents the largest collection of pharmaceutical purchasers in the United States. While many of these individuals already have supplemental drug insurance coverage, nearly 11 million pay cash prices for pharmaceuticals, which have recently soared by nearly three times the inflation rate (Lueck and Horvath, 2002).

A substantial and controversial hurdle facing the prescription drug benefit is financing. The United States Congressional Budget Office estimates that the cost of the Medicare drug benefit will be approximately $850 billion over 10 years (Kaiser Daily Health Policy Report, 2005). However, the benefit has also created the largest ever coalition of prescription drug buying power in the United States. Such a coalition could extract price benefits equal to or greater than those received by the Medicaid program or the Veteran's Administration systems. The latter organizations have, in the past, most favored customer status from the US pharmaceutical industry. As suggested by this study's results, the implementation of pharmacy benefit schemes targeted to directly influence patient drug selection among the elderly, and ultimately pharmaceutical market share, could give Medicare PDPs the bargaining power required to command price reductions to minimize overall costs. This potential buying power would make a prescription drug benefit economically feasible. However, if the benefit is structured in such a fashion that a large cohort of beneficiaries cannot get access to important treatments, the benefit may not be politically feasible.

The ability to aggregate purchasing power of Medicare beneficiaries would be especially critical in the statins market. Cholesterol-lowering agents make up a large portion of many elderly individuals' drug bills. Moreover, in 2000, among managed care firms serving Medicare beneficiaries, three of the top four drugs ranked in terms of annual per member costs were statins: Lipitor, Zocor, and Pravachol (Novartis, 2001). These data suggest that increased purchasing power may decrease Medicare payments for statins in the future.

Conclusion

If an insurer wants its enrollees to use specific drugs, then this study confirms that consumer behavior is affected by both price (copayments) and non-price methods, controlling for copayments, at the plan level. This suggests that drug insurance benefit incentives are effective at influencing demand, and that copayments allocate drugs among the insured in the same way that prices allocate goods among buyers in a market. Interestingly, since it appears that copayments influence the choice of a statin, one may wonder if improper financial incentives lead to less appropriate and effective care (Mays *et al.*, 2001). It is possible that health plans rely too heavily on financial inducements and ignore medical considerations, although these results do not suggest that this occurs among statins.

Other scholars have pondered the question of health plan efficiency in terms of common inpatient, surgical procedures such as an appendectomy (Arnould *et al.*, 1984). Can this study argue that drug benefit structures are an efficient method of influencing consumer behavior? This is unclear without a more accurate picture of other steering methods and costs to insurers that may impact their bottom-lines. However, results suggest that Lipitor and Zocor, the leading statins in terms of efficacy, are most affected by managed insurance incentives. Patients appear most sensitive to copayment ratio changes for these drugs compared to others in the alternative set as well as more affected by non-pecuniary rationing when copayment levels are held constant across plan type.

Contrary to much public opinion and debate, it appears that the relevant price for many individuals is not set by drug firms but by insurers. With this knowledge, health plans have significant bargaining power in terms of negotiating discounts from manufacturers. Since copayment levels appear to matter in the choice of a drug, insurers can influence consumer behavior and may be capable of shifting market share, to some extent, from one statin to another. This issue is one which deserves further attention as it appears, from anecdotal evidence, that this behavior occurs among actors in the industry.

Of course, it is possible that this sample is not entirely representative and there is still some selection bias in terms of who receives treatment. The behavior of patients treated with statins may be fundamentally different from those not using them. Traditionally, these features could be controlled for by applying a two-stage methodology where the likelihood of being prescribed a statin is studied prior to the multinomial logit (MNL) step. Although this step could be performed for patients with some prior evidence of coronary heart disease (CHD), it is expected that those patients not treated with statins are probably in better health than their counterparts, on average, and not displaying enough signs of CHD progression to warrant use.

As pharmaceutical technology advances into the twenty-first century, larger prescription drug expenditures by consumers, insurers, and governments are certain to follow. In the class of statins alone there is a new blockbuster drug offered by AstraZeneca, rosuvastatin (Crestor), on the horizon which is expected to be more effective at reducing low density lipoprotein-cholesterol (LDL) and increasing high density lipoprotein-cholesterol (HDL) than its predecessors (Stender *et al.*, 2005). Moreover, an additional new drug agent, Ezetimibe, has displayed significant ability to inhibit the absorption of cholesterol (Gupta *et al.*, 2002). If past pricing behavior by drug companies is a predictor of future drug prices, these innovators will be costly and their use will be highly managed by insurers wishing to minimize their own costs. Moreover, the entrance of generic versions of Mevacor and Pravachol into the choice set will add an additional level of complexity to patients' choice problem. In addition, the market for statin treatment in the foreseeable future is expected to nearly triple in size as doctors begin to adopt the NCEP's newest cholesterol-lowering standards. As the market expands, the newest statin and its forebears will compete fiercely to capture a sizeable share of the lucrative market. Also, this study suggests that the copayments imposed by health plans and other non-price steering tactics will have a strong influence on the choice of the newest statin relative to the existing alternatives in the market.

Appendices

Appendix A: statin national drug codes

National drug codes (NDCs) are assigned by the Federal Drug Administration in the United States to reflect the product manufacturer, type of drug, and package size. The following NDCs were used in this study to search for claims of the statins of interest.

Lescol (Fluvastatin)

00078017605	00078017615	00078023405	00078023415	54569382100
54569382101	54868332900	55175300203	55289074060	

Lipitor (Atorvastatin)

00071015523	00071015534	00071015540	00071015623	00071015640
00071015723	54569446600	54569446700	54868393400	55175532503
55175532509				

Mevacor (Lovastatin)

54569061300	54569061301	54569061302	54569061303	54569061304
54569325600	54569325601	54569801100	54868068601	54868068602
54868068603	54868068604	54868108700	54868108701	54868196800
55175504606	55289040030	00006073061	00006073128	00006073137
00006073161	00006073178	00006073182	00006073194	00006073261
00006073282	00006073294			

Pravachol (Pravastatin)

00003015450	00003015451	00003017850	00003017851	00003019450
00003515405	00003515406	00003517805	00003517806	00003517875
00003519410	54569371500	54569371501	54569371502	54569371503
54569384000	54569407100	54569434600	54569851000	54569851001
54569859800	54868228801	54868228802	54868327000	54868327001
55175539003	55289010430			

Zocor (Simvastatin)

00006054361	00006072628	00006072654	00006072661	00006073528
00006073554	00006073561	00006073582	00006073587	00006074028
00006074061	00006074082	00006074087	00006074961	00006358928
54569418000	54569418001	54569440300	54569440400	54868263901
54868310400				

Appendix B: the Charlson comorbidity index

The index can range from zero to ten with weights assigned in the following manner:

Conditions	ICD-9 codes	weight
Myocardial infarct	410, 411	1
Congestive heart failure	398, 402, 428	1
Peripheral vascular disease	440–447	1
Dementia	290, 291, 294	1
Cerebrovascular disease	430–433, 435	1
Chronic pulmonary disease	491, 492, 493	1
Connective tissue disease	710, 714, 725	1
Ulcer disease	531–534	1
Mild liver disease	571, 573	1
Hemiplegia	342, 434, 436, 437	2
Moderate or severe renal disease	403, 404, 580–586	2
Diabetes	250	2
Leukemia	204–208	2
Lymphoma	200, 202, 203	2
Any tumor	140–195	2
Moderate or severe liver disease	070, 570, 572	3
Metastatic solid tumor	196–199	4

Appendix C: main multivariate regression results

Table C1 Estimates for choice of Lescol relative to Pravachol

N=44,642	Estimate	Std error	Z	P>|z|	90% confidence interval	
Les/prava copay	−0.876*	0.265	−3.300	0.001	−1.312	−0.439
Lip/prava copay	−0.681*	0.230	−2.960	0.003	−1.060	−0.303
Meva/prava copay	1.415*	0.288	4.910	0.000	0.941	1.890
Zoc/prava copay	−0.861	0.456	−1.890	0.059	1.612	−0.111
Age 45–55	0.015	0.074	0.200	0.843	−0.108	0.137
Age 55–60	0.129	0.080	1.620	0.106	−0.002	0.260
Age > 60	0.031	0.081	0.390	0.699	−0.102	0.165
Gender	−0.193*	0.046	−4.230	0.000	−0.268	−0.118
Northeast	−0.348*	0.080	−4.350	0.000	−0.480	−0.216
Midwest	−0.380*	0.066	−5.740	0.000	−0.488	−0.271
West	−0.146	0.092	−1.580	0.114	−0.297	0.006
Diabetes	−0.149#	0.072	−2.070	0.038	−0.267	−0.031
Hypertension	−0.190#	0.088	−2.170	0.030	−0.335	−0.046
Respiratory symptoms	0.367*	0.117	3.130	0.002	0.174	0.560
Cardiac dysrhythmias	−0.010	0.127	−0.080	0.939	−0.219	0.199
HMO enrollee	0.717*	0.225	3.190	0.001	0.348	1.087
PPO enrollee	0.600*	0.156	3.850	0.000	0.343	0.856
POS enrollee	0.201	0.863	0.230	0.816	−1.219	1.621
HMO*copayment	−0.036	0.024	−1.470	0.143	−0.076	0.004
PPO*copayment	−0.096*	0.020	−4.680	0.000	−0.129	−0.062
POS*copayment	0.010	0.095	0.110	0.914	−0.146	0.166

(*continued*)

Table C1 Continued

N=44,642	Estimate	Std error	Z	P>|z|	90% confidence interval	
Other cholesterol drugs	−0.215	0.153	−1.410	0.158	−0.466	0.036
Primary therapy	0.356*	0.052	6.850	0.000	0.271	0.442
Constant	0.225	0.555	0.410	0.685	−0.688	1.138

Notes
* (#, +) denotes significance denoted at 1 percent (5%, 10%) level.
MNL results (Log-odds ratio coefficients).

Table C2 Estimates for choice of Lipitor relative to Pravachol

N=44,642	Estimate	Std error	Z	P>|z|	90% confidence interval	
Les/Prava copay	0.107	0.190	0.560	0.574	−0.205	0.418
Lip/Prava copay	−1.649*	0.160	−10.290	0.000	−1.912	−1.385
Meva/Prava copay	0.282	0.238	1.180	0.236	−0.110	0.674
Zoc/prava copay	−2.637*	0.323	−8.170	0.000	−3.168	−2.107
Age 45 to 55	−0.045	0.047	−0.960	0.339	−0.123	0.033
Age 55 to 60	−0.056	0.051	−1.100	0.271	−0.140	0.028
Age > 60	−0.185*	0.051	−3.620	0.000	−0.270	−0.101
Gender	−0.019	0.029	−0.660	0.510	−0.067	0.029
Northeast	−0.040	0.054	−0.740	0.461	−0.129	0.049
Midwest	−0.088#	0.043	−2.040	0.042	−0.158	−0.017
West	−0.162*	0.062	−2.640	0.008	−0.263	−0.061
Diabetes	0.297*	0.042	7.120	0.000	0.228	0.366
Hypertension	−0.277*	0.060	−4.630	0.000	−0.376	−0.179
Respiratory symptoms	0.065	0.069	0.950	0.342	−0.048	0.179
Cardiac dysrhythmias	0.255*	0.083	3.080	0.002	0.119	0.391
HMO enrollee	−3.002*	0.296	−10.150	0.000	−3.488	−2.516
PPO enrollee	−0.768*	0.111	−6.950	0.000	−0.950	−0.586
POS enrollee	−0.887	0.687	−1.290	0.197	−2.017	0.243
HMO*copayment	0.297*	0.025	12.140	0.000	0.257	0.338
PPO*copayment	0.134*	0.014	9.360	0.000	0.110	0.158
POS*copayment	0.123	0.075	1.630	0.104	−0.001	0.247
Other cholesterol drugs	0.028	0.088	0.310	0.754	−0.117	0.172
Primary therapy	−0.254*	0.037	−6.940	0.000	−0.314	−0.194
Constant	4.787*	0.365	13.100	0.000	4.186	5.388

Note
* (#, +) denotes significance denoted at 1 percent (5%, 10%) level.

Table C3 Estimates for choice of Mevacor relative to Pravachol

N=44,642	Estimate	Std error	Z	P>|z|	90% confidence interval	
Les/Prava copay	−0.064	0.287	−0.220	0.823	−0.536	0.408
Lip/Prava copay	−0.110	0.228	−0.480	0.628	−0.485	0.264
Meva/Prava copay	−0.522	0.469	−1.110	0.266	−1.293	0.250
Zoc/Prava copay	−0.121	0.410	−0.300	0.767	−0.795	0.552

Table C3 Continued

N=44,642	Estimate	Std error	Z	P>|z|	90% confidence interval	
Age 45–55	0.317*	0.094	3.380	0.001	0.163	0.471
Age 55–60	0.661*	0.096	6.850	0.000	0.502	0.820
Age > 60	0.834*	0.095	8.770	0.000	0.678	0.990
Gender	−0.016	0.047	−0.340	0.735	−0.093	0.062
Northeast	0.314*	0.091	3.470	0.001	0.165	0.463
Midwest	−0.171#	0.071	−2.400	0.016	−0.288	−0.054
West	−0.054	0.104	−0.520	0.603	−0.225	0.117
Diabetes	−0.058	0.070	−0.840	0.403	−0.173	0.056
Hypertension	0.117	0.098	1.190	0.234	−0.045	0.278
Respiratory symptoms	−0.324*	0.115	−2.820	0.005	−0.512	−0.135
Cardiac dysrhythmias	0.135	0.113	1.200	0.228	−0.050	0.321
HMO enrollee	−0.466	0.291	−1.600	0.109	−0.945	0.013
PPO enrollee	1.384*	0.163	8.470	0.000	1.116	1.653
POS enrollee	14.377*	2.540	5.660	0.000	10.199	18.555
HMO*copayment	0.006	0.027	0.210	0.834	−0.039	0.051
PPO*copayment	−0.185*	0.023	−8.000	0.000	−0.223	−0.147
POS*copayment	−1.661*	0.289	−5.750	0.000	−2.136	−1.186
Other cholesterol drugs	0.187	0.132	1.420	0.154	−0.029	0.404
Primary therapy	0.413*	0.056	7.420	0.000	0.321	0.504
Constant	−0.876	0.624	−1.400	0.160	−1.902	0.151

Note
* (#, +) denotes significance denoted at 1 percent (5%, 10%) level.

Table C4 Estimates for choice of Zocor relative to Pravachol

N=44,642	Estimate	Std error	Z	P>|z|	90% confidence interval	
Les/Prava copay	−0.496*	0.185	−2.680	0.007	−0.800	−0.191
Lip/Prava copay	0.209	0.149	1.400	0.163	−0.037	0.454
Meva/Prava copay	0.732*	0.212	3.450	0.001	0.383	1.082
Zoc/Prava copay	−2.639*	0.309	8.530	0.000	−3.147	−2.130
Age 45–55	0.219*	0.050	4.380	0.000	0.137	0.302
Age 55–60	0.368*	0.053	6.890	0.000	0.280	0.456
Age > 60	0.334*	0.053	6.270	0.000	0.247	0.422
Gender	0.039	0.029	1.320	0.185	−0.009	0.087
Northeast	−0.155*	0.053	−2.940	0.003	−0.242	−0.068
Midwest	−0.365*	0.042	−8.640	0.000	−0.434	−0.295
West	−0.531*	0.065	−8.200	0.000	−0.638	−0.425
Diabetes	−0.046	0.044	−1.050	0.295	−0.117	0.026
Hypertension	0.197*	0.061	3.250	0.001	0.097	0.297
Respiratory symptoms	−0.158#	0.067	−2.370	0.018	−0.268	−0.048
Cardiac dysrhythmias	−0.355*	0.080	−4.460	0.000	−0.486	−0.224
HMO enrollee	1.369*	0.151	9.040	0.000	1.120	1.618
PPO enrollee	0.217#	0.109	2.000	0.045	0.039	0.396
POS enrollee	13.024*	1.102	11.820	0.000	11.212	14.836
HMO*copayment	−0.119*	0.016	−7.600	0.000	−0.144	−0.093
PPO*copayment	0.006	0.014	0.400	0.691	−0.018	0.029

(*continued*)

Table C4 Continued

N=44,642	Estimate	Std error	Z	P>|z|	90% confidence interval	
POS*copayment	−1.401*	0.122	−11.460	0.000	−1.602	−1.200
Other cholesterol drugs	−0.339*	0.094	−3.590	0.000	−0.494	−0.184
Primary therapy	0.005	0.035	0.140	0.889	−0.053	0.063
Constant	2.630*	0.359	7.330	0.000	2.040	3.220

Note
* (#, +) denotes significance denoted at 1 percent (5%, 10%) level.

Marginal effects estimates

Table C5 Marginal effects estimates for choice of Lescol

N=44,642	Estimate	Std error	Z	P>|z|	90% confidence interval	
Les/Prava copay	−0.041*	0.013	−3.200	0.001	−0.063	−0.020
Lip/Prava copay	−0.007	0.012	−0.640	0.524	−0.027	0.012
Meva/Prava copay	0.060*	0.014	4.460	0.000	0.038	0.083
Zoc/Prava copay	0.066*	0.023	2.880	0.004	0.028	0.104
Age 45–55	−0.004	0.004	−1.100	0.272	−0.010	0.001
Age 55–60	−0.002	0.004	−0.570	0.569	−0.009	0.004
Age > 60	−0.005	0.004	−1.280	0.200	−0.012	0.001
Gender	−0.012*	0.002	−4.870	0.000	−0.016	−0.008
Northeast	−0.016*	0.003	−4.530	0.000	−0.022	−0.010
Midwest	−0.011*	0.003	−3.480	0.001	−0.017	−0.006
West	0.006	0.005	1.230	0.220	−0.002	0.014
Diabetes	−0.013*	0.003	−4.240	0.000	−0.018	−0.008
Hypertension	−0.010#	0.004	−2.330	0.020	−0.017	−0.003
Respiratory symptoms	0.026*	0.008	3.520	0.000	0.014	0.039
Cardiac dysrhythmias	−0.001	0.006	−0.080	0.934	−0.011	0.010
HMO enrollee	0.020	0.013	1.510	0.130	−0.002	0.041
PPO enrollee	0.041*	0.010	4.170	0.000	0.025	0.058
POS enrollee	−0.083*	0.011	−7.640	0.000	−0.101	−0.065
HMO*copayment	−0.006*	0.001	−4.580	0.000	−0.008	−0.004
PPO*copayment	−0.008*	0.001	−7.960	0.000	−0.010	−0.006
POS*copayment	0.034*	0.005	7.000	0.000	0.026	0.042
Other cholesterol drugs	−0.007	0.007	−0.930	0.354	−0.018	0.005
Primary therapy	0.027*	0.003	8.520	0.000	0.021	0.032

Note
* (#, +) denotes significance denoted at 1 percent (5%, 10%) level.

Table C6 Marginal effects estimates for choice of Lipitor

N=44,642	Estimate	Std error	Z	P>|z|	90% confidence interval	
Les/Prava copay	0.108*	0.031	3.470	0.001	0.057	0.159
Lip/Prava copay	−0.388*	0.029	−13.380	0.000	−0.436	−0.340

Table C6 Continued

N=44,642	Estimate	Std error	Z	P>|z|	90% confidence interval	
Meva/Prava copay	−0.050	0.046	−1.100	0.272	−0.125	0.025
Zoc/Prava copay	−0.246*	0.057	−4.350	0.000	−0.340	−0.153
Age 45–55	−0.045*	0.008	−5.520	0.000	−0.058	−0.031
Age 55–60	−0.075*	0.008	−9.050	0.000	−0.088	−0.061
Age > 60	−0.100*	0.008	−12.320	0.000	−0.114	−0.087
Gender	−0.005	0.005	−1.000	0.317	−0.013	0.003
Northeast	0.011	0.009	1.290	0.196	−0.003	0.025
Midwest	0.038*	0.007	5.380	0.000	0.026	0.049
West	0.029*	0.011	2.760	0.006	0.012	0.047
Diabetes	0.080*	0.007	11.220	0.000	0.069	0.092
Hypertension	−0.085*	0.010	−8.660	0.000	−0.102	−0.069
Respiratory symptoms	0.032*	0.012	2.690	0.007	0.012	0.051
Cardiac dysrhythmias	0.102*	0.015	6.670	0.000	0.077	0.127
HMO enrollee	−0.420*	0.011	−38.310	0.000	−0.438	−0.402
PPO enrollee	−0.225*	0.015	−14.660	0.000	−0.251	−0.200
POS enrollee	−0.653*	0.031	−21.180	0.000	−0.704	−0.602
HMO*copayment	0.084*	0.005	16.430	0.000	0.076	0.092
PPO*copayment	0.035*	0.003	14.060	0.000	0.031	0.040
POS*copayment	0.237*	0.018	13.290	0.000	0.208	0.267
Other cholesterol drugs	0.048*	0.016	3.050	0.002	0.022	0.074
Primary therapy	−0.073*	0.006	−12.830	0.000	−0.083	−0.064

Note
* (#, +) denotes significance denoted at 1 percent (5%, 10%) level.

Table C7 Marginal effects estimates for choice of Mevacor

N=44,642	Estimate	Std error	Z	P>|z|	90% confidence interval	
Les/Prava copay	0.007	0.012	0.550	0.581	−0.013	0.027
Lip/Prava copay	0.023#	0.010	2.340	0.019	0.007	0.039
Meva/Prava copay	−0.048#	0.022	−2.230	0.025	−0.084	−0.013
Zoc/Prava copay	0.094*	0.018	5.350	0.000	0.065	0.122
Age 45–55	0.012*	0.005	2.760	0.006	0.005	0.020
Age 55–60	0.029*	0.005	5.300	0.000	0.020	0.038
Age > 60	0.044*	0.006	7.530	0.000	0.034	0.053
Gender	−0.001	0.002	−0.260	0.798	−0.004	0.003
Northeast	0.022*	0.005	4.750	0.000	0.014	0.029
Midwest	0.001	0.003	0.360	0.719	−0.004	0.006
West	0.010#	0.005	1.960	0.050	0.002	0.019
Diabetes	−0.007*	0.003	−2.600	0.009	−0.012	−0.003
Hypertension	0.007+	0.004	1.670	0.096	0.000	0.015
Respiratory symptoms	−0.014*	0.004	−3.380	0.001	−0.021	−0.007
Cardiac dysrhythmias	0.007	0.005	1.420	0.157	−0.001	0.016
HMO enrollee	−0.029*	0.006	−4.730	0.000	−0.039	−0.019
PPO enrollee	0.103*	0.014	7.620	0.000	0.081	0.125
POS enrollee	0.275	0.281	0.980	0.329	−0.188	0.737
HMO* copayment	−0.003#	0.001	−2.320	0.020	−0.005	−0.001
PPO* copayment	−0.011*	0.001	−11.270	0.000	−0.013	−0.010

(*continued*)

Table C7 Continued

N=44,642	Estimate	Std error	Z	P>|z|	90% confidence interval	
POS* copayment	−0.057*	0.012	−4.840	0.000	−0.077	−0.038
Other cholesterol drugs	0.017#	0.007	2.340	0.019	0.005	0.029
Primary therapy	0.026*	0.003	8.670	0.000	0.021	0.031

Note
* (#, +) denotes significance denoted at 1 percent (5%, 10%) level.

Table C8 Marginal effects estimates for choice of Pravachol

N=44,642	Estimate	Std error	Z	P>|z|	90% confidence interval	
Les/Prava copay	0.034	0.024	1.410	0.157	−0.006	0.073
Lip/Prava copay	0.097*	0.020	4.900	0.000	0.064	0.129
Meva/Prava copay	−0.073*	0.028	−2.630	0.008	−0.119	−0.027
Zoc/Prava copay	0.336*	0.040	8.470	0.000	0.271	0.401
Age 45 to 55	−0.014#	0.006	−2.310	0.021	−0.024	−0.004
Age 55 to 60	−0.027*	0.006	−4.380	0.000	−0.038	−0.017
Age > 60	−0.020*	0.006	−3.050	0.002	−0.030	−0.009
Gender	0.001	0.004	0.270	0.791	−0.005	0.007
Northeast	0.012+	0.007	1.740	0.082	0.001	0.024
Midwest	0.034*	0.006	6.030	0.000	0.024	0.043
West	0.046*	0.009	4.930	0.000	0.031	0.062
Diabetes	−0.015*	0.005	−2.810	0.005	−0.023	−0.006
Hypertension	0.004	0.008	0.580	0.562	−0.008	0.017
Respiratory symptoms	0.004	0.009	0.420	0.676	−0.011	0.018
Cardiac dysrhythmias	0.000	0.010	0.020	0.988	−0.017	0.017
HMO enrollee	−0.054*	0.015	−3.730	0.000	−0.078	−0.030
PPO enrollee	0.000	0.013	0.030	0.975	−0.022	0.022
POS enrollee	−0.248*	0.035	−7.100	0.000	−0.306	−0.191
HMO*copayment	−0.011*	0.002	−4.560	0.000	−0.014	−0.007
PPO*copayment	−0.006*	0.002	−3.290	0.001	−0.009	−0.003
POS*copayment	0.094*	0.013	7.300	0.000	0.073	0.115
Other cholesterol drugs	0.018	0.012	1.470	0.142	−0.002	0.038
Primary therapy	0.006	0.005	1.300	0.193	−0.002	0.014

Note
* (#, +) denotes significance denoted at 1 percent (5%, 10%) level.

Table C9 Marginal effects estimates for choice of Zocor

N=44,642	Estimate	Std error	Z	P>|z|	90% confidence interval	
Les/Prava copay	−0.107*	0.030	−3.580	0.000	−0.157	−0.058
Lip/Prava copay	0.276*	0.026	10.640	0.000	0.233	0.318
Meva/Prava copay	0.111*	0.037	3.000	0.003	0.050	0.172
Zoc/Prava copay	−0.249*	0.054	−4.640	0.000	−0.337	−0.161
Age 45–55	0.050*	0.009	5.690	0.000	0.036	0.065
Age 55–60	0.076*	0.009	8.0.0	0.000	0.060	0.091

Table C9 Continued

N=44,642	Estimate	Std. error	Z	P>|z|	90% confidence interval	
Age > 60	0.081*	0.009	8.590	0.000	0.066	0.097
Gender	0.016*	0.005	3.340	0.001	0.008	0.024
Northeast	−0.029*	0.008	−3.670	0.000	−0.043	−0.016
Midwest	−0.061*	0.007	−9.030	0.000	−0.072	−0.050
West	−0.092*	0.010	−9.560	0.000	−0.108	−0.076
Diabetes	−0.046*	0.007	−6.690	0.000	−0.057	−0.034
Hypertension	0.083*	0.011	7.740	0.000	0.065	0.101
Respiratory symptoms	−0.047*	0.011	−4.470	0.000	−0.065	−0.030
Cardiac dysrhythmias	−0.109*	0.012	−9.240	0.000	−0.129	−0.090
HMO enrollee	0.484*	0.021	22.730	0.000	0.449	0.519
PPO enrollee	0.080*	0.019	4.260	0.000	0.049	0.111
POS enrollee	0.709#	0.278	2.550	0.011	0.252	1.167
HMO*copayment	−0.065*	0.004	−18.130	0.000	−0.071	−0.059
PPO*copayment	−0.010*	0.002	−4.190	0.000	−0.014	−0.006
POS*copayment	−0.308*	0.020	−15.080	0.000	−0.341	−0.274
Other cholesterol drugs	−0.077*	0.015	−5.230	0.000	−0.101	−0.053
Primary therapy	0.014#	0.006	2.510	0.012	0.005	0.024

Note
* (#, +) denotes significance denoted at 1 percent (5%, 10%) level.

Appendix D: ICD-9 codes of interest

ICD-9-CM Codes used to identify conditions of interest

Code	Condition	Description
272.0	Hypercholesterolemia	Elevated levels of cholesterol
272.1	Hyperglyceridemia	Elevated triglyceride levels
272.2	Hyperlipidemia	Elevated cholesterol and
272.4		triglyceride levels
410.xx	Myocardial infarction	Heart attack
412.xx		
411.xx	Ischemic heart disease	Narrowed heart arteries
414.xx		
413.xx	Angina pectoris	Recurring pain or discomfort in the chest
429.2	Cardiovascular disease, unspecified	Dysfunctional conditions of the heart, arteries, and veins

Appendix E: multivariate results—health status

Multivariate regression result for patients with evidence of CHD

Table E1 Estimates for choice of Lescol relative to Pravachol

N=34,607	Estimate	Std error	Z	P>|z|	90% confidence interval	
Les/Prava copay	−0.757#	0.329	−2.300	0.022	−1.299	−0.215
Lip/Prava copay	−0.597#	0.271	−2.200	0.028	−1.042	−0.151

(*continued*)

Table E1 Continued

N=34,607	Estimate	Std error	Z	P>|z|	90% confidence interval	
Meva/Prava copay	0.999*	0.385	2.600	0.009	0.366	1.633
Zoc/Prava copay	−1.063⁺	0.603	−1.760	0.078	−2.055	−0.071
Age 45–55	0.006	0.093	0.070	0.948	−0.147	0.159
Age 55–60	0.109	0.098	1.110	0.265	−0.052	0.270
Age > 60	−0.003	0.100	−0.030	0.977	−0.167	0.161
Gender	−0.247*	0.054	−4.570	0.000	−0.336	−0.158
Northeast	−0.351*	0.103	−3.430	0.001	−0.520	−0.183
Midwest	−0.339*	0.079	−4.300	0.000	−0.469	−0.210
West	−0.146	0.110	−1.330	0.185	−0.326	0.035
Diabetes	−0.102	0.081	−1.260	0.209	−0.236	0.032
Hypertension	−0.171	0.109	−1.560	0.118	−0.350	0.009
Respiratory symptoms	0.233⁺	0.140	1.670	0.096	0.003	0.463
Cardiac dysrhythmias	0.027	0.145	0.190	0.852	−0.212	0.266
HMO enrollee	0.625#	0.279	2.240	0.025	0.165	1.085
PPO enrollee	0.471#	0.185	2.550	0.011	0.168	0.775
POS enrollee	−1.666	1.099	−1.520	0.129	−3.474	0.141
HMO*copayment	−0.018	0.030	−0.590	0.556	−0.066	0.031
PPO*copayment	−0.067*	0.024	−2.800	0.005	−0.107	−0.028
POS*copayment	0.208⁺	0.120	1.730	0.083	0.010	0.405
Other cholesterol drugs	−0.200	0.175	−1.150	0.252	−0.487	0.087
Constant	0.641	0.699	0.920	0.359	−0.508	1.791

Notes
* (#, +) denotes significance denoted at 1 percent (5%, 10%) level.
MNL Results (Log-odds ratio coefficients).

Table E2 Estimates for choice of Lipitor relative to Pravachol

N=34,607	Estimate	Std error	Z	P>|z|	90% confidence interval	
Les/Prava copay	0.124	0.219	0.560	0.572	−0.237	0.484
Lip/Prava copay	−1.578*	0.183	−8.630	0.000	−1.879	−1.277
Meva/Prava copay	0.323	0.264	1.220	0.223	−0.112	0.758
Zoc/Prava copay	−3.121*	0.370	−8.430	0.000	−3.730	−2.512
Age 45–55	−0.020	0.056	−0.360	0.722	−0.111	0.072
Age 55–60	−0.058	0.059	−0.980	0.325	−0.156	0.039
Age > 60	−0.182*	0.059	−3.070	0.002	−0.280	−0.085
Gender	−0.027	0.033	−0.830	0.404	−0.081	0.027
Northeast	−0.096	0.065	−1.470	0.140	−0.203	0.011
Midwest	−0.085⁺	0.049	−1.750	0.081	−0.165	−0.005
West	−0.144#	0.070	−2.080	0.038	−0.259	−0.030
Diabetes	0.308*	0.046	6.680	0.000	0.232	0.383
Hypertension	−0.213*	0.070	−3.030	0.002	−0.329	−0.098
Respiratory symptoms	0.034	0.080	0.420	0.673	−0.098	0.165
Cardiac dysrhythmias	0.201#	0.090	2.230	0.026	0.052	0.349
HMO enrollee	−3.920*	0.407	−9.630	0.000	−4.589	−3.251
PPO enrollee	−0.880*	0.125	−7.050	0.000	−1.085	−0.674
POS enrollee	−1.147	0.850	−1.350	0.177	−2.545	0.252
HMO*copayment	0.371*	0.032	11.490	0.000	0.318	0.425

Table E2 Continued

N=34,607	Estimate	Std error	Z	P>|z|	90% confidence interval	
PPO*copayment	0.152*	0.016	9.420	0.000	0.126	0.179
POS*copayment	0.152	0.093	1.620	0.104	−0.002	0.305
Other cholesterol drugs	0.069	0.098	0.710	0.478	−0.091	0.230
Constant	5.125*	0.425	12.050	0.000	4.425	5.825

Note
* (#, +) denotes significance denoted at 1 percent (5%, 10%) level.

Table E3 Estimates for choice of Mevacor relative to Pravachol

N=34,607	Estimate	Std error	Z	P>|z|	90% confidence interval	
Les/Prava copay	−0.418	0.335	−1.250	0.212	−0.968	0.133
Lip/Prava copay	−0.171	0.264	−0.650	0.517	−0.606	0.264
Meva/Prava copay	−1.266*	0.381	−3.320	0.001	−1.893	−0.640
Zoc/Prava copay	0.156	0.490	0.320	0.750	−0.650	0.962
Age 45–55	0.329*	0.115	2.850	0.004	0.139	0.519
Age 55–60	0.678*	0.118	5.740	0.000	0.484	0.872
Age > 60	0.824*	0.117	7.040	0.000	0.632	1.017
Gender	−0.009	0.055	−0.160	0.870	−0.099	0.081
Northeast	0.499*	0.108	4.600	0.000	0.320	0.677
Midwest	−0.094	0.083	−1.120	0.261	−0.231	0.043
West	−0.124	0.123	−1.000	0.316	−0.326	0.079
Diabetes	−0.043	0.079	−0.540	0.588	−0.172	0.087
Hypertension	−0.091	0.124	−0.730	0.466	−0.295	0.114
Respiratory symptoms	−0.291#	0.139	−2.090	0.037	−0.519	−0.062
Cardiac dysrhythmias	0.236+	0.128	1.840	0.066	0.025	0.446
HMO enrollee	−0.490	0.380	−1.290	0.197	−1.116	0.135
PPO enrollee	1.511*	0.194	7.770	0.000	1.191	1.831
POS enrollee	17.915*	1.716	10.440	0.000	15.093	20.736
HMO*copayment	0.011	0.035	0.330	0.740	−0.045	0.068
PPO*copayment	−0.205*	0.028	7.240	0.000	−0.251	−0.158
POS*copayment	−2.055*	0.192	−10.700	0.000	−2.371	−1.739
Other cholesterol drugs	0.241	0.149	1.610	0.106	−0.004	0.486
Constant	−0.119	0.596	−0.200	0.842	−1.099	0.862

Note
* (#, +) denotes significance denoted at 1 percent (5%, 10%) level.

Table E4 Estimates for choice of Zocor relative to Pravachol

N=34,607	Estimate	Std error	Z	P>|z|	90% confidence interval	
Les/Prava copay	−0.464#	0.213	−2.180	0.029	−0.815	−0.114
Lip/Prava copay	0.027	0.168	0.160	0.871	−0.250	0.304
Meva/Prava copay	0.867*	0.245	3.540	0.000	0.464	1.271
Zoc/Prava copay	−2.713*	0.355	−7.640	0.000	−3.297	−2.129

(*continued*)

Table E4 Continued

N=34,607	Estimate	Std error	Z	P>|z|	90% confidence interval	
Age 45–55	0.261*	0.060	4.370	0.000	0.163	0.359
Age 55–60	0.368*	0.063	5.840	0.000	0.264	0.472
Age > 60	0.357*	0.063	5.670	0.000	0.254	0.461
Gender	0.038	0.033	1.150	0.252	−0.017	0.093
Northeast	−0.138#	0.063	−2.180	0.029	−0.243	−0.034
Midwest	−0.385*	0.048	−8.020	0.000	−0.464	−0.306
West	−0.501*	0.073	−6.890	0.000	−0.621	−0.381
Diabetes	−0.025	0.048	−0.520	0.602	−0.104	0.054
Hypertension	0.196*	0.071	2.750	0.006	0.079	0.313
Respiratory symptoms	−0.206*	0.078	−2.640	0.008	−0.335	−0.078
Cardiac dysrhythmias	−0.289*	0.087	−3.310	0.001	−0.433	−0.145
HMO enrollee	1.135*	0.181	6.280	0.000	0.838	1.433
PPO enrollee	0.278#	0.122	2.270	0.023	0.076	0.479
POS enrollee	13.490*	1.386	9.730	0.000	11.210	15.770
HMO*copayment	−0.104*	0.018	−5.710	0.000	−0.134	−0.074
PPO*copayment	−0.002	0.016	−0.100	0.918	−0.028	0.025
POS*copayment	−1.457*	0.154	−9.470	0.000	−1.710	−1.204
Other cholesterol drugs	−0.332*	0.105	−3.160	0.002	−0.505	−0.159
Constant	2.738*	0.416	6.580	0.000	2.054	3.423

Note
* (#, +) denotes significance denoted at 1 percent (5%, 10%) level.

Marginal effects estimates for patients with evidence of CHD

Table E5 Marginal effects estimates for choice of Lescol

N=34,607	Estimate	Std error	Z	P>|z|	90% confidence interval	
Les/Prava copay	−0.032#	0.015	−2.140	0.032	−0.056	−0.007
Lip/Prava copay	0.001	0.013	0.110	0.910	−0.019	0.022
Meva/Prava copay	0.032+	0.018	1.820	0.070	0.003	0.061
Zoc/Prava copay	0.061#	0.028	2.130	0.033	0.014	0.108
Age 45–55	−0.005	0.004	−1.210	0.227	−0.012	0.002
Age 55–60	−0.003	0.005	−0.580	0.564	−0.010	0.005
Age > 60	−0.006	0.004	−1.390	0.163	−0.013	0.001
Gender	−0.013*	0.003	−4.970	0.000	−0.018	−0.009
Northeast	−0.014*	0.004	−3.440	0.001	−0.021	−0.007
Midwest	−0.008#	0.004	−2.280	0.023	−0.014	−0.002
West	0.005	0.005	0.860	0.392	−0.004	0.013
Diabetes	−0.011*	0.003	−3.250	0.001	−0.016	−0.005
Hypertension	−0.008+	0.005	−1.690	0.091	−0.016	0.000
Respiratory symptoms	0.017#	0.008	2.210	0.027	0.004	0.030
Cardiac dysrhythmias	0.001	0.007	0.160	0.871	−0.010	0.013
HMO enrollee	0.028+	0.017	1.660	0.098	0.000	0.055
PPO enrollee	0.030*	0.010	2.960	0.003	0.013	0.047
POS enrollee	−0.106*	0.017	−6.220	0.000	−0.134	−0.078
HMO*copayment	−0.007*	0.001	−4.420	0.000	−0.009	−0.004

Table E5 Continued

N=34,607	Estimate	Std error	Z	P>|z|	90% confidence interval	
PPO*copayment	−0.006*	0.001	−5.590	0.000	−0.008	−0.004
POS*copayment	0.041*	0.005	8.210	0.000	0.033	0.049
Other cholesterol drugs	−0.007	0.007	−0.890	0.374	−0.019	0.006

Note
* (#, +) denotes significance denoted at 1 percent (5%, 10%) level.

Table E6 Marginal effects estimates for choice of Lipitor

N=34,607	Estimate	Std error	Z	P>|z|	90% confidence interval	
Les/Prava copay	0.113*	0.037	3.060	0.002	0.052	0.173
Lip/Prava copay	−0.358*	0.033	−10.770	0.000	−0.413	−0.303
Meva/Prava copay	−0.036	0.046	−0.780	0.438	−0.112	0.040
Zoc/Prava copay	−0.358*	0.065	−5.480	0.000	−0.465	−0.250
Age 45–55	−0.045*	0.010	−4.570	0.000	−0.061	−0.029
Age 55–60	−0.076*	0.010	−7.680	0.000	−0.093	−0.060
Age > 60	−0.104*	0.010	−10.340	0.000	−0.120	−0.087
Gender	−0.006	0.005	−1.090	0.274	−0.015	0.003
Northeast	−0.008	0.011	−0.790	0.429	−0.026	0.009
Midwest	0.039*	0.008	4.800	0.000	0.026	0.052
West	0.032*	0.012	2.640	0.008	0.012	0.052
Diabetes	0.080*	0.008	10.070	0.000	0.067	0.093
Hypertension	−0.070*	0.012	−5.890	0.000	−0.090	−0.050
Respiratory symptoms	0.034#	0.014	2.490	0.013	0.012	0.057
Cardiac dysrhythmias	0.079*	0.017	4.790	0.000	0.052	0.106
HMO enrollee	−0.454*	0.011	−41.290	0.000	−0.472	−0.436
PPO enrollee*	0.258	0.018	−14.330	0.000	−0.288	−0.229
POS enrollee*	−0.642*	0.032	−20.060	0.000	−0.694	−0.589
HMO*copayment*	0.101	0.007	14.310	0.000	0.089	0.112
PPO*copayment*	0.041	0.003	13.390	0.000	0.036	0.046
POS*copayment*	0.258	0.017	15.390	0.000	0.231	0.286
Other cholesterol drugs*	0.057	0.018	3.170	0.002	0.027	0.086

Note
* (#, +) denotes significance denoted at 1 percent (5%, 10%) level.

Table E7 Marginal effects estimates for choice of Mevacor

N=34,607	Estimate	Std error	Z	P>|z|	90% confidence interval	
Les/Prava copay	−0.011	0.013	−0.850	0.395	−0.033	0.011
Lip/Prava copay	0.021#	0.011	2.010	0.044	0.004	0.039
Meva/Prava copay	−0.080*	0.015	−5.280	0.000	−0.104	−0.055
Zoc/Prava copay	0.110*	0.019	5.640	0.000	0.078	0.142
Age 45–55	0.011#	0.005	2.140	0.033	0.003	0.020
Age 55–60	0.028*	0.006	4.490	0.000	0.018	0.038

(*continued*)

Table E7 Continued

N=34,607	Estimate	Std error	Z	P>|z|	90% confidence interval	
Age > 60	0.039*	0.007	6.010	0.000	0.029	0.050
Gender	0.000	0.002	0.050	0.959	−0.004	0.004
Northeast	0.032*	0.006	5.500	0.000	0.022	0.041
Midwest	0.004	0.003	1.330	0.184	−0.001	0.010
West	0.005	0.005	0.930	0.350	−0.004	0.014
Diabetes	−0.007#	0.003	−2.370	0.018	−0.011	−0.002
Hypertension	−0.003	0.005	−0.670	0.502	−0.011	0.005
Respiratory symptoms	−0.010#	0.005	−2.070	0.038	−0.019	−0.002
Cardiac dysrhythmias	0.012#	0.006	1.990	0.047	0.002	0.022
HMO enrollee	−0.021#	0.009	−2.500	0.012	−0.035	−0.007
PPO enrollee	0.109*	0.016	6.800	0.000	0.082	0.135
POS enrollee	0.804*	0.094	8.540	0.000	0.649	0.958
HMO*copayment	−0.004*	0.001	−2.930	0.003	−0.007	−0.002
PPO*copayment	−0.012*	0.001	−10.310	0.000	−0.014	−0.010
POS*copayment	−0.072*	0.006	−13.030	0.000	−0.081	−0.063
Other cholesterol drugs	0.017#	0.008	2.200	0.028	0.004	0.030

Note
* (#, +) denotes significance denoted at 1 percent (5%, 10%) level.

Table E8 Marginal effects estimates for choice of Pravachol

N=34,607	Estimate	Std error	Z	P>|z|	90% confidence interval	
Les/Prava copay	0.031	0.028	1.100	0.271	−0.015	0.077
Lip/Prava copay	0.108*	0.022	4.850	0.000	0.072	0.145
Meva/Prava copay	−0.073#	0.033	−2.230	0.026	−0.127	−0.019
Zoc/Prava copay	0.378*	0.047	8.110	0.000	0.301	0.454
Age 45–55	−0.018#	0.007	−2.440	0.015	−0.029	−0.006
Age 55–60	−0.026*	0.007	−3.530	0.000	−0.038	−0.014
Age > 60	−0.019*	0.007	−2.660	0.008	−0.031	−0.007
Gender	0.002	0.004	0.460	0.644	−0.005	0.009
Northeast	0.013	0.009	1.500	0.134	−0.001	0.027
Midwest	0.033*	0.006	5.200	0.000	0.023	0.043
West	0.044*	0.011	4.100	0.000	0.026	0.061
Diabetes	−0.018*	0.006	−3.160	0.002	−0.028	−0.009
Hypertension	0.003	0.009	0.370	0.709	−0.012	0.018
Respiratory symptoms	0.010	0.011	0.930	0.355	−0.008	0.027
Cardiac dysrhythmias	−0.001	0.011	−0.100	0.919	−0.020	0.018
HMO enrollee	−0.024	0.020	−1.200	0.232	−0.058	0.009
PPO enrollee	0.006	0.015	0.410	0.681	−0.019	0.031
POS enrollee	−0.230*	0.034	−6.750	0.000	−0.286	−0.174
HMO*copayment	−0.018*	0.003	−6.180	0.000	−0.023	−0.013
PPO*copayment	−0.008*	0.002	−3.700	0.000	−0.011	−0.004
POS*copayment	0.094*	0.016	5.710	0.000	0.067	0.120
Other cholesterol drugs	0.013	0.014	0.960	0.335	−0.009	0.035

Note
* (#, +) denotes significance denoted at 1 percent (5%, 10%) level.

Table E9 Marginal effects estimates for choice of Zocor

N=34,607	Estimate	Std error	Z	P>|z|	90% confidence interval	
Les/Prava copay	-0.100*	0.034	-2.950	0.003	-0.156	-0.044
Lip/Prava copay	0.227*	0.029	7.810	0.000	0.179	0.275
Meva/Prava copay	0.157*	0.040	3.880	0.000	0.090	0.223
Zoc/Prava copay	-0.190*	0.060	-3.190	0.001	-0.289	-0.092
Age 45–55	0.057*	0.011	5.350	0.000	0.039	0.074
Age 55–60	0.077*	0.011	6.900	0.000	0.059	0.096
Age > 60	0.089*	0.011	7.820	0.000	0.070	0.108
Gender	0.017*	0.005	3.190	0.001	0.008	0.026
Northeast	-0.022#	0.010	-2.300	0.021	-0.038	-0.006
Midwest	-0.068*	0.008	-8.830	0.000	-0.081	-0.055
West	-0.085*	0.011	-8.030	0.000	-0.103	-0.068
Diabetes	-0.044*	0.007	-5.960	0.000	-0.057	-0.032
Hypertension	0.078*	0.012	6.350	0.000	0.058	0.098
Respiratory symptoms	-0.051*	0.012	-4.170	0.000	-0.071	-0.031
Cardiac dysrhythmias	-0.091*	0.013	-7.130	0.000	-0.112	-0.070
HMO enrollee	0.472*	0.029	16.400	0.000	0.424	0.519
PPO enrollee	0.113*	0.023	4.990	0.000	0.076	0.150
POS enrollee	0.174+	0.093	1.870	0.062	0.021	0.327
HMO*copayment	-0.072*	0.005	-14.900	0.000	-0.080	-0.064
PPO*copayment	-0.016*	0.003	-5.360	0.000	-0.020	-0.011
POS*copayment	-0.321*	0.025	-13.000	0.000	-0.362	-0.280
Other cholesterol drugs	-0.080*	0.016	-5.030	0.000	-0.107	-0.054

Note
* (#, +) denotes significance denoted at 1 percent (5%, 10%) level.

Multivariate regression results for patients without evidence of CHD

Table E10 Estimates for choice of Lescol relative to Pravachol

N = 10,035	Estimate	Std error	Z	P>|z|	90% confidence interval	
Les/Prava copay	-1.197#	0.482	-2.490	0.013	-1.989	-0.405
Lip/Prava copay	-0.950#	0.452	-2.100	0.036	-1.694	-0.206
Meva/Prava copay	1.779*	0.530	3.360	0.001	0.908	2.651
Zoc/Prava copay	-0.236	0.781	-0.300	0.762	-1.521	1.048
Age 45–55	0.020	0.126	0.160	0.875	-0.187	0.227
Age 55–60	0.186	0.142	1.310	0.191	-0.048	0.420
Age > 60	0.109	0.145	0.750	0.452	-0.129	0.347
Gender	-0.037	0.087	-0.420	0.676	-0.180	0.107
Northeast	-0.337#	0.133	-2.530	0.012	-0.556	-0.117
Midwest	-0.464*	0.130	-3.570	0.000	-0.677	-0.250
West	-0.170	0.172	-0.990	0.323	-0.452	0.113
Diabetes	-0.283+	0.154	-1.840	0.066	-0.537	-0.030
Hypertension	-0.185	0.153	-1.210	0.226	-0.436	0.066
Respiratory symptoms	0.788*	0.226	3.480	0.000	0.416	1.161
Cardiac dysrhythmias	-0.233	0.300	-0.780	0.438	-0.727	0.261
HMO enrollee	1.214*	0.392	3.090	0.002	0.568	1.859

(continued)

Table E10 Continued

N = 10,035	Estimate	Std error	Z	P>|z|	90% confidence interval	
PPO enrollee	0.972*	0.333	2.920	0.003	0.425	1.518
POS enrollee	1.867	1.282	1.460	0.145	−0.241	3.975
HMO*copayment	−0.100#	0.045	−2.230	0.026	−0.173	−0.026
PPO*copayment	−0.183*	0.045	−4.110	0.000	−0.256	−0.110
POS*copayment	−0.156	0.142	−1.100	0.270	−0.389	0.077
Other cholesterol drugs	−0.289	0.320	−0.910	0.365	−0.815	0.236
Constant	0.031	0.951	0.030	0.974	−1.533	1.594

Note
* (#, +) denotes significance denoted at 1 percent (5%, 10%) level.
MNL results (Log-odds ratio coefficients).

Table E11 Estimates for choice of Lipitor relative to Pravachol

N = 10,035	Estimate	Std error	Z	P>|z|	90% confidence interval	
Les/Prava copay	−0.006	0.380	−0.020	0.987	−0.631	0.618
Lip/Prava copay	−1.739*	0.347	−5.000	0.000	−2.310	−1.167
Meva/Prava copay	0.109	0.542	0.200	0.840	−0.782	1.001
Zoc/Prava copay	−1.116+	0.660	−1.690	0.091	−2.203	−0.030
Age 45–55	−0.108	0.091	−1.190	0.236	−0.258	0.042
Age 55–60	−0.029	0.103	−0.280	0.781	−0.198	0.141
Age > 60	−0.183+	0.104	−1.750	0.080	−0.354	−0.011
Gender	0.012	0.064	0.190	0.853	−0.093	0.117
Northeast	0.144	0.102	1.410	0.157	−0.023	0.311
Midwest	−0.066	0.094	−0.700	0.482	−0.221	0.089
West	−0.238+	0.134	−1.780	0.076	−0.459	−0.018
Diabetes	0.278*	0.100	2.790	0.005	0.114	0.442
Hypertension	−0.413*	0.116	−3.560	0.000	−0.604	−0.222
Respiratory symptoms	0.176	0.143	1.240	0.216	−0.058	0.411
Cardiac dysrhythmias	0.412+	0.222	1.850	0.064	0.047	0.777
HMO enrollee	−1.345*	0.436	−3.090	0.002	−2.061	−0.628
PPO enrollee	−0.507#	0.258	−1.960	0.050	−0.931	−0.082
POS enrollee	−0.410	1.092	−0.380	0.708	−2.207	1.387
HMO*copayment	0.148*	0.042	3.550	0.000	0.079	0.216
PPO*copayment	0.077#	0.033	2.340	0.019	0.023	0.131
POS*copayment	0.067	0.120	0.550	0.579	−0.131	0.264
Other cholesterol drugs	−0.168	0.212	−0.790	0.428	−0.516	0.180
Constant	3.411*	0.727	4.690	0.000	2.216	4.607

Note
* (#, +) denotes significance denoted at 1 percent (5%, 10%) level.

Table E12 Estimates for choice of Mevacor relative to Pravachol

N = 10,035	Estimate	Std error	Z	P>|z|	90% confidence interval	
Les/Prava copay	0.606	0.535	1.130	0.257	−0.274	1.486
Lip/Prava copay	−0.055	0.446	−0.120	0.901	−0.789	0.678

Table E12 Continued

N = 10,035	Estimate	Std error	Z	P>|z|	90% confidence interval	
Meva/Prava copay	0.932	0.931	1.000	0.317	−0.600	2.464
Zoc/Prava copay	−0.986	0.738	−1.340	0.181	−2.200	0.228
Age 45–55	0.286[+]	0.162	1.770	0.078	0.019	0.552
Age 55–60	0.632*	0.173	3.660	0.000	0.348	0.916
Age > 60	0.864*	0.168	5.150	0.000	0.588	1.140
Gender	−0.023	0.093	−0.250	0.805	−0.177	0.131
Northeast	0.018	0.151	0.120	0.905	−0.231	0.267
Midwest	−0.321[#]	0.137	−2.350	0.019	−0.546	−0.097
West	0.115	0.193	0.600	0.550	−0.202	0.433
Diabetes	−0.162	0.153	−1.060	0.288	−0.413	0.089
Hypertension	0.373[#]	0.185	2.010	0.044	0.068	0.678
Respiratory symptoms	−0.292	0.223	−1.310	0.191	−0.658	0.075
Cardiac dysrhythmias	0.146	0.248	0.590	0.556	−0.262	0.554
HMO enrollee	−0.362	0.462	−0.780	0.433	−1.121	0.397
PPO enrollee	1.261*	0.334	3.780	0.000	0.712	1.810
POS enrollee	9.044	6.281	1.440	0.150	−1.287	19.374
HMO*copayment	−0.004	0.047	−0.090	0.932	−0.082	0.074
PPO*copayment	−0.164*	0.045	−3.670	0.000	−0.238	−0.091
POS*copayment	−1.068	0.707	−1.510	0.130	−2.231	0.094
Other cholesterol drugs	0.003	0.284	0.010	0.991	−0.463	0.470
Constant	−1.594	1.133	−1.410	0.160	−3.457	0.270

Note
* (#, +) denotes significance denoted at 1 percent (5%, 10%) level.

Table E13 Estimates for choice of Zocor relative to Pravachol

N = 10,035	Estimate	Std error	Z	P>|z|	90% confidence interval	
Les/Prava copay	−0.721[#]	0.380	−1.900	0.058	−1.346	−0.096
Lip/Prava copay	0.852*	0.325	2.620	0.009	0.317	1.386
Meva/Prava copay	0.528	0.425	1.240	0.215	−0.172	1.228
Zoc/Prava copay	−2.533*	0.632	−4.010	0.000	−3.572	−1.494
Age 45–55	0.101	0.093	1.080	0.280	−0.053	0.254
Age 55–60	0.395*	0.103	3.820	0.000	0.225	0.565
Age > 60	0.266	0.104	2.570	0.010	0.095	0.437
Gender	0.046	0.062	0.750	0.455	−0.055	0.147
Northeast	−0.173[+]	0.097	−1.790	0.074	−0.332	−0.014
Midwest	−0.268*	0.090	−2.970	0.003	−0.417	−0.120
West	−0.687*	0.145	−4.740	0.000	−0.925	−0.449
Diabetes	−0.140	0.102	−1.370	0.172	−0.308	0.028
Hypertension	0.211[+]	0.119	1.780	0.075	0.016	0.407
Respiratory symptoms	−0.041	0.132	−0.310	0.754	−0.258	0.175
Cardiac dysrhythmias	−0.545[#]	0.210	−2.590	0.010	−0.891	−0.198
HMO enrollee	1.914*	0.291	6.580	0.000	1.436	2.393
PPO enrollee	0.137	0.254	0.540	0.591	−0.282	0.555
POS enrollee	12.831*	1.723	7.440	0.000	9.996	15.665

(continued)

Table E13 Continued

N = 10,035	Estimate	Std error	Z	P>|z|	90% confidence interval	
HMO*copayment	−0.151*	0.031	−4.810	0.000	−0.203	−0.100
PPO*copayment	0.025	0.033	0.760	0.446	−0.029	0.080
POS*copayment	−1.359*	0.191	−7.120	0.000	−1.673	−1.045
Other cholesterol drugs	−0.356+	0.215	−1.660	0.097	−0.709	−0.003
Constant	2.180*	0.724	3.010	0.003	0.990	3.370

Note
* (#, +) denotes significance denoted at 1 percent (5%, 10%) level.

Marginal effects estimates for patients without evidence of CHD

Table E14 Marginal effects estimates for choice of Lescol

N = 10,035	Estimate	Std error	Z	P>|z|	90% confidence interval	
Les/Prava copay	−0.071#	0.030	−2.330	0.020	−0.121	−0.021
Lip/Prava copay	−0.057+	0.029	−1.950	0.051	−0.105	−0.009
Meva/Prava copay	0.111*	0.035	3.190	0.001	0.054	0.168
Zoc/Prava copay	0.097+	0.050	1.940	0.053	0.015	0.180
Age 45–55	−0.001	0.008	−0.090	0.929	−0.014	0.013
Age 55–60	−0.002	0.009	−0.260	0.795	−0.017	0.013
Age > 60	−0.002	0.009	−0.220	0.828	−0.017	0.013
Gender	−0.004	0.006	−0.790	0.431	−0.014	0.005
Northeast	−0.023*	0.008	−2.980	0.003	−0.036	−0.010
Midwest	−0.022*	0.008	−2.880	0.004	−0.035	−0.010
West	0.012	0.012	1.010	0.312	−0.008	0.033
Diabetes	−0.022*	0.008	−2.630	0.009	−0.035	−0.008
Hypertension	−0.013	0.010	−1.390	0.163	−0.029	0.002
Respiratory symptoms	0.071*	0.022	3.150	0.002	0.034	0.107
Cardiac dysrhythmias	−0.016	0.017	−0.930	0.351	−0.043	0.012
HMO enrollee	0.016	0.026	0.620	0.534	−0.026	0.058
PPO enrollee	0.087*	0.032	2.760	0.006	0.035	0.139
POS enrollee	−0.066*	0.022	−3.050	0.002	−0.101	−0.030
HMO*copayment	−0.006#	0.003	−2.210	0.027	−0.011	−0.002
PPO*copayment	−0.016*	0.003	−5.250	0.000	−0.021	−0.011
POS*copayment	0.036*	0.012	3.120	0.002	0.017	0.056
Other cholesterol drugs	−0.007	0.020	−0.340	0.734	−0.040	0.026

Note
* (#, +) denotes significance denoted at 1 percent (5%, 10%) level.

Table E15 Marginal effects estimates for choice of Lipitor

N = 10,035	Estimate	Std error	Z	P>|z|	90% confidence interval	
Les/Prava copay	0.101#	0.057	1.760	0.078	0.007	0.195
Lip/Prava copay	−0.438*	0.053	−8.230	0.000	−0.525	−0.350

Table E15 Continued

N = 10,035	Estimate	Std error	Z	P>|z|	90% confidence interval	
Meva/Prava copay	−0.100	0.116	−0.860	0.389	−0.291	0.091
Zoc/Prava copay	0.086	0.115	0.750	0.453	−0.103	0.275
Age 45–55	−0.040*	0.014	−2.900	0.004	−0.062	−0.017
Age 55–60	−0.068*	0.014	−4.730	0.000	−0.091	−0.044
Age > 60	−0.086*	0.014	−6.010	0.000	−0.110	−0.063
Gender	−0.002	0.010	−0.160	0.871	−0.017	0.014
Northeast	0.059*	0.015	3.980	0.000	0.034	0.083
Midwest	0.034#	0.014	2.380	0.017	0.011	0.058
West	0.022	0.022	1.010	0.310	−0.014	0.058
Diabetes	0.089*	0.016	5.380	0.000	0.062	0.116
Hypertension	−0.109*	0.018	−6.210	0.000	−0.138	−0.080
Respiratory symptoms	0.022	0.023	0.950	0.343	−0.016	0.060
Cardiac dysrhythmias	0.161*	0.045	3.530	0.000	0.086	0.235
HMO enrollee	−0.326*	0.021	−15.810	0.000	−0.360	−0.292
PPO enrollee	−0.160*	0.030	−5.420	0.000	−0.209	−0.111
POS enrollee	−0.634*	0.090	−7.030	0.000	−0.782	−0.485
HMO*copayment	0.051*	0.007	7.010	0.000	0.039	0.063
PPO*copayment	0.021*	0.005	4.500	0.000	0.013	0.028
POS*copayment	0.196*	0.035	5.620	0.000	0.139	0.253
Other cholesterol drugs	0.011	0.035	0.320	0.752	−0.046	0.068

Note
* (#, +) denotes significance denoted at 1 percent (5%, 10%) level.

Table E16 Marginal effects estimates for choice of Mevacor

N = 10,035	Estimate	Std error	Z	P>|z|	90% confidence interval	
Les/Prava copay	0.060#	0.028	2.170	0.030	0.014	0.105
Lip/Prava copay	0.013	0.022	0.590	0.558	−0.024	0.050
Meva/Prava copay	0.031	0.054	0.570	0.570	−0.058	0.119
Zoc/Prava copay	0.026	0.036	0.740	0.458	−0.032	0.085
Age 45–55	0.017+	0.009	1.790	0.074	0.001	0.032
Age 55–60	0.029*	0.011	2.580	0.010	0.011	0.048
Age > 60	0.056*	0.013	4.220	0.000	0.034	0.078
Gender	−0.003	0.005	−0.520	0.600	−0.010	0.005
Northeast	0.004	0.008	0.540	0.590	−0.009	0.017
Midwest	−0.009	0.007	−1.300	0.195	−0.020	0.002
West	0.032#	0.014	2.280	0.023	0.009	0.056
Diabetes	−0.010	0.007	−1.450	0.146	−0.021	0.001
Hypertension	0.026#	0.011	2.450	0.014	0.009	0.044
Respiratory symptoms	−0.022#	0.009	−2.340	0.019	−0.038	−0.007
Cardiac dysrhythmias	0.012	0.014	0.860	0.391	−0.011	0.034
HMO enrollee	−0.051*	0.009	−5.630	0.000	−0.066	−0.036
PPO enrollee	0.099*	0.029	3.370	0.001	0.051	0.147
POS enrollee	0.016	0.061	0.260	0.791	−0.084	0.116
HMO*copayment	0.001	0.002	0.520	0.600	−0.003	0.005

(*continued*)

Table E16 Continued

N = 10,035	Estimate	Std error	Z	P>|z|	90% confidence interval	
PPO*copayment	−0.011*	0.002	−4.700	0.000	−0.015	−0.007
POS*copayment	−0.030	0.039	−0.760	0.447	−0.094	0.035
Other cholesterol drugs	0.014	0.018	0.820	0.413	−0.014	0.043

Note
* (#, +) denotes significance denoted at 1 percent (5%, 10%) level.

Table E17 Marginal effects estimates for choice of Pravachol

N = 10,035	Estimate	Std error	Z	P>|z|	90% confidence interval	
Les/Prava copay	0.057	0.047	1.230	0.220	−0.019	0.134
Lip/Prava copay	0.044	0.041	1.070	0.286	−0.024	0.111
Meva/Prava copay	−0.074	0.052	−1.410	0.159	−0.160	0.012
Zoc/Prava copay	0.232*	0.076	3.070	0.002	0.108	0.356
Age 45–55	−0.005	0.011	−0.420	0.676	−0.023	0.014
Age 55–60	−0.033*	0.012	−2.850	0.004	−0.053	−0.014
Age > 60	−0.021+	0.012	−1.740	0.081	−0.041	−0.001
Gender	−0.003	0.008	−0.360	0.717	−0.016	0.010
Northeast	0.008	0.013	0.640	0.523	−0.013	0.029
Midwest	0.031#	0.012	2.540	0.011	0.011	0.051
West	0.059*	0.020	2.910	0.004	0.026	0.092
Diabetes	−0.002	0.012	−0.130	0.895	−0.022	0.019
Hypertension	0.003	0.014	0.210	0.835	−0.020	0.026
Respiratory symptoms	−0.016	0.016	−1.030	0.302	−0.043	0.010
Cardiac dysrhythmias	0.004	0.027	0.160	0.871	−0.040	0.048
HMO enrollee	−0.109*	0.019	−5.760	0.000	−0.141	−0.078
PPO enrollee	−0.023	0.029	−0.770	0.440	−0.070	0.025
POS enrollee	−0.295*	0.097	−3.050	0.002	−0.453	−0.136
HMO*copayment	0.004	0.004	0.940	0.348	−0.003	0.011
PPO*copayment	−0.001	0.004	−0.290	0.774	−0.008	0.006
POS*copayment	0.098*	0.021	4.750	0.000	0.064	0.132
Other cholesterol drugs	0.037	0.027	1.360	0.175	−0.008	0.082

Note
* (#, +) denotes significance denoted at 1 percent (5%, 10%) level.

Table E18 Marginal effects estimates for choice of Zocor

N = 10,035	Estimate	Std error	Z	P>|z|	90% confidence interval	
Les/Prava copay	−0.147#	0.064	−2.290	0.022	−0.253	−0.041
Lip/Prava copay	0.438*	0.060	7.270	0.000	0.339	0.537
Meva/Prava copay	0.032	0.078	0.410	0.680	−0.096	0.160
Zoc/Prava copay	−0.442*	0.117	−3.760	0.000	−0.635	−0.249
Age 45–55	0.029+	0.017	1.710	0.088	0.001	0.056

Table E18 Continued

N = 10,035	Estimate	Std error	Z	P>|z|	90% confidence interval	
Age 55–60	0.074*	0.018	4.020	0.000	0.044	0.104
Age > 60	0.053*	0.018	2.930	0.003	0.023	0.083
Gender	0.011	0.010	1.110	0.268	−0.006	0.028
Northeast	−0.048*	0.015	−3.170	0.002	−0.073	−0.023
Midwest	−0.034#	0.015	−2.290	0.022	−0.059	−0.010
West	−0.126*	0.026	−4.910	0.000	−0.168	−0.084
Diabetes	−0.055*	0.017	−3.190	0.001	−0.084	−0.027
Hypertension	0.093*	0.023	4.060	0.000	0.055	0.131
Respiratory symptoms	−0.054#	0.022	−2.410	0.016	−0.091	−0.017
Cardiac dysrhythmias	−0.161*	0.029	−5.470	0.000	−0.209	−0.113
HMO enrollee	0.471*	0.051	9.300	0.000	0.387	0.554
PPO enrollee	−0.003	0.040	−0.080	0.933	−0.069	0.063
POS enrollee	0.978*	0.055	17.910	0.000	0.888	1.068
HMO*copayment	−0.050*	0.006	−8.090	0.000	−0.060	−0.040
PPO*copayment	0.007	0.005	1.400	0.161	−0.001	0.015
POS*copayment	−0.300*	0.030	−9.880	0.000	−0.350	−0.250
Other cholesterol drugs	−0.056	0.038	−1.470	0.141	−0.118	0.006

Note
* (#, +) denotes significance denoted at 1 percent (5%, 10%) level.

Appendix F: multivariate results—copayment estimation

Multivariate regression results for monthly copayment estimation

Table F1 Estimates for choice of Lescol relative to Pravachol

N = 44,625	Estimate	Std error	Z	P>|z|	90% confidence interval	
Les/Prava copay	−0.758#	0.376	−2.020	0.044	−1.376	−0.140
Lip/Prava copay	−0.791+	0.438	−1.810	0.071	−1.511	−0.070
Meva/Prava copay	1.864*	0.482	3.860	0.000	1.070	2.657
Zoc/Prava copay	−1.988*	0.740	−2.680	0.007	−3.205	−0.770
Age 45–55	0.005	0.075	0.060	0.951	−0.119	0.128
Age 55–60	0.108	0.080	1.340	0.181	−0.025	0.240
Age > 60	−0.001	0.082	−0.010	0.994	−0.136	0.134
Gender	−0.192*	0.046	−4.190	0.000	−0.267	−0.116
Northeast	−0.442*	0.083	−5.350	0.000	−0.578	−0.306
Midwest	−0.401*	0.068	−5.870	0.000	−0.514	−0.289
West	−0.164+	0.093	−1.770	0.076	−0.316	−0.012
Diabetes	−0.145#	0.072	−2.020	0.043	−0.263	−0.027
Hypertension	−0.140	0.089	−1.580	0.114	−0.286	0.006
Respiratory symptoms	0.322*	0.121	2.660	0.008	0.123	0.522
Cardiac dysrhythmias	−0.041	0.126	−0.320	0.748	−0.249	0.167
HMO enrollee	−0.116	0.211	−0.550	0.584	−0.463	0.232
PPO enrollee	0.425*	0.165	2.580	0.010	0.154	0.696
POS enrollee	0.166	0.932	0.180	0.859	−1.367	1.699
HMO*copayment	0.059#	0.026	2.280	0.023	0.016	0.101

(*continued*)

Table F1 Continued

N = 44,625	Estimate	Std error	Z	P>|z|	90% confidence interval	
PPO*copayment	−0.079*	0.020	−4.020	0.000	−0.112	−0.047
POS*copayment	0.008	0.100	0.080	0.939	−0.156	0.171
Other cholesterol drugs	−0.209	0.153	−1.370	0.171	−0.460	0.042
Primary therapy	0.367*	0.052	7.030	0.000	0.281	0.452
Constant	0.890	0.656	1.360	0.175	-0.190	1.970

Note
* (#, +) denotes significance denoted at 1 percent (5%, 10%) level.
MNL results (Log-odds ratio coefficients).

Table F2 Estimates for choice of Lipitor relative to Pravachol

N = 44,625	Estimate	Std error	Z	P>|z|	90% confidence interval	
Les/Prava copay	−0.089	0.248	−0.360	0.720	−0.496	0.319
Lip/Prava copay	−0.504+	0.274	−1.840	0.066	−0.955	−0.054
Meva/Prava copay	−0.048	0.335	−0.140	0.885	−0.599	0.502
Zoc/Prava copay	−3.507*	0.449	−7.810	0.000	−4.246	−2.769
Age 45–55	−0.061	0.048	−1.280	0.200	−0.139	0.017
Age 55–60	−0.094+	0.051	−1.840	0.066	−0.179	−0.010
Age > 60	−0.235*	0.052	−4.540	0.000	−0.320	−0.150
Gender	−0.018	0.029	−0.610	0.540	−0.066	0.030
Northeast	−0.102+	0.054	−1.880	0.060	−0.192	−0.013
Midwest	−0.119*	0.044	−2.720	0.007	−0.192	−0.047
West	−0.194*	0.062	−3.120	0.002	−0.296	−0.092
Diabetes	0.303*	0.042	7.260	0.000	0.234	0.372
Hypertension	−0.143#	0.060	−2.370	0.018	−0.242	−0.044
Respiratory symptoms	−0.028	0.071	−0.400	0.688	−0.145	0.088
Cardiac dysrhythmias	−0.016	0.080	−0.210	0.837	−0.148	0.115
HMO enrollee	−3.291*	0.281	−11.710	0.000	−3.754	−2.829
PPO enrollee	−0.852*	0.112	−7.630	0.000	−1.036	−0.669
POS enrollee	0.128	0.645	0.200	0.842	−0.933	1.189
HMO*copayment	0.331*	0.026	12.970	0.000	0.289	0.373
PPO*copayment	0.123*	0.013	9.160	0.000	0.101	0.145
POS*copayment	0.009	0.069	0.120	0.902	−0.105	0.122
Other cholesterol drugs	0.020	0.088	0.230	0.819	−0.125	0.165
Primary therapy	−0.245*	0.037	−6.700	0.000	−0.305	−0.185
Constant	5.006*	0.408	12.260	0.000	4.335	5.678

Note
* (#, +) denotes significance denoted at 1 percent (5%, 10%) level.

Table F3 Estimates for choice of mevacor relative to Pravachol

N = 44,625	Estimate	Std error	Z	P>|z|	90% confidence interval	
Les/Prava copay	0.100	0.399	0.250	0.803	−0.556	0.756
Lip/Prava copay	−1.705*	0.450	−3.790	0.000	−2.444	−0.965

Table F3 Continued

N = 44,625	Estimate	Std error	Z	P>|z|	90% confidence interval	
Meva/Prava copay	−0.306	0.477	−0.640	0.522	−1.090	0.479
Zoc/Prava copay	0.106	0.657	0.160	0.871	−0.974	1.187
Age 45–55	0.287*	0.093	3.080	0.002	0.134	0.440
Age 55–60	0.637*	0.096	6.640	0.000	0.479	0.795
Age > 60	0.815*	0.095	8.600	0.000	0.659	0.970
Gender	−0.014	0.047	−0.300	0.765	−0.091	0.063
Northeast	0.016	0.087	0.180	0.853	−0.127	0.159
Midwest	−0.082	0.072	−1.140	0.253	−0.201	0.036
West	−0.019	0.103	−0.180	0.854	−0.188	0.150
Diabetes	−0.056	0.070	−0.800	0.425	−0.170	0.059
Hypertension	0.091	0.100	0.910	0.361	−0.073	0.255
Respiratory symptoms	−0.227#	0.114	−1.990	0.047	−0.415	−0.039
Cardiac dysrhythmias	0.254#	0.114	2.230	0.026	0.066	0.442
HMO enrollee	−1.423*	0.291	−4.890	0.000	−1.902	−0.944
PPO enrollee	0.770*	0.156	4.920	0.000	0.512	1.027
POS enrollee	12.442*	1.619	7.680	0.000	9.778	15.105
HMO*copayment	0.144*	0.030	4.870	0.000	0.095	0.193
PPO*copayment	−0.067*	0.018	−3.620	0.000	−0.097	−0.036
POS*copayment	−1.396*	0.178	−7.850	0.000	−1.689	−1.104
Other cholesterol drugs	0.217+	0.131	1.650	0.099	0.001	0.433
Primary therapy	0.415*	0.055	7.490	0.000	0.324	0.506
Constant	0.173	0.610	0.280	0.777	−0.830	1.175

Note
* (#, +) denotes significance denoted at 1 percent (5%, 10%) level.

Table F4 Estimates for choice of Zocor relative to Pravachol

N = 44,625	Estimate	Std error	Z	P>|z|	90% confidence interval	
Les/Prava copay	−0.465+	0.245	−1.900	0.057	−0.868	−0.063
Lip/Prava copay	−0.063	0.268	−0.230	0.815	−0.504	0.379
Meva/Prava copay	1.795*	0.348	5.150	0.000	1.222	2.367
Zoc/Prava copay	−3.044*	0.447	−6.810	0.000	−3.779	−2.310
Age 45–55	0.186*	0.051	3.670	0.000	0.103	0.269
Age 55–60	0.331*	0.054	6.110	0.000	0.242	0.420
Age > 60	0.300*	0.054	5.540	0.000	0.211	0.389
Gender	0.038	0.029	1.290	0.196	−0.010	0.086
Northeast	−0.264*	0.054	−4.910	0.000	−0.352	−0.175
Midwest	−0.409*	0.044	−9.340	0.000	−0.481	−0.337
West	−0.547*	0.067	−8.220	0.000	−0.656	−0.437
Diabetes	−0.053	0.044	−1.220	0.221	−0.125	0.018
Hypertension	0.340*	0.062	5.530	0.000	0.239	0.442
Respiratory symptoms	−0.387*	0.070	−5.560	0.000	−0.501	−0.273
Cardiac dysrhythmias	−0.244*	0.079	−3.100	0.002	−0.374	−0.115
HMO enrollee	−0.534*	0.158	−3.380	0.001	−0.794	−0.274
PPO enrollee	0.431*	0.108	4.000	0.000	0.254	0.609
POS enrollee	18.912*	1.189	15.900	0.000	16.956	20.868
HMO*copayment	0.098*	0.018	5.350	0.000	0.068	0.129

(*continued*)

Table F4 Continued

N = 44,625	Estimate	Std error	Z	P>|z|	90% confidence interval	
PPO*copayment	−0.028#	0.013	−2.070	0.038	−0.049	−0.006
POS*copayment	−2.028*	0.129	−15.690	0.000	−2.241	−1.815
Other cholesterol drugs	−0.347*	0.095	−3.640	0.000	−0.504	−0.190
Primary therapy	0.019	0.036	0.540	0.588	−0.039	0.078
Constant	2.291*	0.427	5.360	0.000	1.588	2.993

Note
* (#, +) denotes significance denoted at 1 percent (5%, 10%) level.

Marginal effects estimates for monthly copayment estimation

Table F5 Marginal effects estimates for choice of Lescol

N = 44,625	Estimate	Std error	Z	P>|z|	90% confidence interval	
Les/Prava copay	−0.031+	0.018	−1.710	0.088	−0.062	−0.001
Lip/Prava copay	−0.027	0.022	−1.250	0.211	−0.062	0.008
Meva/Prava copay	0.069*	0.022	3.150	0.002	0.033	0.105
Zoc/Prava copay	0.028	0.037	0.760	0.448	−0.033	0.090
Age 45–55	−0.003	0.004	−0.920	0.359	−0.010	0.003
Age 55–60	−0.002	0.004	−0.440	0.658	−0.008	0.005
Age > 60	−0.005	0.004	−1.260	0.207	−0.012	0.002
Gender	−0.011*	0.002	−4.710	0.000	−0.015	−0.007
Northeast	−0.016*	0.004	−4.470	0.000	−0.022	−0.010
Midwest	−0.011*	0.003	−3.310	0.001	−0.017	−0.006
West	0.006	0.005	1.170	0.243	−0.002	0.014
Diabetes	−0.013*	0.003	−4.150	0.000	−0.018	−0.008
Hypertension	−0.012*	0.004	−2.990	0.003	−0.019	−0.006
Respiratory symptoms	0.031*	0.008	3.890	0.000	0.018	0.044
Cardiac dysrhythmias	0.002	0.007	0.300	0.762	−0.009	0.013
HMO enrollee	0.061*	0.017	3.490	0.000	0.032	0.090
PPO enrollee	0.028*	0.010	2.870	0.004	0.012	0.044
POS enrollee	−0.100*	0.018	−5.410	0.000	−0.130	−0.069
HMO*copayment	−0.006*	0.001	−5.160	0.000	−0.009	−0.004
PPO*copayment	−0.006*	0.001	−6.310	0.000	−0.008	−0.005
POS*copayment	0.048*	0.005	9.230	0.000	0.040	0.057
Other cholesterol drugs	−0.006	0.007	−0.870	0.386	−0.018	0.006
Primary therapy	0.026*	0.003	8.270	0.000	0.021	0.032

Note
* (#, +) denotes significance denoted at 1 percent (5%, 10%) level.

Table F6 Marginal effects estimates for choice of Lipitor

N = 44,625	Estimate	Std error	Z	P>|z|	90% confidence interval	
Les/Prava copay	0.054	0.041	1.310	0.189	−0.013	0.121
Lip/Prava copay	−0.057	0.043	−1.350	0.178	−0.128	0.013
Meva/Prava copay	−0.275*	0.056	−4.920	0.000	−0.367	−0.183

Table F6 Continued

N = 44,625	Estimate	Std error	Z	P>|z|	90% confidence interval	
Zoc/Prava copay	−0.377*	0.077	−4.900	0.000	−0.504	−0.251
Age 45–55	−0.043*	0.008	−5.320	0.000	−0.057	−0.030
Age 55–60	−0.079*	0.008	−9.400	0.000	−0.092	−0.065
Age > 60	−0.107*	0.008	−12.670	0.000	−0.121	−0.093
Gender	−0.004	0.005	−0.920	0.356	−0.012	0.003
Northeast	0.018#	0.009	2.110	0.035	0.004	0.033
Midwest	0.035*	0.007	4.890	0.000	0.023	0.046
West	0.023#	0.011	2.140	0.032	0.005	0.040
Diabetes	0.083*	0.007	11.480	0.000	0.071	0.095
Hypertension	−0.075*	0.010	−7.500	0.000	−0.091	−0.058
Respiratory symptoms	0.037*	0.012	3.140	0.002	0.018	0.056
Cardiac dysrhythmias	0.021	0.014	1.500	0.134	−0.002	0.044
HMO enrollee	−0.381*	0.014	−26.400	0.000	−0.405	−0.357
PPO enrollee	−0.248*	0.015	−16.210	0.000	−0.273	−0.223
POS enrollee	−0.600*	0.034	−17.570	0.000	−0.656	−0.544
HMO*copayment	0.060*	0.005	12.880	0.000	0.052	0.067
PPO*copayment	0.035*	0.002	14.210	0.000	0.031	0.039
POS*copayment	0.288*	0.014	19.950	0.000	0.265	0.312
Other cholesterol drugs	0.046*	0.016	2.910	0.004	0.020	0.072
Primary therapy	−0.074*	0.006	−12.960	0.000	−0.084	−0.065

Note
* (#, +) denotes significance denoted at 1 percent (5%, 10%) level.

Table F7 Marginal effects estimates for choice of Mevacor

N = 44,625	Estimate	Std error	Z	P>|z|	90% confidence interval	
Les/Prava copay	0.018	0.018	1.000	0.316	−0.012	0.049
Lip/Prava copay	−0.074*	0.021	−3.580	0.000	−0.108	−0.040
Meva/Prava copay	−0.056*	0.021	−2.670	0.008	−0.090	−0.021
Zoc/Prava copay	0.140*	0.030	4.600	0.000	0.090	0.190
Age 45–55	0.013*	0.005	2.660	0.008	0.005	0.021
Age 55–60	0.031*	0.006	5.380	0.000	0.022	0.040
Age > 60	0.047*	0.006	7.650	0.000	0.037	0.057
Gender	0.000	0.002	−0.210	0.830	−0.004	0.003
Northeast	0.010#	0.004	2.260	0.024	0.003	0.017
Midwest	0.007#	0.003	2.200	0.028	0.002	0.013
West	0.014#	0.006	2.490	0.013	0.005	0.024
Diabetes	−0.007*	0.003	−2.590	0.010	−0.012	−0.003
Hypertension	0.001	0.005	0.190	0.847	−0.007	0.008
Respiratory symptoms	−0.005	0.005	−1.050	0.293	−0.013	0.003
Cardiac dysrhythmias	0.021*	0.007	3.080	0.002	0.010	0.032
HMO enrollee	−0.023*	0.009	−2.640	0.008	−0.037	−0.009
PPO enrollee	0.050*	0.010	5.080	0.000	0.034	0.067
POS enrollee	−0.002	0.002	−0.710	0.479	−0.006	0.002
HMO*copayment	−0.001	0.001	−0.870	0.383	−0.003	0.001
PPO*copayment	−0.005*	0.001	−6.170	0.000	−0.006	−0.004

(*continued*)

Table F7 Continued

N = 44,625	Estimate	Std error	Z	P>|z|	90% confidence interval	
POS*copayment	−0.033*	0.008	−4.360	0.000	−0.045	−0.020
Other cholesterol drugs	0.020#	0.008	2.570	0.010	0.007	0.033
Primary therapy	0.027*	0.003	8.660	0.000	0.022	0.032

Note
*(#, +) denotes significance denoted at 1 percent (5%, 10%) level.

Table F8 Marginal effects estimates for choice of Pravachol

N = 44,625	Estimate	Std error	Z	P>|z|	90% confidence interval	
Les/Prava copay	0.040	0.031	1.290	0.198	−0.011	0.092
Lip/Prava copay	0.059+	0.035	1.670	0.095	0.001	0.116
Meva/Prava copay	−0.122*	0.044	−2.790	0.005	−0.193	−0.050
Zoc/Prava copay	0.418*	0.057	7.270	0.000	0.323	0.512
Age 45 to 55	−0.010+	0.006	−1.720	0.085	−0.020	0.000
Age 55 to 60	−0.022*	0.006	−3.530	0.000	−0.033	−0.012
Age > 60	−0.014#	0.006	−2.340	0.020	−0.024	−0.004
Gender	0.001	0.004	0.260	0.798	−0.005	0.007
Northeast	0.027*	0.007	3.630	0.000	0.015	0.039
Midwest	0.037*	0.006	6.510	0.000	0.028	0.046
West	0.049*	0.010	5.080	0.000	0.033	0.064
Diabetes	−0.015*	0.005	−2.840	0.004	−0.023	−0.006
Hypertension	−0.012+	0.007	−1.680	0.092	−0.025	0.000
Respiratory symptoms	0.023#	0.010	2.360	0.018	0.007	0.038
Cardiac dysrhythmias	0.013	0.010	1.230	0.219	−0.004	0.030
HMO enrollee	0.209*	0.033	6.330	0.000	0.155	0.263
PPO enrollee	0.001	0.013	0.090	0.929	−0.021	0.023
POS enrollee	−0.294*	0.036	−8.190	0.000	−0.353	−0.235
HMO*copayment	−0.028*	0.003	−10.520	0.000	−0.033	−0.024
PPO*copayment	−0.004*	0.002	−2.700	0.007	−0.007	−0.002
POS*copayment	0.135*	0.013	10.570	0.000	0.114	0.156
Other cholesterol drugs	0.018	0.012	1.470	0.142	−0.002	0.038
Primary therapy	0.004	0.005	0.950	0.343	−0.003	0.012

Note
* (#, +) denotes significance denoted at 1 percent (5%, 10%) level.

Table F9 Marginal effects estimates for choice of Zocor

N = 44,625	Estimate	Std error	Z	P>|z|	90% confidence interval	
Les/Prava copay	−0.081#	0.039	−2.070	0.038	−0.145	−0.017
Lip/Prava copay	0.100#	0.041	2.460	0.014	0.033	0.167
Meva/Prava copay	0.383*	0.054	7.050	0.000	0.294	0.473
Zoc/Prava copay	−0.208*	0.074	−2.820	0.005	−0.330	−0.087
Age 45 to 55	0.045*	0.009	5.020	0.000	0.030	0.059
Age 55 to 60	0.072*	0.010	7.510	0.000	0.056	0.088

Table F9 Continued

N = 44,625	Estimate	Std error	Z	P>|z|	90% confidence interval	
Age > 60	0.079*	0.010	8.100	0.000	0.063	0.095
Gender	0.015*	0.005	3.240	0.001	0.008	0.023
Northeast	−0.038*	0.008	−4.740	0.000	−0.052	−0.025
Midwest	−0.068*	0.007	−9.760	0.000	−0.079	−0.056
West	−0.092*	0.010	−9.200	0.000	−0.108	−0.075
Diabetes	−0.048*	0.007	−7.120	0.000	−0.059	−0.037
Hypertension	0.099*	0.011	9.220	0.000	0.081	0.117
Respiratory symptoms	−0.085*	0.010	−8.310	0.000	−0.102	−0.068
Cardiac dysrhythmias	−0.056*	0.012	−4.600	0.000	−0.077	−0.036
HMO enrollee	0.134*	0.032	4.230	0.000	0.082	0.186
PPO enrollee	0.168*	0.019	8.690	0.000	0.137	0.200
POS enrollee	0.995*	0.002	472.300	0.000	0.992	0.999
HMO*copayment	−0.024*	0.003	−7.470	0.000	−0.029	−0.019
PPO*copayment	−0.019*	0.002	−7.950	0.000	−0.023	−0.015
POS*copayment	−0.439*	0.022	−19.740	0.000	−0.475	−0.402
Other cholesterol drugs	−0.078*	0.015	−5.270	0.000	−0.102	−0.054
Primary therapy	0.016*	0.006	2.790	0.005	0.007	0.026

Note
* (#, +) denotes significance denoted at 1 percent (5%, 10%) level.

Multivariate regression results for the "Visual Inspection" copayment estimation method

Table F10 Estimates for choice of Lescol relative to Pravachol

N = 44,625	Estimate	Std error	Z	P>|z|	90% confidence interval	
Les/Prava copay	−0.595	0.612	−0.970	0.331	−1.602	0.412
Lip/Prava copay	−1.093#	0.430	−2.540	0.011	−1.801	−0.386
Meva/Prava copay	2.929#	1.427	2.050	0.040	0.583	5.275
Zoc/Prava copay	−0.074	0.502	−0.150	0.883	−0.900	0.753
Age 45–55	0.030	0.074	0.410	0.682	−0.092	0.153
Age 55–60	0.146+	0.080	1.830	0.067	0.015	0.277
Age > 60	0.047	0.081	0.580	0.565	−0.086	0.180
Gender	−0.191*	0.046	−4.180	0.000	−0.266	−0.116
Northeast	−0.320*	0.079	−4.040	0.000	−0.450	−0.190
Midwest	−0.402*	0.065	−6.220	0.000	−0.509	−0.296
West	−0.158+	0.092	−1.720	0.085	−0.310	−0.007
Diabetes	−0.144#	0.072	−2.010	0.045	−0.262	−0.026
Hypertension	−0.185#	0.091	−2.030	0.042	−0.335	−0.035
Respiratory symptoms	0.379*	0.114	3.330	0.001	0.192	0.566
Cardiac dysrhythmias	−0.175	0.115	−1.520	0.129	−0.364	0.015
HMO enrollee	0.618*	0.225	2.750	0.006	0.249	0.988
PPO enrollee	0.549*	0.148	3.710	0.000	0.305	0.792
POS enrollee	0.153	0.323	0.470	0.635	−0.379	0.685
HMO*copayment	−0.009	0.023	−0.390	0.699	−0.046	0.029
PPO*copayment	−0.075*	0.015	−4.930	0.000	−0.100	−0.050

(continued)

Table F10 Continued

N = 44,625	Estimate	Std error	Z	P>|z|	90% confidence interval	
POS*copayment	0.022	0.031	0.720	0.471	−0.028	0.073
Other cholesterol drugs	−0.221	0.153	−1.450	0.147	−0.472	0.030
Primary therapy	0.363*	0.052	6.970	0.000	0.278	0.449
Constant	−2.094	1.670	−1.250	0.210	−4.841	0.653

Notes
* (#, +) denotes significance denoted at 1 percent (5%, 10%) level.
MNL results (Log-odds ratio coefficients).

Table F11 Estimates for choice of Lipitor relative to Pravachol

N = 44,625	Estimate	Std error	Z	P>|z|	90% confidence interval	
Les/Prava copay	0.974*	0.380	2.570	0.010	0.350	1.599
Lip/Prava copay	−1.013*	0.288	−3.520	0.000	−1.487	−0.540
Meva/Prava copay	−1.429	0.902	−1.580	0.113	−2.912	0.054
Zoc/Prava copay	0.612	0.372	1.650	0.100	0.001	1.224
Age 45–55	−0.036	0.047	−0.760	0.444	−0.113	0.041
Age 55–60	−0.042	0.050	−0.840	0.402	−0.125	0.041
Age > 60	−0.172*	0.050	−3.410	0.001	−0.255	−0.089
Gender	−0.024	0.029	−0.840	0.402	−0.072	0.023
Northeast	0.065	0.052	1.260	0.208	−0.020	0.150
Midwest	−0.228*	0.042	−5.480	0.000	−0.297	−0.160
West	−0.149#	0.061	−2.450	0.014	−0.248	−0.049
Diabetes	0.296*	0.042	7.120	0.000	0.228	0.364
Hypertension	−0.185*	0.058	−3.190	0.001	−0.281	−0.090
Respiratory symptoms	0.058	0.067	0.860	0.388	−0.052	0.168
Cardiac dysrhythmias	−0.192*	0.073	−2.610	0.009	−0.312	−0.071
HMO enrollee	−1.399*	0.227	−6.160	0.000	−1.772	−1.025
PPO enrollee	−0.273*	0.094	−2.900	0.004	−0.428	−0.118
POS enrollee	−0.162	0.218	−0.740	0.457	−0.520	0.196
HMO*copayment	0.112*	0.021	5.350	0.000	0.078	0.147
PPO*copayment	0.045*	0.010	4.550	0.000	0.029	0.061
POS*copayment	0.044#	0.021	2.130	0.033	0.010	0.078
Other cholesterol drugs	0.000	0.087	0.000	0.999	−0.143	0.144
Primary therapy	−0.263*	0.036	−7.270	0.000	−0.323	−0.204
Constant	1.789+	0.964	1.860	0.063	0.204	3.374

Note
* (#, +) denotes significance denoted at 1 percent (5%, 10%) level.

Table F12 Estimates for choice of Mevacor relative to Pravachol

N = 44,625	Estimate	Std error	Z	P>|z|	90% confidence interval	
Les/Prava copay	0.822	0.581	1.410	0.158	−0.135	1.778
Lip/Prava copay	−1.823*	0.436	−4.180	0.000	−2.540	−1.106
Meva/Prava copay	3.467#	1.365	2.540	0.011	1.223	5.712
Zoc/Prava copay	−0.311	0.526	−0.590	0.554	−1.177	0.554

Table F12 Continued

N = 44,625	Estimate	Std error	Z	P>|z|	90% confidence interval	
Age 45– 55	0.334*	0.092	3.610	0.000	0.182	0.486
Age 55–60	0.694*	0.095	7.290	0.000	0.537	0.850
Age > 60	0.861*	0.094	9.180	0.000	0.706	1.015
Gender	−0.010	0.047	−0.220	0.829	−0.088	0.067
Northeast	0.077	0.086	0.900	0.370	−0.064	0.219
Midwest	−0.016	0.069	−0.230	0.820	-0.130	0.098
West	0.041	0.102	0.410	0.683	−0.126	0.208
Diabetes	−0.051	0.070	−0.730	0.465	−0.166	0.064
Hypertension	−0.078	0.097	−0.800	0.423	−0.237	0.082
Respiratory symptoms	0.101	0.109	0.930	0.354	−0.079	0.281
Cardiac dysrhythmias	0.088	0.104	0.840	0.400	−0.084	0.260
HMO enrollee	−0.689#	0.302	−2.280	0.022	−1.185	−0.193
PPO enrollee	0.008	0.152	0.050	0.960	−0.243	0.258
POS enrollee	−0.002	0.472	0.000	0.997	−0.778	0.774
HMO*copayment	0.067#	0.027	2.510	0.012	0.023	0.111
PPO*copayment	0.022	0.016	1.420	0.156	−0.004	0.048
POS*copayment	−0.024	0.045	−0.540	0.590	−0.099	0.050
Other cholesterol drugs	0.232+	0.131	1.770	0.076	0.017	0.448
Primary therapy	0.409*	0.055	7.400	0.000	0.318	0.500
Constant	−3.910#	1.563	−2.500	0.012	−6.482	−1.339

Note
* (#, +) denotes significance denoted at 1 percent (5%, 10%) level.

Table F13 Estimates for choice of Zocor relative to Pravachol

N = 44,625	Estimate	Std error	Z	P>|z|	90% confidence interval	
Les/Prava copay	0.769#	0.377	2.040	0.041	0.150	1.389
Lip/Prava copay	0.814*	0.291	2.800	0.005	0.335	1.293
Meva/Prava copay	0.773	0.886	0.870	0.383	−0.684	2.229
Zoc/Prava copay	0.200	0.373	0.540	0.592	−0.413	0.812
Age 45 to 55	0.227*	0.049	4.660	0.000	0.147	0.307
Age 55 to 60	0.397*	0.052	7.610	0.000	0.311	0.482
Age > 60	0.360*	0.052	6.920	0.000	0.274	0.445
Gender	0.040	0.029	1.360	0.174	−0.008	0.088
Northeast	−0.252*	0.052	−4.870	0.000	−0.337	−0.167
Midwest	−0.355*	0.041	−8.590	0.000	−0.423	−0.287
West	−0.501*	0.063	−7.970	0.000	−0.605	−0.398
Diabetes	−0.044	0.043	−1.000	0.316	−0.115	0.028
Hypertension	−0.017	0.057	−0.290	0.771	−0.111	0.078
Respiratory symptoms	0.142#	0.065	2.170	0.030	0.035	0.250
Cardiac dysrhythmias	−0.362*	0.073	−4.960	0.000	−0.483	−0.242
HMO enrollee	0.271	0.185	1.460	0.144	−0.034	0.576
PPO enrollee	−0.319*	0.100	−3.200	0.001	−0.483	−0.155
POS enrollee	−0.341	0.217	−1.580	0.115	−0.698	0.015
HMO*copayment	−0.008	0.018	−0.440	0.658	−0.038	0.022
PPO*copayment	0.078*	0.010	7.590	0.000	0.061	0.095

(continued)

Table F13 Continued

N = 44,625	Estimate	Std error	Z	P>|z|	90% confidence interval	
POS*copayment	0.095*	0.021	4.600	0.000	0.061	0.129
Other cholesterol drugs	−0.325*	0.093	−3.500	0.000	−0.478	−0.172
Primary therapy	0.019	0.035	0.530	0.593	−0.039	0.077
Constant	−2.150#	0.951	−2.260	0.024	−3.714	−0.586

Note
* (#, +) denotes significance denoted at 1 percent (5%, 10%) level.

Marginal effects for the "Visual Inspection" copayment estimation method

Table F14 Marginal effects estimates for choice of Lescol

N = 44,642	Estimate	Std error	Z	P>|z|	90% confidence interval	
Les/Prava copay	−0.073#	0.031	−2.350	0.019	−0.124	−0.022
Lip/Prava copay	−0.051#	0.020	−2.470	0.013	−0.084	−0.017
Meva/Prava copay	0.167#	0.070	2.380	0.017	0.052	0.282
Zoc/Prava copay	−0.020	0.023	−0.880	0.382	−0.059	0.018
Age 45–55	−0.003	0.004	−0.970	0.333	−0.009	0.002
Age 55–60	−0.002	0.004	−0.600	0.547	−0.009	0.004
Age > 60	−0.005	0.004	−1.310	0.191	−0.011	0.001
Gender	−0.011*	0.002	−4.780	0.000	−0.015	−0.007
Northeast	−0.014*	0.003	−4.010	0.000	−0.019	−0.008
Midwest	−0.010*	0.003	−3.200	0.001	−0.015	−0.005
West	0.004	0.005	0.830	0.408	−0.004	0.012
Diabetes	−0.013*	0.003	−4.200	0.000	−0.018	−0.008
Hypertension	−0.006	0.004	−1.320	0.188	−0.013	0.001
Respiratory symptoms	0.018*	0.007	2.710	0.007	0.007	0.029
Cardiac dysrhythmias	0.001	0.006	0.210	0.835	−0.008	0.011
HMO enrollee	0.067*	0.018	3.670	0.000	0.037	0.097
PPO enrollee	0.051*	0.010	4.880	0.000	0.034	0.068
POS enrollee	0.020	0.017	1.210	0.228	−0.007	0.048
HMO*copayment	−0.003*	0.001	−3.010	0.003	−0.005	−0.001
PPO*copayment	−0.007*	0.001	−9.080	0.000	−0.008	−0.006
POS*copayment	−0.002	0.001	−1.180	0.236	−0.004	0.001
Other cholesterol drugs	−0.007	0.007	−0.960	0.339	−0.018	0.005
Primary therapy	0.026*	0.003	8.510	0.000	0.021	0.031

Note
* (#, +) denotes significance denoted at 1 percent (5%, 10%) level.

Table F15 Marginal effects estimates for choice of Lipitor

N = 44,642	Estimate	Std error	Z	P>|z|	90% confidence interval	
Les/Prava copay	0.123+	0.066	1.850	0.064	0.014	0.232
Lip/Prava copay	−0.281*	0.045	−6.310	0.000	−0.354	−0.208
Meva/Prava copay	−0.559*	0.146	−3.840	0.000	−0.799	−0.320

Table F15 Continued

N = 44,642	Estimate	Std error	Z	P>|z|	90% confidence interval	
Zoc/Prava copay	0.123#	0.060	2.060	0.039	0.025	0.222
Age 45–55	−0.045*	0.008	−5.800	0.000	−0.057	−0.032
Age 55–60	−0.078*	0.008	−9.770	0.000	−0.091	−0.065
Age > 60	−0.103*	0.008	−12.900	0.000	−0.116	−0.090
Gender	−0.006	0.005	−1.340	0.181	−0.014	0.001
Northeast	0.053*	0.008	6.380	0.000	0.039	0.066
Midwest	0.001	0.007	0.220	0.826	−0.010	0.013
West	0.028*	0.010	2.690	0.007	0.011	0.044
Diabetes	0.080*	0.007	11.360	0.000	0.069	0.092
Hypertension	−0.035*	0.009	−3.740	0.000	−0.050	−0.020
Respiratory symptoms	−0.016	0.011	−1.480	0.138	−0.033	0.002
Cardiac dysrhythmias	0.001	0.013	0.100	0.922	−0.020	0.022
HMO enrollee	−0.276*	0.020	−13.730	0.000	−0.309	−0.243
PPO enrollee	−0.037#	0.016	−2.350	0.019	−0.064	−0.011
POS enrollee	0.001	0.027	0.060	0.956	−0.042	0.045
HMO*copayment	0.026*	0.003	7.970	0.000	0.021	0.031
PPO*copayment	0.001	0.002	0.800	0.422	−0.001	0.004
POS*copayment	−0.002	0.002	−0.850	0.394	−0.006	0.002
Other cholesterol drugs	0.039#	0.015	2.550	0.011	0.014	0.064
Primary therapy	−0.078*	0.006	−13.960	0.000	−0.087	−0.069

Note
* (#, +) denotes significance denoted at 1 percent (5%, 10%) level.

Table F16 Marginal effects estimates for choice of Mevacor

N = 44,642	Estimate	Std error	Z	P>|z|	90% confidence interval	
Les/Prava copay	0.010	0.026	0.380	0.706	−0.033	0.053
Lip/Prava copay	−0.084*	0.021	−4.020	0.000	−0.118	−0.050
Meva/Prava copay	0.178*	0.063	2.810	0.005	0.074	0.281
Zoc/Prava copay	−0.031	0.023	−1.370	0.172	−0.068	0.006
Age 45–55	0.013*	0.005	2.750	0.006	0.005	0.021
Age 55–60	0.031*	0.007	4.610	0.000	0.020	0.042
Age > 60	0.046*	0.008	5.800	0.000	0.033	0.059
Gender	0.000	0.002	−0.090	0.932	−0.004	0.003
Northeast	0.008#	0.004	1.990	0.046	0.001	0.015
Midwest	0.012*	0.003	3.420	0.001	0.006	0.017
West	0.016*	0.006	2.650	0.008	0.006	0.025
Diabetes	−0.007#	0.003	−2.410	0.016	−0.012	−0.002
Hypertension	0.000	0.004	0.110	0.911	−0.007	0.008
Respiratory symptoms	0.000	0.005	0.000	0.997	−0.008	0.008
Cardiac dysrhythmias	0.017*	0.006	2.790	0.005	0.007	0.027
HMO enrollee	−0.021#	0.009	−2.340	0.019	−0.036	−0.006
PPO enrollee	0.010	0.007	1.290	0.197	−0.003	0.022
POS enrollee	0.009	0.023	0.390	0.699	−0.029	0.047
HMO*copayment	0.001	0.001	1.320	0.187	0.000	0.003
PPO*copayment	−0.001	0.001	−1.370	0.170	−0.002	0.000
POS*copayment	−0.004#	0.002	−2.350	0.019	−0.007	−0.001

(*continued*)

Table F16 Continued

N = 44,642	Estimate	Std error	Z	P>|z|	90% confidence interval	
Other cholesterol drugs	0.021#	0.008	2.470	0.014	0.007	0.035
Primary therapy	0.027*	0.004	5.990	0.000	0.019	0.034

Note
* (#, +) denotes significance denoted at 1 percent (5%, 10%) level.

Table F17 Marginal effects estimates for choice of Pravachol

N = 44,642	Estimate	Std error	Z	P>|z|	90% confidence interval	
Les/Prava copay	−0.107#	0.047	−2.290	0.022	−0.184	−0.030
Lip/Prava copay	0.040	0.037	1.080	0.278	−0.021	0.101
Meva/Prava copay	−0.019	0.114	−0.170	0.865	−0.206	0.168
Zoc/Prava copay	−0.046	0.047	−0.980	0.328	−0.123	0.031
Age 45–55	−0.015#	0.006	−2.540	0.011	−0.025	−0.005
Age 55–60	−0.030*	0.006	−4.900	0.000	−0.040	−0.020
Age > 60	−0.022*	0.006	−3.510	0.000	−0.032	−0.012
Gender	0.001	0.004	0.310	0.756	−0.005	0.007
Northeast	0.013+	0.007	1.890	0.058	0.002	0.024
Midwest	0.040*	0.005	7.350	0.000	0.031	0.049
West	0.041*	0.009	4.590	0.000	0.027	0.056
Diabetes	−0.015*	0.005	−2.890	0.004	−0.023	−0.006
Hypertension	0.015#	0.008	1.990	0.047	0.003	0.027
Respiratory symptoms	−0.017#	0.008	−2.070	0.039	−0.030	−0.003
Cardiac dysrhythmias	0.036*	0.010	3.470	0.001	0.019	0.053
HMO enrollee	0.034	0.027	1.250	0.212	−0.011	0.079
PPO enrollee	0.029#	0.013	2.300	0.022	0.008	0.050
POS enrollee	0.029	0.029	1.010	0.313	−0.018	0.077
HMO*copayment	−0.007*	0.003	−2.750	0.006	−0.011	−0.003
PPO*copayment	−0.007*	0.001	−5.590	0.000	−0.009	−0.005
POS*copayment	−0.008*	0.003	−3.070	0.002	−0.013	−0.004
Other cholesterol drugs	0.018	0.012	1.500	0.133	−0.002	0.038
Primary therapy	0.006	0.005	1.260	0.209	−0.002	0.013

Note
* (#, +) denotes significance denoted at 1 percent (5%, 10%) level.

Table F18 Marginal effects estimates for choice of Zocor

N = 44,642	Estimate	Std error	Z	P>|z|	90% confidence interval	
Les/Prava copay	0.048	0.066	0.720	0.469	−0.061	0.156
Lip/Prava copay	0.375*	0.045	8.300	0.000	0.301	0.449
Meva/Prava copay	0.235+	0.142	1.650	0.099	0.001	0.468
Zoc/Prava copay	−0.026	0.060	−0.430	0.665	−0.124	0.073
Age 45–55	0.050*	0.008	5.920	0.000	0.036	0.064
Age 55–60	0.079*	0.009	8.500	0.000	0.064	0.094
Age > 60	0.084*	0.010	8.720	0.000	0.068	0.100
Gender	0.016*	0.005	3.490	0.000	0.009	0.024

Table F18 Continued

N = 44,642	Estimate	Std error	Z	P>|z|	90% confidence interval	
Northeast	−0.060*	0.008	−7.970	0.000	−0.073	−0.048
Midwest	−0.043*	0.007	−6.560	0.000	−0.054	−0.032
West	−0.088*	0.009	−9.720	0.000	−0.103	−0.073
Diabetes	−0.046*	0.007	−6.740	0.000	−0.057	−0.034
Hypertension	0.025*	0.009	2.710	0.007	0.010	0.041
Respiratory symptoms	0.015	0.010	1.400	0.162	−0.003	0.032
Cardiac dysrhythmias	−0.055*	0.012	−4.720	0.000	−0.075	−0.036
HMO enrollee	0.196*	0.034	5.850	0.000	0.141	0.252
PPO enrollee	−0.052*	0.017	−3.100	0.002	−0.080	−0.025
POS enrollee	−0.060#	0.026	−2.330	0.020	−0.102	−0.018
HMO*copayment	−0.017*	0.003	−6.060	0.000	−0.022	−0.013
PPO*copayment	0.013*	0.002	7.370	0.000	0.010	0.016
POS*copayment	0.016*	0.002	6.740	0.000	0.012	0.020
Other cholesterol drugs	−0.072*	0.017	−4.110	0.000	−0.100	−0.043
Primary therapy	0.019*	0.006	3.250	0.001	0.009	0.029

Note
* (#, +) denotes significance denoted at 1 percent (5%, 10%) level.

Appendix G: mathematical exposition from Chapter 6

The information in this appendix also appears in McFadden (1981).

Choice probability assumptions

The choice probability $P(k \mid \mathbf{B}, \mathbf{s})$ specifies the probability of choosing any option $k \in \mathrm{K}$, given that a selection must be made from a choice set $\mathbf{B} \in B$ and the decisionmaker has characteristics $\mathbf{s} \in \mathrm{S}$. Choice probabilities are assumed to satisfy the following two conditions:

> **PCS 1:** Choice probabilities are nonnegative and sum to one, with $P(\mathbf{B} \mid \mathbf{B}, \mathbf{s}) = 1$.[31]
> **PCS 2:** Choice probabilities depend only on the measured attributes of alternatives and individual characteristics; if $\mathbf{B} = (k_1, \ldots, k_i)$ and $\mathbf{B}' = (k_1', \ldots, k_j')$ have $\mathbf{z}_k = \xi(k_j) = \xi(k_j')$ for $j = 1, \ldots, l$, then $P(k_j \mid \mathbf{B}, \mathbf{s}) = P(k'_j \mid \mathbf{B}', \mathbf{s})$.

Assumptions imposed on μ

For, $\mathbf{B} = \{k_1, \ldots, k_l\} \in B$, μ^B is a probability measure that represents the manner in which the demand for statins is distributed throughout the population among decisionmakers when faced with the choice set $\mathbf{B}$ with the following assumptions are imposed on μ:

> **RUM 1:** The restrictions of μ to the space of utility values on a finite set of alternatives $\mathbf{B} \in B$ depends only on the measured attributes of those

alternatives;   if $\mathbf{B} = (k_1 \ldots, k_l)$ and $\mathbf{B}' = (k'_1 \ldots, k'_l)$ have $z_k = \xi(k_j) = \xi(k'_j)$ for $j = 1, \ldots, l$, then $\mu^B = \mu^{B'}$.

Thus, probability measures for the sets $\mathbf{B}$ and $\mathbf{B}'$ are not dependent on the ordering of the alternatives in the sets, but only on the attributes as mapped by ξ. The distribution of tastes does not change from one set to another because utility valuations are only predicated upon the attributes of the alternatives.

RUM 2: The probability of "ties" is zero; $\mu(\langle UER^k | u(k_1 = u(k_2) \rangle, \mathbf{s}) = 0$.

The last assumption states that the choice of an alternative in the family of sets $\mathbf{B}$ is determined by utility maximization.

RUM 3: Each RUM (K, Z, ξ, S, μ) and family of choice sets $\mathbf{B} \in B$ generates a probability choice system (K, Z, ξ, B, S, P) via the following mapping: for $\mathbf{B} = (k_1, \ldots, k_l) \in B$, $\mathbf{s} \in \mathbf{S}$, and $j = 1, \ldots, l$, $P(k_1 | \mathbf{B}, \mathbf{s} = \mu(\langle U \in \mathbf{R}^K | U(k_1) \leq U(k_j)$ for $j = 1, \ldots l \rangle, \mathbf{s})$. (G.1)

The assumption **RUM 2** guarantees that there is almost always a unique utility-maximizing alternative, so that (G.1) is well-defined, with $P(\mathbf{B} | \mathbf{B}, \mathbf{s}) = 1$.

The direct utility assumption

If an individual's total consumption is represented by a vector $\mathbf{x}$ of divisible commodities and the choice of a discrete alternative k (a drug in the statins class) which has a vector of measured attributes $\mathbf{w}$. The individual has a utility function $\tilde{U}: \tilde{\mathbf{X}} \times \mathbf{W} \times \mathbf{K} \rightarrow [0,1]$, where $\tilde{\mathbf{X}} \times \mathbf{W}$ is the space of pairs of vectors $(\mathbf{x}, \mathbf{w})$. Consumers' utility function is assumed to satisfy the direct utility (**DU**) assumption.

DU: $\tilde{\mathbf{X}}$ is the nonnegative orthant of a finite-dimensional real vector space, and $\mathbf{W}$ is a closed set in a finite-dimensional real vector space. The utility function $\tilde{U}(.,.,k)$ is continuous on $\tilde{\mathbf{X}} \times \mathbf{W}$ for each $k \in$ K. $\tilde{U}$ $(.,\mathbf{w}, k)$ is twice continuously differentiable on $\tilde{\mathbf{X}}$, with $\partial \tilde{U}/\partial \mathbf{x} \geq 0$ and $\partial \tilde{U}/\partial \mathbf{x}| > 0$, and is strictly differentially quasi-concave, for each $\mathbf{w} \in$ $\mathbf{W}$ and $k \in$ K.

Properties of indirect utility

The indirect utility function (6.1) has the following indirect utility (**IU**) properties:

IU 1: For $\mathbf{h} > 0$, y-q > 0, $\mathbf{w} \in$ W, $k \in$ K and $\tilde{U}$ satisfying DU, $V(y\text{-}q, \mathbf{h}, \mathbf{w}, k; \tilde{U})$ is continuous in (y-q, $\mathbf{h}$, $\mathbf{w}$), twice continuously differentiable and homogeneous of degree zero in (y-q, $\mathbf{h}$), strictly differentiably quasi-convex in $\mathbf{h}$, and has $\partial V/\partial(y\text{-}q) > 0$.

As one might expect, $\partial V/\partial (y - q) > 0$ suggests that smaller copayments (cost of alternative), all other factors held constant, increase indirect utility to a decisionmaker since there is more income remaining to purchase other commodities.

IU 2: (Roy's Identity): The maximum of $\tilde{U}(\mathbf{x},\mathbf{w}, k)$ subject to $\mathbf{h}\cdot\mathbf{x} \leq y - q$ is achieved at a unique vector $\mathbf{x} = X(y\text{-}q, \mathbf{h}, \mathbf{w}, k; \tilde{U})$ which satisfies

$$\mathbf{X}(y - q, \mathbf{h}, k; \tilde{U}) = -\frac{\partial V/\partial \mathbf{h}}{\partial V/\partial y}.$$

Notes

1 Introduction

1 Almost 65 million Americans have one or more types of cardiovascular disease (American Heart Association, 2003).

3 Coronary heart disease and the statins

2 Cholesterol quintiles are assigned as follows: < 181 mg/dl, 182–202, 203–220, 221–244, and >245.

3 Ischemia is defined as a localized tissue anemia due to obstruction of the inflow of arterial blood.

4 In a 1997 report, the UK Department of Public Health recommended that patients with an annual CHD risk of 3 percent or more be considered as potential candidates for statin therapy. The NCEP ATP III study states that a 10-year risk of 20 percent or more is equivalent to CHD.

5 Nerve dysfunction resulting in temporary loss of movement due to inflammation of nerves.

4 Economic differentiation among statins

6 The MEPS database is publicly available on the internet.

7 Data for 1999 reflects only the first three quarters.

5 The structure of demand for prescription drugs

8 This figure represents the retail value of the product samples given to office-based physicians.

9 At the same time, this does not dismiss the possibility that patients switch statin treatment because of a within plan change in copayments.

6 The economics of drug demand

10 Chapter 5 argues physicians have a more accurate idea of patients' costs than in the past.

11 Theoretically, a choice set available to decisionmakers may be smaller if access to one or more drugs in the class was limited due to insurer restrictions such as closed formularies.

12 It is also possible that patients are informed of price differentials by pharmacists at the point of purchase. Either way, a health care professional is alerting the consumer to copayment differences.

13 In this study, copayments are the only drug attributes measured. However, other economic variables that are considered patient specific characteristics include insurance type and interaction terms between insurer type and copayment level.
14 For a complete mathematical exposition, see Appendix G.
15 See RUM 6.1–6.3 in Appendix G.
16 This structure is outlined in McFadden (1981).
17 See the Direct Utility Assumption in Appendix G.
18 See the Indirect Utility properties in Appendix G.

7 Econometric specification of prescription drug choice

19 To be exact, the MNL coefficients represent the impact on the log odds ratios of the choice probabilities. However, marginal effects on the probabilities of choice can be calculated and are presented later in the section.
20 The remainder of the discussion of IIA borrows from Horowitz and Savin's 2001 paper.
21 Crawford *et al.* (1998) show this is true for a case where all regressors are variable for each individual. The same can be shown to hold for this case where some regressors (drug attributes) do not vary from individual to individual.

8 Data

22 These plans make payments on a per patient rather than per service basis for covered procedures.
23 Codes and brief definitions can be found in Appendix D.
24 There were no Medicare eligible retirees in the statin monotherapy final sample.
25 See Hellerstein (1998) and O'Connor *et al.* (1999) for examples and Frech (1977) for a review.
26 For patients with an initial statin fill in 1997, medical utilization is measured for 1997 only.
27 The national drug code list for these drugs is extensive, especially for niacin, and not presented here.

9 Descriptive statistics

28 Cardiac dysrhythmias are abnormal rhythms of the heart and cause symptoms such as palpitations or dizziness; they cause the heart to pump less efficiently.

10 Multivariate regression results

29 To test this difference, it was assumed that the covariance across marginal effects was zero.

11 Multivariate sensitivity analyses

30 These data is not displayed in Table 11.1 because the incidence rates are small and these conditions do not appear as explanatory variables in multivariate regressions.

Appendices

31 Let $P(\mathbf{C}|\mathbf{B}, 5) = \Sigma_{k\epsilon C} P(k|\mathbf{B}, 5)$.

Bibliography

Acevedo, Monica; Sprecher, Dennis L.; Lauer, Michael S.; Franci, Gary. "Routine Statin Treatment after Acute Coronary Syndromes?" *American Heart Journal*, 143(6), 2002: 940–942.

Adams, Chris. "Some Drug Firms Seem to Evade Medicare Price-Reporting Rules." *The Wall Street Journal*, February 24, 2003: A3.

Aikin, Kathryn J. "Direct-to-Consumer Advertising of Prescription Drugs: Physician Survey Primary Results." Division of Drug Marketing, Advertising and Communications, Federal Drug Administration, January 13, 2003, available at www.fda.gov

American Heart Association. *Heart Disease and Stroke Statistics—2003 Update*. Dallas, TX: American Heart Association, 2002.

American Heart Association. *2002 Heart and Stroke Statistical Update*. Dallas, TX: American Heart Association, 2003.

Anderson, J.L.; Carlquist, J.F.; Muhlestein, J.B.; Horne, B.D.; Elmer, S.P. "Evaluation of C-reactive Protein, an Inflammatory Marker, and Infectious Serology as Risk Factors for Coronary Artery Disease and Myocardial Infarction." *Journal of the American College of Cardiology*, 32, 1998: 35–41.

Andrews, Thomas C.; Ballantyne, Christie M.; Hsia, Judith A.; Kramer, Jeffrey H. *American Journal of Medicine*, 111, 2001: 185–191.

Arnould, Richard J.; Debrock, Lawrence W.; Pollard, John W. "Do HMOs Produce Specific Services More Efficiently?" *Inquiry*, 21, Fall 1984: 243–253.

Ashraf, Talat; Hay, Joel W.; Pitt, Bertram; Wittels, Ellison; Crouse, John; Davidson, Michael; Furberg, Curt D.; Radican, Larry. "Cost-Effectiveness of Pravastatin in Secondary Prevention of Coronary Heart Disease." *American Journal of Cardiology*, 78, 1996, 409–414.

Attanasio, Ermanno; Russo, Pierluigi; Allen, Shannon E. "Cost-minimization Analysis of Simvastatin Versus Atorvastatin for Maintenance Therapy in Patients with Coronary or Peripheral Vascular Disease." *Clinical Therapeutics*, 23(2), 2001: 276–283.

Ballantyne, Christie M.; Andrews, Thomas C.; Hsia, Judith A.; Kramer, Jeffrey H.; Shear, Charles. "Correlation of Non-High-Density Lipoprotein Cholesterol with Apolipoprotein B: Effect of 5 Hydroxymethylglutaryl Coenzyme A Reductase Inhibitors on Non-High-Density Lipoprotein Cholesterol Levels." *American Journal of Cardiology*, 88, 2001: 265–269.

Barry, M; Heerey, Adrienne. "Cost-effectiveness of Statins for the Secondary Prevention of Coronary Heart Disease in Ireland." *Irish Medical Journal*, 95(5), May 2002: 133–135.

Baycol Recall Center. "Baycol Recall Overview." Internet document and website, available at http://www.baycol-recall-center.com/, 2002 (accessed on September 21, 2002).

Ben-Akiva, Moshe; Lerman, Steven R. *Multinomial Choice.* In: *Discrete Choice Analysis: Theory and Application to Travel Demand.* Cambridge, MA: MIT Press, 1985.

Bennett, Max D. "Health Insurance and Price Distortions." PhD Dissertation, John Hopkins University, 1973.

Bennett, Max D. "Influence of Health Insurance on Patterns of Care: Maternity Hospitalization." *Inquiry*, 12, 1975: 59–66.

Berndt, Ernst R., "The U.S. Pharmaceutical Industry: Why Major Growth in Times of Cost Containment?" *Health Affairs*, 20(2), March/April 2001: 100–114.

Birch, Stephen. "Relationship Between Increasing Prescription Charges and Consumption in Groups not Exempt from Charges." *Journal of the Royal College of General Practitioners*, 36, 1986: 154–156.

Boston Consulting Group. "The Changing Environment for U.S. Pharmaceuticals." April 1993.

Brian, Earl W.; Gibbens, Stephen F. "California's Medi-Cal Copayment Experiment." *Medical Care*, 1974, 12(12) supplement: 1–56.

Burton, Thomas M. "Backlash Rises Against Flashy Ads for Prescription Pharmaceuticals." *The Wall Street Journal*, March 13, 2002: B3.

Caro, J.; Klittich, W.; McGuire A.; Ford, I.; Pettitt, D.; Norrie, J.; Shepherd, J. for the WOSCOPS Economic Analysis Committee. "International Economic Analysis of Primary Prevention of Cardiovascular Disease with Pravastatin in WOSCOPS." *European Heart Journal*, 20, 1999: 263–268.

Chaiyakunapruk, Natorn; Boudreau, Denise; Ramsey, Scoot D. "Pharmaco-Economic Impact of HMG-CoA Reductase Inhibitors in type 2 Diabetes." *Journal of Cardiovascular Risk*, 8, 2000: 127–132.

Charlson, M.E.; Pompei, P.; Ales, K.L.; McKenzie, C.R. "A New Method of Classifying Prognostic Comorbidity in Longitudinal Studies: Development and Validation." *Journal of Chronic Disorders*, 40(5), 1987: 373–383.

Chew, Lisa D.; O'Young, Theresa S.; Hazlet, Thomas K.; Bradley, Katharine A.; Maynard, Charles; Lessler, Daniel S. "A Physician Survey of the Effect of Drug Sample Availability on Physician's Behavior." *Journal of General Internal Medicine*, 15, 2000: 478–483.

Ching, Andrew T. "Consumer Learning and Heterogeneity: Dynamics of Demand for Prescription Drugs after Patent Expiration." Mimeo, April 2002.

Cobos, Albert; Jovell, Albert J.; Garcia-Altes, Anna; Garcias-Closas, Reina; Serra-Majem, Lluis. "Which Statin is Most Efficient for the Treatment of Hypercholesterolemia? A Cost-effectiveness Analysis." *Clinical Therapeutics*, 21(11), 1999: 1924–1936.

Constantinides, P. "Plaque Hemorrhages, Their Genesis and Their Role in Supraplaque Thrombosis and Atherogenesis." In: Glagov, S.; Newman, W.P.; Schaffer, S. eds, *Pathobiology of the Human Atherosclerotic Plaque*. New York, NY: Springer-Verlag; 1990: 393–411.

Cook, Anna; Kornfield, Thomas; Gold, Marsha. "The Role of PBMs in Managing Drug Costs: Implications for a Medicare Drug Benefit." *Mathematica Policy Research, Inc. report*, January 2000.

Coscelli, Andrea. "The Importance of Doctors' and Patients' Preferences in the Prescription Decision." *Journal of Industrial Economics*, 48(3), September 2000: 349–369.

Coulson, Edward N.; Stuart, Bruce C. "Insurance Choice and the Demand for Prescription Drugs." *Southern Economic Journal*, 61(4), April 1995: 1146–1157.

Coulson, Edward N.; Terza, Joseph V.; Neslusan, Cheryl A.; Stuart, Bruce C. "Estimating the Moral-Hazard Effect of Supplemental Medical Insurance in the Demand for Prescription Drugs by the Elderly." *American Economic Review*, 85(2), May 1995: 122–126.

Crawford, David L.; Pollak, Robert A.; Vella, Francis. "Simple Inference in Multinomial and Ordered Logit." *Econometric Reviews*, 17(3), 1998: 289–299.

Crouch, Michael A. "Effective Use of Statins to Prevent Coronary Heart Disease." *American Family Physician*, 63(2), January 15, 2000: 309–320.

Crouse, John Robert; Byington, Robert Patrick; Bond, M. Gene; Espeland, Mark Andrew; Craven, Timothy Edward; Sprinkle, Janine Worthy; McGovern, Mark Edward; Furberg, Curt Daniel. "Pravastatin, Lipids, and Atherosclerosis in the Carotid Arteries (PLAC-II)." *American Journal of Cardiology*, 75, 1995: 455–459.

Dart, Anthony; Jerums, George; Nicholson, Geoffrey; d'Emden, Michael; Hamilton-Craig, Ian; Tallis, George; Best, James; West, Malcolm; Sullivan, David; Bracs, Peter; Black, Donald. "A multicenter, Double-Blind, One-Year Study Comparing Safety and Efficacy of Atorvastatin versus Simvastatin in Patients with Hypercholesterolemia." *American Journal of Cardiology*, 80, 1997: 39–44.

Davidson, Michael H.; Stein, Evan; Dujovne, Carlos A.; Hunninghake, Donald B.; Weiss, Stuart R.; Knopp, Robert H.; Illingworth, D. Roger; Mitchel, Yale B.; Melino, Micael R.; Zupkis, Robert V.; Dobrinska, Michael R.; Amin, Raju D.; Tobert, Jonathan A. "The Efficacy and Six-Week Tolerability of Simvastatin 80 and 160 mg/Day." *American Journal of Cardiology*, 79, 1997: 38–42.

Davies, M.J. "A Macro and Micro View of Coronary Vascular Insult in Ischemic Heart Disease." *Circulation*, 82(2) Supplement, 1990: II-38–II-46.

DeVries, Andrea. "Affecting Physician Prescribing Behavior: Factors Influencing the Success of a Pharmacy Intervention." University of Minnesota Division of Health Services Research and Policy Research Brief, 8(5), June 2001.

Downs, John R.; Clearfield, Michael; Weis, Stephen; Shapiro, Deborah R.; Beere, Polly A.; Langendorfer, Alexandra; Stein, Evan A.; Kruyer, William; Gotto, Antonio M. Jr. "Primary Prevention of Acute Coronary Events with Lovastatin in Men and Women with Average Cholesterol Levels." *Journal of the American Medical Association*, 279, 1998: 1615–1622.

Dranove, David; White, William D. "Agency and the Organization of Health Care Delivery." *Inquiry*, 24, Winter 1987: 405–415.

Dranove, David; Shanley, Mark; White, William D. "Price and Concentration in Hospital Markets: The Switch from Patient-driven to Payer-driven Competition." *Journal of Law and Economics*, 36, April 1993: 179–204.

Dubois, Robert W.; Chawla, Anita; Neslusan, Cheryl A.; Smith, Mark W.; Wade, Sally. "Explaining Drug Spending Trends: Does Perception Match Reality?" *Health Affairs*, 19(2), March/April 2000: 231–239.

Ellison, Sara Fisher; Cockburn, Iain; Griliches, Zvi; Hausman, Jerry. "Characteristics of Demand for Pharmaceutical Products: An Examination of Four Cephalosporins." *RAND Journal of Economics*, 28(3), Autumn 1997: 426–446.

Escarce, Jose J.; Kapur, Kanika; Joyce, Geoffrey F.; Van Vorst, Krista A. "Medical Care Expenditures Under Gatekeeper and Point-of-Service Arrangments." *Health Services Research*, 36(6), December 2001, Part I: 1037–1057.

Evans, Marc; Rees, Alan. "The Myotoxicity of Statins." *Current Opinion in Lipidology*, 13, 2002: 415–420.

Falger, Paul R.J. "If Cardiac Patients Benefit from Statins, Why Not Commonly Prescribe Them and Follow up Their Use?" *European Journal of Internal Medicine*, 12, 2001: 475–476.

Farmer, John A.; Torre-Amione, Guillermo. "Comparative Tolerability of the HMG-CoA Reductase Inhibitors." *Drug Safety*, 23(3), 2000: 197–213.

Feely, J.; McGettigan, P.; Kelly, A. "Growth in Use of Statins After Trials not Targeted to Most Appropriate Patients." *Journal of Clinical Pharmacology and Therapeutics*, 67(4), 2000: 438–441.

Findlay, S.D. "Direct-to-Consumer Promotion of Prescription Drugs: Economic Implications for Patients, Payers and Providers." *Pharmacoeconomics*, 19(2), 2001: 109–119.

Findlay, Steven; Sherman, Daniel; Chockley, Nancy; Watkins, Suzanne. *Prescription Drug Expenditures in 2001*. National Institute for Health Care Management, Washington, DC, May 2002, available at www.nihcm.org/spending2001.pdf (accessed on October 12, 2002).

Frech, H.E. III. "The Demand for Medical Care: A Survey." Report to the Bureau of Health Planning and Resources Development Health Resources Administration; United States Department of Health, Education and Welfare: March 1977.

Frolkis, Joseph P.; Zyzanski, Stephen J.; Schwartz, Jonathan M.; Suhan, Pamela S. "Physician Noncompliance with the 1993 National Cholesterol Education Program (NCEP-ATPII) Guidelines." *Ciculation*, 98, 1998: 851–855.

Gaist, D.; Jeppesen, U.; Anderson, M.; Garcia Rodriguez, L.A.; Hallas, J.; Sindrup, S.H. "Statins and Risk of Polyneuropathy: A Case-Control Study." *Neurology*, 58, 2002: 1333–1337.

Ganz, David A.; Kuntz, Karen M; Jacobson, Gretchen A.; Avorn, Jerry. "Cost-effectiveness of 3-Hydroxy-3-Methylglutaryl Coenzyme A Reductase Inhibitor Therapy in Older Patients with Myocardial Infarction." *Annuals of Internal Medicine*, 132, 2000: 780–787.

Gianfrancesco, Frank; Manning, Beatrice; Wang, Ruey-hua. "Effects of Prescription to OTC Switches on Out-of-Pocket Health Care Costs and Utilization." *Drug Benefit Trends*, 14(3), 2002: 13–30.

Gold, Marthe R.; Russell, Louise B.; Siegel, Joanna E.; Weinstein, Milton C. (eds) *Cost-Effectiveness in Health and Medicine*. New York: Oxford University Press, 1996.

Goldman, Lee; Goldman, Paula; Williams, Lawrence W.; Weinstein, Milton C. "Cost-effectiveness Considerations in the Treatment of Heterozygous Familial Hypercholesterolemia with Medications." *American Journal of Cardiology*, 72, 1993: 75D–79D.

Goldman, Lee; Weinstein, Milton C.; Goldman, Paula; Williams, Lawrence W. "Cost-effectiveness of HMG-CoA Reductase Inhibition for Primary and Secondary Prevention of Coronary Heart Disease." *Journal of the American Medical Association*, 265, 1991: 1145–1151.

Gordon, Tavia; Castelli, William P.; Hjortland, Marthana C.; Kannel, William B.; Dawber, Thomas R. "High Density Lipoprotein As a Protective Factor Against Coronary Heart Disease." *American Journal of Medicine*, 62, May 1977: 707–714.

Gotto, Antonio. "Statins: Powerful Drugs for Lowering Cholesterol; Advice for Patients." *Circulation*, 105, 2002: 1514–1516.

Gotto, Antonio M.; Grundy, Scott M. "Lowering LDL Cholesterol: Questions from Recent Meta-Analyses and Subset Analyses of Clinical Trial Data." *Circulation*, 99, March 2, 1999: 1–7.

Gotto, Antonio M.; Kuller, Lewis H. "Eligibility for Lipid-Lowering Drug Therapy in Primary Prevention: How do the Adult Treatment Panel II and Adult Treatment Panel III Guidelines Compare?" *Circulation*, 105, 2002: 136–139.

Grabowski, Henry. "The Role of Cost-Effectiveness Analysis in Managed-Care Decisions." *Pharmacoeconomics*, 14(1) Supplement, 1998: 16–24.

Grabowski, Henry G.; Vernon John M. "Brand Loyalty, Entry, and Price Competition in Pharmaceuticals after the 1984 Drug Act." *Journal of Law and Economics*, 35(2), October 1992: 331–350.

Grace, Karen A.; Swiecki, Jennifer; Hyatt, Richard; Gibbs, Henry; Jones, David L.; Sheikh, Munazza; Spain, John; Manevi, Kent W., Viola, Rebecca; Taylor, Allen J. "Implementation of a Therapeutic Inter-change Clinic for HMG-CoA Reductase Inhibitors." *American Journal of Health System Pharmacy*, 59, June 1, 2002: 1077–1082.

Gross, David. *Trends In The Costs, Coverage, And Use Of Prescription Drugs By Medicare Beneficiaries*. Public Policy Institute, Washington, DC: AARP, July 2001, available at http://research.aarp.org/health/dd63_trends.html (accessed on June 24, 2002).

Grover, Steven A.; Coupal, Louis; Paquet, Steeve; Zowall, Hanna. "Cost-Effectiveness of 3-hydroxy-3-methylglutaryl-coenzyme A Reductase Inhibitors in the Secondary Prevention of Cardiovascular Disease." *Archives of Internal Medicine*, 159, March 22, 1999: 593–600.

Grover, Steven A.; Coupal, Louis; Paquet, Steeve; Zowall, Hanna; Alexander, Charles M.; Weiss, Thomas W.; Gomes, Daniel R.J. "How Cost-effective if the Treatment of Dyslipideia in Patients with Diabetes but Without Cardiovascular Disease?" *Diabetes Care*, 24(1), January 2001: 45–50.

Grover, Steven A.; Ho, Vivian; Lavoie, Frederic; Coupal, Louis; Zowall, Hanna; Pilote, Lousie. "The Importance of Indirect Costs in Primary Cardiovascular Disease Prevention: Can we Save lives and Money with Statins?" *Archives of Internal Medicine*, 163, 2003: 333–339.

Grundy, Scott M. "Primary Prevention of Coronary Heart Disease: Integrating Risk Assessment with Intervention." *Circulation*, 100, 1999: 988–998.

Grundy, Scott M.; Balady, Gary J.; Criqui, Michael H.; Fletcher, Gerald; Greenland, Philip; Hiratzka, Loren F.; Houston-Miller, Nancy; Kris-Etherton, Penny; Krumholz, Harlan M.; LaRosa, John; Ockene Ira S.; Pearson, Thomas A.; Reed, James; Washington, Reginald; Smith, Sidney C. "Guide to Primary Prevention of Cardiovascular Diseases: A Statement for Healthcare Professionals from the Task Force on Risk Reduction." *Circulation*, 95(9), 6 May 1997: 2329–2331.

Grundy, Scott M.; Benjamin, Ivor J.; Burke, Gregory L.; Chait, Alan; Eckel, Robert; Howard, Barbara V.; Mitch, William; Smith, Sidney C.; Sowers, James R. "Diabetes and Cardiovascular Disease: A Statement for Healthcare Professionals from the American Heart Association." *Circulation*, 100, 1999: 1134–1146.

Grundy, Scott M.; Pasternak, Richard; Greenland, Philip; Smith, Sidney Jr.; Fuster, Valentin. "Assessment of Cardiovascular Risk by use of Multiple-risk-factor Assessment Equations: A Statement for Healthcare Professionals from the American Heart Association and the American College of Cardiology." *Circulation*, 100, 1999: 1481–1492.

Gupta, Eric K.; Ito, Matthew. "Ezetimibe: The first in a Novel Class of Selective Cholesterol-Absorption Inhibitors." *Heart Disease*, 4(6), 2002: 399–409.

Harris, Brian L.; Stergachis, Andy; Ried, L. Douglas. "The Effect of Drug Co Payments on Utilization and Cost of Pharmaceuticals in a Health Maintenance Organization." *Medical Care*, October 1990, 28(10): 907–917.

Harris, Gardiner; Lueck, Sarah. "Drug Makers Unite on Discounts for Elderly to Ease Confusion." *Wall Street Journal*, April 10, 2002: A3.

Hausman, Jerry; McFadden, Daniel. "Specification Tests for the Multinomial Logit Model." *Econometrica*, 52(5), September 1984: 1219–1240.

Haverkate, F; Thompson, S.G.; Pyke, S.D.M.; Gallimore, J.R.; Pepys, M.B. for the European Concerted Action on Thrombosis and Disabilities: Angina Pectoris Study

Group. "Production of C-reactive Protein and Risk of Coronary Events in Stable and Unstable Angina." *Lancet*, 349, 1997: 462–466.

Hay, Joel W.; Wittels, Ellison H.; Gotto, Antonio M. "An Economic Evaluation of Lovastatin for Cholesterol Lowering and Coronary Artery Disease Reduction." *American Journal of Cardiology*, 67, 1991: 789–796.

Heart Protection Study (HPS) Collaborative Group. MRC/BHF Heart Protection Study of cholesterol lowering with simvastatin in 20,536 high-risk individuals: a randomised placebo-controlled trial. *Lancet* 2002; 360: 7–22.

Hellerstein, Judith K. "The Importance of the Physician in the Generic Versus Trade-Name Prescription Decision." *RAND Journal of Economics*, 29(1), Spring 1998: 108–136.

Hoerger, Thomas J.; Bala, Mohan V.; Bray, Jeremy W.; Wilcosky, Timothy C.; LaRosa, John. "Treatment Patterns and Distribution of Low-Density Lipoprotein Cholesterol Levels in Treatment-Eligible United States Adults." *American Journal of Cardiology*, 82, 1998: 61–65.

Horowitz, Joel L.; Savin N.E. "Binary Response Models: Logits, Probits and Semiparametrics." *Journal of Economic Perspectives*, 15(4), Fall 2001: 43–56.

Hunningkake, Donald B. "Postdischarge Lipid Management of Coronary Artery Disease Patients According to the New National Cholesterol Education Program Guidelines." *American Journal of Cardiology*, 88(8A), October 18, 2001: 37K–41K.

Hunningkake, Donald; Insull, William, Knopp, Robert; Davidson, Michael; Lohrbauer, Leif; Jones, Peter; Kafonek, Stephanie. "Comparison of the Efficacy of Atorvastatin Versus Cerivastatin in Primary Hypercholesterolemia." *American Journal of Cardiology*, 88, 2001: 635–639.

Huse, Daniel M.; Russell, Mason W.; Miller, Jeffrey D.; Kraemer, Dale F.; D'Agostino, Ralph B.; Ellison, R. Curtis; Hartz, Stuart C. "Cost-effectiveness of Statins." *American Journal of Cardiology*, 82, 1998: 1357–1363.

Jacobson, Terry A. "Cost-effectiveness of 3-Hydroxy-3-Methylglutaryl-Coenzyme A (HMG-CoA) Reductase Inhibitor Therapy in the Managed Care Era." *American Journal of Cardiology*, 78(6) Supplement, 1996: 32–41.

Johnson, Richard E.; Goodman, Michael J.; Hornbrook Mark C.; Eldredge, Michael B. "The Effect of Increased Prescription Drug Cost-Sharing on Medical Care Utilization and Expenses of Elderly Health Maintenance Organization Members." *Medical Care*, 1997, 35(11): 1119–1131.

Jones, John D. "Easier to Swallow: Strategies for Managing Pharmaceutical Costs." *Risk Management*, February 1996: 42–47.

Jones, Peter; Kafonek, Stephanie; Laurora, Irene; Hunningkake, Donald. "Comparative Dose Efficacy Study of Atorvastatin Versus Simvastatin, Pravastatin, Lovastatin, and Fluvastatin in Patients with Hypercholesterolemia (The CURVES Study)." *American Journal of Cardiology*, 81, 1998: 582–587.

Jonsson, B.; Cook, J.R.; Pederson, T.R. "The Cost-effectiveness of Lipid Lowering in Patients with Diabetes: Results From the 4S Trials." *Diabetologia*, 42, 1999: 1293–1301.

Joyce, Geoffrey F.; Escarce, Jose J.; Solomon, Matthew D.; Goldman, Dana P. "Employer Drug Benefit Plans and Spending on Prescription Drugs." *Journal of the American Medical Association*, 288(14), October 9, 2002: 1733–1739.

Kaiser Daily Health Policy Report. "Medicare Drug Benefit to Cost $849B Over 10 Years, CBO Says." at: http://www.kaisernetwork.org/daily_reports/rep_index.cfm?hint=3&DR_ID=28497 (accessed on March 7, 2005).

Kaiser Family Foundation. *Employer Health Benefits 2001 Annual Survey.* Section Six: Market Share of Health Plans, 2001.

Kaiser Family Foundation. *Prescription Drug Trends: A Chartbook Update* (Publication No. 3112), Menlo Park, CA: November 2001.

Kessler, John M. "Lipid-lowering Drugs, Cost-effectiveness Data, and the Formulary System: A health Systems Perspective." *American Heart Journal*, 137, 1999: S111–S114.

Kmietowicz, Zosia. "Statins are the New Aspirin, Oxford Researchers say." *British Medical Journal*, 323, 17 November, 2001: 1145.

Knapp, David A. "Paying for Outpatient Prescription Drugs and Related Services in Programs." *Medical Care Review*, August 1971, 826–859.

Kreling, David. "What Strategies can States use to Control Costs and How Effective are they?" Wisconsin Family Impact Seminar Briefing Report: 1–12, 2000, available at http://www.uwex.edu/ces/familyimpact/fis16kreling.htm (accessed on June 18, 2002).

Kuntz K.M.; Tsevat J.; Goldman L.; and Weinstein M.C.; 1996. Costeffectiveness of routine coronary angiography after acute myocardial infarction. *Circulation,* 94: 957–65.

Kuntz, Karen M.; Tsevat, Joel; Goldman, Lee; Weinstein, Milton C. "Cost-effectiveness of Routine Coronary Angiography After Acute Myocardial Infarction." *Circulation*, 94, 1999: 957–965.

Lamarche, Benoit; Moorjani, Sital; Lupien, Paul J.; Cantin, Bernard; Bernard, Paul-Marie; Dagenais, Gilles R.; Despres, Jean-Pierre. "Apolipoprotein A-I and B Levels and the Risk of Ischemic Heart Disease During a Five-Year Follow-up of Men in the Quebec Cardiovascular Study." *Circulation* 94, 1996: 273–278.

Lancaster, Kelvin. *Consumer Demand: A New Approach.* New York: Columbia University Press, 1971.

Landers, Peter. "States Jointly Seek Drug Discounts Under Medicaid." *Wall Street Journal*, February 20, 2003: D3.

Lavers, R.J. "Prescription Charges, the Demand for Prescriptions and Morbidity." *Applied Economics*, 21, 1989: 1043–1052.

Law, M.R. "Lowering Heart Disease Risk with Cholesterol Reduction: Evidence from Observational Studies and Clinical Trials." *European Heart Journal Supplements*, 1 Supplement S, 1999: S3–S8.

Lemaitre, Rozenn N.; Psaty, Bruce M.; Heckbert, Susan R.; Kronmal, Richard A.; Newman, Anne B.; Burke, Gregory L. "Therapy with Hydroxymethylglutaryl Coenzyme A Reductase Inhibitors (Statins) and Associated Risk of Incident Cardiovascular Events in Older Adults." *Archives of Internal Medicine*, 162, June 24, 2002: 1395–1400.

Levy, Roy. *The Pharmaceutical Industry: A Discussion of Competitive and Antitrust Issues in an Environment of Change*, Bureau of Economics Staff Report, Federal Trade Commission, March 1999.

Lewis, Nancy J.W.; Patwell, John T.; Briesacher, Becky A. "The Role of Insurance Claims Databases in Drug Therapy Outcomes Research." *Pharmacoeconomics*, 4(5), 1993: 323–330.

Liebman, Milton. "DTC's Role in the Statin Bonanza." *Medical Marketing and Media*, November 2001: 86–92.

Liebowitz, Arleen; Manning, Willard G.; Newhouse, Joseph P. "The Demand for Prescription Drugs as a Function of Cost-Sharing." *Social Science and Medicine*, 21(10), 1985, 1063–1069.

Lim, Stephen S.; Vos, Theo; Peeters, Anna; Liew, Danny; McNeil, John J. "Cost-effectiveness of prescribing statins according to Pharmaceutical Benefits Scheme criteria." *Medical Journal of Australia*, 175, 2001: 459–464.

Lipid Research Clinics Program. "The Lipid Research Clinics Coronary Primary Prevention Trial results. I. Reduction in the Incidence of Coronary Heart Disease." *Journal of the American Medical Association*, 251, 1984a: 351–364.

Lipid Research Clinics Program. "The Lipid Research Clinics Coronary Primary Prevention Trial results. II. The Relationship of Reduction in Incidence of Coronary Heart Disease to Cholesterol Lowering." *Journal of the American Medical Association*, 251, 1984b: 365–374.

LIPID Study Group, The "Long-term Effectiveness and Safety of Pravastatin in 9014 Patients with Coronary Heart Disease and Average Cholesterol Concentrations: The LIPID Trial Follow-up." *Lancet*, 359, 2002: 1379–1387.

Lipton, Helene L.; Kreling, David H.; Collins, Ted; Hertz, Karen C. "Pharmacy Benefit Management Companies: Dimensions of Performance." *Annual Review of Public Health*, 20, 1999: 361–401.

Long-term Intervention with Pravastatin in Ischaemic Disease (LIPID) Study Group, The "Prevention of Cardiovascular Events and Death with Pravastatin in Patients with Coronary Heart Disease and a Broad Range of Initial Cholesterol Levels." *New England Journal of Medicine*, 339(19), November 5, 1998: 1349–1357.

Lu, Z. John, and William S. Comanor, "Strategic Pricing of New Pharmaceuticals." *The Review of Economics and Statistics*, 80(1), February 1998, 108–118.

Lueck, Sarah; Horvath, Stephanie. "Prices of Prescription Drugs Used by Seniors Soared in 2001." *Wall Street Journal*, June 25, 2002: B4.

Lundin, Douglas. "Moral Hazard in Physician Prescription Behavior." *Journal of Health Economics*, 19, 2000: 639–662.

Lyles, Alan; Luce, Bryan R.; Rentz, Anne M. "Managed Care Pharmacy, Socioeconomic Assessments and Drug Adoption Decisions." *Social Science and Medicine*, 45(4), 1997: 511–521.

Lyles, Alan; Palumbo, Franci B. "The Effect of Managed Care on Prescription Drug Costs and Benefits." *Pharmacoeconomics*, 15(2), February 1999: 129–140.

McAlister, Finlay A.; Lawson, Fiona M.E.; Teo, Koon K.; Armstrong, Paul W. "Randomised Trials of Secondary Prevention Programmes in Coronary Heart Disease: Systematic Review." *British Medical Journal*, 323, 2001: 957–962.

McCloskey, Amanda. *Failing America's Seniors: Private Health Plans Provide Inadequate Rx Drug Coverage*. Washington, DC: Families USA, May 2002, available at www.familiesusa.org (accessed on November 15, 2002).

McFadden, Daniel L. "Conditional Logit Analysis of Qualitative Choice Behavior." In: Zarembka, Paul ed., *Frontiers of Econometrics*. New York: Academic Press, 1973: 105–142.

McFadden, Daniel L. "Econometric Models of Probabilistic Choice." In: Charles F. Manski and Daniel L. McFadden eds, *Structural Analysis of Discrete Data and Econometric Applications*. Cambridge: MIT Press, 1981: 198–223.

McFadden, Daniel L. "Economic Choices." *American Economic Review*, 91(3), 2001: 351–378.

McKenney, James M. "New Cholesterol Guidelines, New Treatment Challenges." *Pharmacotherapy*, 22(7), 2002: 853–863.

Maclaine, G.D.H.; Patel, H. "A Cost-effectiveness Model of Alternative Statins to Achieve Target LDL-cholesterol Levels." *International Journal of Clinical Practice*, 55(4), 2001: 243–249.

Maddala, G.S. *Limited-Dependent and Qualitative Variables in Econometrics*. United Kingdom: Cambridge University Press, 1983.

Managed Care Measures. *Cardiovascular Benchmarks*, 2001, available at www. diseasebenchmarks.com/cardiovascular (accessed on May 29, 2002).

Marcelino, Jennifer J.; Feingold, Kenneth R. "Inadequate Treatment with HMG-CoA Reductase Inhibitors by Health Care Providers." *American Journal of Medicine*, 100, 1996: 605–610.

Mark, Daniel B.; Hlatky, Mark A.; Califf Robert M.; Naylor, C. David; Lee, Kerry L.; Armstrong, Paul W.; Barbash, Gabriel; White, Harvey; Simoons, Marteen L.; Nelson, Charlotte L.; Clapp-Channing, Nancy; Knight, David; Harrell Jr., Frank E.; Simes, John; Topol, Eric J. "Cost-effectiveness of Thrombolytic Therapy with Tissue Plasminogen Activator as Compared with Streptokinase for Acute Myocardial Infarction." *New England Journal of Medicine*, 332, 1995: 1418–1424.

Martinez, Barbara. "Rx for Margins: Hired to Cut Costs, Firms Find Profits in Generic Drugs." *Wall Street Journal*, 31 March 2003: A1.

Maseri A. "Inflammation, Atherosclerosis and Ischemic Events—Exploring the Hidden Side of the Moon." *New England Journal of Medicine*, 336, 1997: 1014–1016.

Mays, Glen P.; Hurley, Robert E.; Grossman, Joy M. "Consumers Face Higher Costs as Health Plans Seek to Control Drug Spending." *Center for Studying Health System Change Issue Brief*, 45, November 2001.

Mendall, M.A.; Patel, P.; Ballam, L.; Strachan, D.; Northfield, T.C. "C-reactive Protein and its Relation to Cardiovascular Risk Factors: A Population-based Cross-sectional Study." *British Medical Journal*, 312, 1996: 1061–1065.

Momani, Aiman; Odedina, Folakemi; Rosenbluth, Sidney; Madhavean, Sursesh. "Drug-Management Strategies: Consumers' Perspectives." *Journal of Managed Care Pharmacy* 6(2), 2000: 122–128.

Mortimer, Rika Onishi. "Demand for Prescription Drugs: The Effects of Managed Care Pharmacy Benefits." Department of Economics, Working Paper 97/258; Berkeley, CA: University of California, November 1997.

Motheral, Brenda R.; Fairman, Kathleen A. "Effect of a Three-Tier Prescription Copay on Pharmaceutical and Other Medical Utilization." *Medical Care*, 39(12), 2001: 1293–1304.

Motheral, Brenda R.; Henderson, Rochelle. "The Effect of a Copay Increase on Pharmaceutical Utilization, Expenditures, and Treatment Continuation." *American Journal of Managed Care*, 5(11), November 1999: 1383–1394.

Mucha, Lisa. "Does the Level of Private Insurance Coverage for Prescription Drugs Matter?" *Association for Health Services Research Abstract* (1998), abstract only.

National Cholesterol Education Program. *Detection, Evaluation, and Treatment of High Blood Cholesterol in Adults (Adult Treatment Panel III)*. National Institutes of Health, National Heart, Lung, and Blood Institute, May 2001.

Nelson, Arthur A.; Reeder, C. Eugene; Dickson, W. Michael. "The Effect of a Medicaid Drug Copayment Program on the Utilization and Cost of Prescription Services." *Medical Care*, 22(8), August 1984: 724–736.

NewsEdge. "Preferred Drugs, Tiered Copayments paying Off." April 25, 2002, avaiable at www.pharmscope.com/news (accessed on June 25, 2002).

Novartis Pharmaceuticals. "Pharmacy Benefit Report: Facts & Figures 2001 Edition." Novartis, East Hanover, NJ, 2001.

O'Brien, Bernie. "The Effect of Patient Charges on the Utilisation of Prescription Medicines." *Journal of Health Economics*, 8, 1989: 109–132.

O'Connor, Gerald T.; Quinton, Hebe B.; Traven, Neal D.; Ramunno, Lawrence D.; Dodds, T. Andrew; Marciniak, Thomas A.; Wennberg, John E. "Geographic Variation in the

Treatment of Acute Myocardial Infraction: The Cooperative Cardiovascular Project." *Journal of the American Medical Association*, 281(7), February 17, 1999: 627–633.

Oster, Gerry; Borok, Gerald M.; Menzin, Joseph; Heyse, Joseph F.; Epstein, Robert S.; Quinn, Virginia; Benson, Victor; Dudl, R. James; Epstein, Arnold M. "Cholesterol-reduction Intervention Study (RIS): A Randomized Trial to Assess Effectiveness in Clinical Practice." *Archives of Internal Medicine*, 156(7), April 8, 1996: 731–739.

Pasternak, Richard C.; Smith, Sidney C.; Bairey-Merz, C. Noel. "ACC/AHA/NHLBI Clinical Advisory on the Use and Safety of Statins." *Journal of the American College of Cardiology*, 40(3), 2002: 567–572.

Paul-Shaheen, P.; Clark, J.D.; Williams, D. "Small Area Analysis: A Review and Analysis of the North American Literature." *Journal of Health Politics, Policy and Law*, 12(4), 1987: 741–809.

P&T Community. "The FDA Announces Labeling Changes on Heart Benefit Associated with Simvastatin." April 16, 2003, available at www.ptcommunity.com (accessed on May 25, 2003).

Pearson, Thomas A. "The Undertreatment of LDL-cholesterol: Addressing the Challenge." *International Journal of Cardiology*, 74, 2000: S23–S28.

Pearson, Thomas A.; Laurora, Irene; Chu, Henry; Kafonek, Stephanie. "The Lipid Treatment Assessment Project (L-TAP): A Multicenter Survey to Evaluate the Percentages of Dyslipidemic Patients Receiving Lipid-Lowering Therapy and Achieving Low-Density Lipoprotein Cholesterol Goals." *Archives of Internal Medicine*, 160, 2000: 459–467.

Pederson, Terje R.; Olsson, Anders G.; Faergeman, Ole; Kjekshus, John; Wedel, Hans; Berg, Kare; Wilhelmsen, Lars; Haghfelt, Torben; Thorgeirsson, Gudmundur; Pyorala, Kalevi; Miettinen, Tatu; Christopersen, Bjorn; Tobert, Jonathan A.; Musliner, Thomas A.; Cook, Thomas J. for The Scandinavian Survival Study Group. "Lipoprotein Changes and Reduction in the Incidence of Major Coronary Heart Disease Events in the Scandinavian Simvastatin Survival Study (4S)." *Circulation*, 97, April 21, 1998: 1453–1460.

Penna, Pete. "Three-tier Copay Systems and Consumer-centric Care." *Journal of Managed Care Pharmacy*, 6(5), 2000: 351–353.

Perlstein, Steve. "Four-tier Approach Injects Consumerism into Drug Benefit." *Managed Care Online*, August 2001, available at www.managedcaremag.com/archives/0108/0108.fourtier.html (accessed on October 20, 2002).

Petitta, Antonio; Ward, Richard E.; Anadan, J.V.; Beis, Sara J.; Johnson, Alan M. "The Cost-Effectiveness Impact of a Preferred Agent HMG-CoA Reductase Inhibitor Policy in a Managed Care Population." *Journal of Managed Care Pharmacy*, 3, 1997: 548–553.

Pharmaceutical Research and Manufacturers of America (PhRMA) *Pharmaceutical Industry Profile 2000: Research for the Millennium*. Washington, DC: 2000.

Phelps, Charles E.; Newhouse, Joseph P. "Coinsurance, the Price of Time, and the Demand for Medical Services." *Review of Economics and Statistics*, 56(3), August 1974: 334–342.

Pitt, Bertram; Mancini, John; Ellis, Stephen G.; Rosman, Howard S.; Park, Jong-Soon; McGovern, Mark E. for the PLAC I. "Pravastatin Limitation of Atherosclerosis in the Coronary Arteries (PLAC I): Reduction in Atherosclerosis Progression and Clinical Events." *Journal of the American College of Cardiology*, 26, 1995: 1133–1139.

Pitt, Bertram; Waters, David; Brown, William V.; van Boven Ad J.; Schwartz, Leonard; Title, Lawrence M.; Eisenberg, Daniel; Shurzinske, Linda; McCormick, Lisa S. for the Atorvastatin versus Revascularization Treatment Investigators. "Aggressive Lipid-lowering Therapy Compared with Angioplasty in Stable Coronary Artery Disease." *New England Journal of Medicine*, 341, 1999: 70–76.

Practice Management Information Corporation. *International Classification of Diseases, 9th revision, Clinical Modification*. Vols 1 and 2. Los Angeles, 1995.

Prosser, Lisa A.; Stinnett, Aaron A.; Goldman, Paula A.; Williams, Lawrence W.; Hunink, Maria G.M.; Goldman, Lee; Weinstein, Milton C. "Cost-effectiveness of Cholesterol-Lowering Therapies According to Selected Patient Characteristics." *Annals of Internal Medicine*, 132 (10), May 16, 2000: 769–779.

Puddu, Paolo; Puddu, Giovanni M.; Muscari, Antonio. "Current Thinking in Statin Therapy." *Acta Cardiology*, 56(4), 2001: 225–231.

Purcell, Herny; Daly; Caroline; Sheppard, Mary; Morell, Jonathan. "Rational Prescribing of Statins." *The Practitioner*, 245, November 2001: 957–963.

Reckless, John P.D. "Cost-Effectiveness of Statins." *Current Opinion in Lipidology*, 11, 2000: 351–356.

Reeder, C.E.; Nelson, Arthur A. "The Differential Impact of Copayment on Drug Use in a Medicaid Population." *Inquiry*, 22, Winter 1985: 396–403.

Reeder, C.E.; Lingle E.W.; Schulz R.M.; Mauch R.P. Jr; Nightengale B.S.; Pedersen C.A.; Watrous M.L.; Zetzl S.E.; "Economic Impact of Cost-Containment Strategies in Third Party Programmes in the US (Part I)." *Pharmacoeconomics*, 4(2), 1993: 92–103.

Reid, Fiana D.A.; Cook, D.G.; Whincup, P.H. "Use of Statins in the Secondary Prevention of Coronary Heart Disease: Is Treatment Equitable?" *Heart*, 88, 2002: 15–19.

Rich, Sheldon J. "Managed Competition and Formulary Decisions." *Journal of Research in Pharmaceutical Economics*, 7(1/2), 1996: 101–108.

Ridker, Paul M.; Glynn, Robert J.; Hennekens, Charles H. "C-Reactive Protein Adds to the Predictive Value of Total and HDL Cholesterol in Determining Risk of First Myocardial Infarction." *Circulation*, 97, 1998: 2007–2011.

Rockson, Stanley G. "Benefits of Lipid-lowering Agents in Stroke and Coronary Heart Disease: Pharmacoeconomics." *Current Atherosclerosis Reports*, 2, 2000: 144–150.

Rossouw, Jacques E. "Clinical Trials of Lipid-Lowering Drugs." In: Rifkind, Basil M., ed. *Drug Treatment of Hyperlipidemia*. New York: Marcel Dekker, 1991: 67.

Rubinstein, Elan. "Employer Strategies in Managing Prescription Drug Costs." *Business and Health*, January 1991, 26–32.

Russell, Mason W.; Huse, Daniel M.; Drowns, Shelley; Hamel, Elizabeth C.; Hartz, Stuart C. "Direct Medical Costs of Coronary Artery Disease in the United States." *American Journal of Cardiology*, 81, 1998: 1110–1115.

Russell, Mason W.; Huse, Daniel M.; Miller, Jeffrey D.; Kraemer, Dale F.; Hartz, Stuart C. "Cost effectiveness of HMG-CoA Reductase Inhibition in Canada." *Canadian Journal of Clinical Pharmacology*, 8(1), Spring 2001: 9–16.

Sacks, Frank M.; Moye, Lemuel A.; Davis, Barry R.; Cole, Thomas G.; Rouleau, Jean L.; Nash, David T.; Pfeffer, Marc A.; Braunwald, Eugene. "Relationship between Plasma LDL Concentrations during Treatment with Pravastatin and Recurrent Coronary Events in the Cholesterol and Recurrent Events Trial." *Circulation*, 97, April 21, 1998: 1446–1452.

Sacks, Frank M.; Pfeffer, Marc A.; Moye, Lemuel A.; Rouleau, Jean L., Rutherford, John D.; Cole, Thomas G.; Brown, Lisa; Warnica, Wayne; Arnold, J. Malcolm O.; Wun, Chaun-Chaun; Davis, Barry R.; Braunwald, Eugene. "The Effect of Pravastatin on Coronary Events after Myocardial Infarction in Patients with Average Cholesterol Levels." *New England Journal of Medicine*, 335(14), October 3, 1996: 1001–1009.

Sax, M.J.; Emigh, R. 1999. Managed Care Formularies in the United States. *Journal of Managed Care Pharmacy* 5(4).

Scandinavian Simvastatin Survival Study Group. "Randomised Trial of Cholesterol Lowering in 4444 Patients with Coronary Heart Disease: The Scandinavian Simvastatin Survival Study (4S)." *Lancet*, 344, November 19, 1994: 1383–1389.

Schwartz, Gregory G.; Olsson, Anders G., Ezekowitz, Michael D.; Ganz, Peter; Oliver, Michael F.; Waters, David, Zeiher, Andreas; Chaitman, Bernard R.; Leslie, Sally; Stern, Theresa. "Effects of Atorvastatin of Early Recurrent Ischemic Events in Acute Coronary Syndromes: A Randomized Controlled Trial (The Myocardial Ischemia Reduction with Aggressive Cholesterol Lowering." *Journal of the American Medical Association*, 285(13), 2001: 1711–1718.

Scott-Levin. Managed Care Formulary Drug Audit. Newtown, PA, 2001.

Scott-Levin. Benefit Design: How it's Changing Managed Care. Newtown, PA, June 2001.

Selby, Joe V.; Ray, G. Thomas; Zhang, Danya; Colby, Chris J. "Excess Costs of Medical Care for Patients with Diabetes in a Managed Care Population." *Diabetes Care*, 20(9), September 1997: 1396–1402.

Shepherd, James. "Economics of Lipid Lowering in Primary Prevention: Lessons from the West of Scotland Coronary Prevention Study." *American Journal of Cardiology*, 87 Supplement, 2001: 19B–22B.

Shepherd, James; Blauw, Gerard J.; Murphy, Michael B.; Bollen, Edward L.E.M.; Buckley, Brendan M.; Cobbe, Stuart M.; Ford, Ian; Gaw, Allan; Hyland, Michael; Jukema, J. Wouter; Kamper, Adriaan M.; Macfarlane, Peter W.; Meinders, A. Edo; Norrie, John; Packard, Christopher J.; Perry, Ivan J.; Stott, David J.; Sweeney, Brian J.; Twomey, Cillian; Westendorp, Rudi G.J. on behalf of the PROSPER study group. "Pravastatin in Elderly Individuals at Risk of Vascular Disease (PROSPER): A Randomised Controlled Trial." *Lancet*, 360, 2002: 1623–1630.

Shepherd, James; Cobbe, Stuart M.; Ford, Ian; Isles, Christopher G.; Lorimer, A. Ross; Macfarlane, Peter W.; McKillop, James H.; Packard, Christopher J. "Prevention of Coronary Heart Disease with Pravastatin in Men with Hypercholesterolemia." *New England Journal of Medicine*, 333(20), November 16, 1995: 1301–1307.

Sloan, Frank A. (ed.) *Valuing Health Care: Costs, Benefits, and Effectiveness of Pharmaceuticals and Other Medical Technologies*. New York: Cambridge University Press, 1995.

Smith, Dean G. "The Effects of Copayments and Generic Substitution on the Use and Costs of Prescription Drugs." *Inquiry*, 30, Summer 1993: 189–198.

Smith, Mickey C.; Garner, Dewey D. "Effects of a Medicaid Program on Prescription Drug Availability and Acquisition." *Medical Care*, 12(7), July 1974: 571–581.

Sonnenberg, Frank A.; Beck, J. Robert. "Markov Models in Medical Decision Making: A Practical Guide." *Medical Decision Making*, 13, 1993: 322–338.

Soumerai, Stephen B.; Avorn, Jerry. "Economic and Policy Analysis of University-based Drug Detailing." *Medical Care*, 24(4), April 1986: 313–331.

Soumerai, Stephen B.; Avorn, Jerry; Ross-Degnan, Dennis; Gortmaker, Steven. "Payment Restrictions for Prescription Drugs Under Medicaid: Effects on Therapy, Cost, and Equity." *New England Journal of Medicine*, 317; August 27, 1987: 550–556.

Spearman, Marshall E.; Summers, Kent; Moore, Virginia; Jacqmin, Robert; Smith, Gary; Groshen, Susan. "Cost-effectiveness of Initial Therapy with 3-hydroxy-3-methyl-glutaryl Coenzyme A Reductase Inhibitors to Treat Hypercholesterolemia in a Primary Care Setting of a Managed Care Organization." *Clinical Therapeutics*, 19(3), 1997: 582–602.

Stafford, Randall S.; Radley, David C. "The Potential of Pill Splitting to Achieve Cost Savings." *American Journal of Managed Care*, 8(8), August 2002: 706–712.

Stamler, Jeremiah; Wentworth, Deborah; Neaton, James D. "Is Relationship between Serum Cholesterol and Risk of Premature Death from Coronary Heart Disease Continuous and Graded?: Findings in 356, 222 Primary Screenees of the Multiple Risk Factor Intervention Trial (MRFIT)." *Journal of the American Medical Association*, 256, 1986: 2823–2828.

Standing Medical Advisory Committee. "The Use of Statins." UK Department of Public Health, May 1997, available at www.doh.gov.uk/cmo/statins2.htm (accessed on June 30, 2002).

Steele, H. "Monopoly and Competition in the Ethical Drug Market." *Journal of Law and Economics*, 5, 1962: 142–143.

Steiner, Robert L. "The Inverse Association between the Margins of Manufacturers and Retailers." *Review of Industrial Organization*, 8, 1993: 717–740.

Steinke, Doug T.; MacDonald, Thomas M.; Davey, Peter G. "The Doctor–Patient Relationship and Prescribing Patterns." *Pharmacoeconomics*, 16(6), December 1999: 599–603.

Steinman, Michael A. "Gifts to Physicians in the Consumer Marketing Era." *Journal of the American Medical Association*, 284(17), November 1, 2000: 2243.

Stender S; Schuster H; Barter P; Watkins C; Kallend D; on behalf of the MERCURY I Study Group. "Comparison of Rosuvastatin with Atorvastatin, Simvastatin and Pravastatin in Achieving Cholesterol Goals and Improving Plasma Lipids in Hypercholesterolaemic Patients with or without the Metabolic Syndrome in the MERCURY I Trial." *Diabetes, Obesity, and Metabolism*, 7(4) July 2005: 430–438.

Stinnett, Aaron A.; Mittleman, Murray A.; Weinstein, Milton C.; Kuntz, Karen M.; Cohen, David J.; Williams, Lawrence W.; Goldman, Paula A.; Stiger, Douglas O.; Hunink, Maria G.M.; Tsevat, Joel; Tosteson, Anna N.A.; Goldman, Lee. "Appendix C: The Cost-Effectiveness of Dietary and Pharmacologic Therapy for Cholesterol Reduction in Adults." In: Marthe R. Gold; Joanna E. Seigel; Lousie B. Russell; Milton C. Weinstein. eds, *Cost-Effectiveness in Health and Medicine*. New York: Oxford University Press, 1996: 349–391.

Strandberg, Timo E.; Vanhanen, Hannu; Tikkanen; Matti J. "Effect of Statins on C-reactive Protein in Patients with Coronary Artery Disease." *Lancet*, 353(9147), 1999: 118–119.

Stuart, Michael E.; Handley, Matthew A.; Chamberlain, Marvin A.; Wallach, Robert W.; Penna, Peter M.; Stergachis, Andy. "Successful Implementation of a Guideline Program for the Rational Use of Lipid-Lowering Drugs." *HMO Practice*, 5(6), 1991: 198–204.

Takeda-Lilly. "The Takeda and Lilly Prescription Drug Benefit Cost and Plan Design Survey Report: 2001 Edition." Wellman publishing, Inc., Albuquerque, New Mexico, 2001.

Temin, Peter. *Taking Your Medicine*. Cambridge, MA: Harvard University Press, 1980.

Train, Kenneth. *Qualitative Choice Analysis: Theory, Econometrics, and an Application to Automobile Demand*. Cambridge, MA: The MIT Press, 1986.

Tsevat J.; Weinstein M.C.; Williams L.W.; Tosteson A.N.; Goldman L. Expected gains in life expectancy from various coronary heart disease risk factor modifications. *Circulation*. 83, 1991: 1194–1201.

Tsevat, Joel; Kuntz, Karen M.; Orav, E. John; Weinstein, Milton C.; Sacks, Frank M.; Goldman, Lee. "Cost-effectiveness of Pravastatin Therapy for Survivors of Myocardial Infarction with Average Cholesterol Levels." *American Heart Journal*, 141, 2001: 727–734.

United States Census Bureau. *Health Insurance Coverage*: 2002.

United States Department of Health and Human Services. "Report to the President: Prescription Drug Coverage, Spending, Utilization, and Prices." April 2000, available at http://www.aspe.hhs.gov/health/reports/drugstudy/ (accessed on August 28, 2000).

van Hout, Ben A.; Simoons, Maarten L. "Cost-effectiveness of HMG Coenzyme Reductase Inhibitors: Whom to treat?" *European Heart Journal*, 22, 2001: 751–761.

Walker, H. *Market Power and Price Levels in the Ethical Drug Industry*. Bloomington, IN: Indiana University Press, 1971.

Wennberg, J.; Gittelsohn, A. "Variations in Medical Care Among Small Areas." *Scientific American*, 246(4), April 1982: 120–134.

West of Scotland Coronary Prevention Group. "West of Scotland Coronary Prevention Study: Identification of High Risk Groups and Comparison with other Cardiovascular Intervention Trials." *Lancet* 348(9038), 1996, 1339–1342.

Winslow, Ron; McGinley, Laurie; Adams, Chris. "States, Insurers Find Prescriptions for High Drug Costs." *The Wall Street Journal*, September 11, 2002: A1.

Wolfe, John R.; Goddeeris, John H. "Adverse Selection, Moral Hazard, and Wealth Effects in the Medigap Insurance Market." *Journal of Health Economics*, 10, 1991: 433–459.

Wosinska, Marta. "Promoting to Multiple Agents: The Case of Direct-to-Consumer Drug Advertising." October 2001, mimeo.

Zachry, Woodie M.; Shepherd, Marvi D.; Hinch, Melvin J.; Wilson, James P., Brown, Carolyn M.; Lawson, Kenneth A. "Relationship between Direct-to-Consumer Advertising and Physician Diagnosing and Prescribing." *American Journal of Health System Pharmacy*, 59(1), 2002: 33–41.

Index

eBooks – at www.eBookstore.tandf.co.uk

A library at your fingertips!

eBooks are electronic versions of printed books. You can store them on your PC/laptop or browse them online.

They have advantages for anyone needing rapid access to a wide variety of published, copyright information.

eBooks can help your research by enabling you to bookmark chapters, annotate text and use instant searches to find specific words or phrases. Several eBook files would fit on even a small laptop or PDA.

NEW: Save money by eSubscribing: cheap, online access to any eBook for as long as you need it.

Annual subscription packages

We now offer special low-cost bulk subscriptions to packages of eBooks in certain subject areas. These are available to libraries or to individuals.

For more information please contact webmaster.ebooks@tandf.co.uk

We're continually developing the eBook concept, so keep up to date by visiting the website.

www.eBookstore.tandf.co.uk

For Product Safety Concerns and Information please contact our EU
representative GPSR@taylorandfrancis.com
Taylor & Francis Verlag GmbH, Kaufingerstraße 24, 80331 München, Germany

www.ingramcontent.com/pod-product-compliance
Ingram Content Group UK Ltd.
Pitfield, Milton Keynes, MK11 3LW, UK
UKHW020947180425
457613UK00019B/560